T0063275

Praise For *Reawaken Your Authentic Self*

"Living from our Authentic Self is life changing. When you embrace the part of you that is already perfect, whole and complete everything falls into place. Divina shows readers how to do just that. This is a must read!"

Christy Whitman New York Times Bestselling author, "The Art of Having It All"

"Divina's unique take on Reawakening Your Authentic Self allows the reader to heal in mind, body and soul. This book is equipped with so many powerful, practical and straight forward lessons, this book allows the reader to walk confidently along the route their true soul desires"

Peggy McColl, New York Times Best Selling Author

It has been my own experience that awakening to your authentic self profoundly and positively changes the course of your life. In this beautiful book, full of practical tools for daily transformation, Divina lovingly shows you the way to your own personal and spiritual evolution.

Fabienne Fredrickson, author of Embrace Your Magnificence

Divina's Reawaken Your Authentic Self is a wondrous and joyous step by step manual to unleash your full potential. I highly recommend this book to anyone who wants to authentically awaken to who they really are.

Brett Dupree, Professional Speaker, Author of Joyous Expansion and Life Coach

Divina's book and coaching program is exceptional and so insightful. Before the coaching I was a hesitant in moving forward with my life purpose and had beliefs holding me back from the love and abundance I deserved, but she put me at ease with her sense of humor and has an uncanny ability getting the results you need. Then after coaching with her, I learned to value myself for the amazing woman I am. The 3 most important results I got in my life are becoming a successful entrepreneur, bringing love in, and receiving the abundance I deserve thanks to Divina and her program.

Stacey Ison, Law of Attraction Life coach

Before working with Divina, my level of energetic frequency was lower and I was much less conscious in my awakening of my authentic self, but then after working with Divina's book, I realized it is a treasure trove of tools and resources for someone, such as myself, that elevated my energetic frequencies in day to day life for a fuller expression of my talents, life purpose and authentic self. It also covers practices that I am implementing for long term results that have heightened my sensitivities and awareness of the influences we let into our lives. The author, Divina Caballo, offers her personal use of diet, exercise and affirmations in such a generous way I feel as if I was given a very expensive gift! Thanks to her openness to share her life work, I have been able to use Awakening Your Authentic Self to continue doing just as the title offers! Thank you, Divina, priceless information! If you have any questions about her work you can contact me on facebook.

Sarah Christensen

Before working with Divina, I had a lot of insecurities about my work as a musician and human being, I lacked confidence and energy on a physical level. Then after working with Divina in my health in my physical diet and I was impressed with the information she offered in this part of the program which was different than anything I offered. It was so instrumental in giving me energy and the mindset part of the program was important to help me stay centered in my new diet changes that affected my expression of my life purpose. The spiritual aspect of the program helped me awaken creativity levels I never new possible especially as a musician.

Benj Clark, musician

Before working with Divina, I was stubborn, and not fully being able to express my authentic self, but after being in the program I realized how much I had changed. This is an absolutely amazing system — filled with lots of wonderful information that teaches about health, happiness, and spiritual well-being and awakening. I have implemented many of the teachings of this program into my life and I really appreciate the results of awakened consciousness, happiness and a greater alignment to my life purpose!!! This holistic program truly represents excellent food for thought and reflection for body, mind and spirit. Thank you to the author for sharing such a treasure with this book.

Shirine Elkis

I purchased the program by Divina and found it to be an excellent system that I really love. This program covers everything that you need to know about how to lead a healthy and vibrant life. It really helps you to uncover who you truly are and how to live an authentic, joyful and fulfilling existence! My life has changed from applying much of what I have learned and I am really grateful that Divina shares so much with the reader about how to attract and create the kind of life you always dreamed of but did not know how or where to begin. I have told all of my family and friends about this fantastic program and how it can change their lives! I can't wait to consume her other products and programs.

Boris Elkis

Divina Caballo has done a great job helping people awaken to their own happiness and authentic self in her new book, "Reawaken Your Authentic Self". She shares openly and from her heart about her own personal awakening and how you can find the answers you are searching for in your own life. She sets up the step by step framework of how you can awaken to who you truly are on all levels. Divina delivers her wisdom in a soulful, heart felt manner and truly has a passion to help others find happiness and connection in an authentic way. She includes the tools she developed for the body, mind and spirit that will assist you in opening and deepening your spiritual connection and awakening. This book that will become your go to guide for awakening to your highest potential, developing a greater spiritual connection and living a healthier, happier, whole life. It is a holistic guidebook with step by step instructions on what to do on all levels of body, mind and spirit to live authentically in happiness and on purpose. Bravo, Divina!

Cyndi Crockett

REAWAKEN
YOUR AUTHENTIC SELF

FULLY AWAKEN & MONETIZE YOUR LIFE PURPOSE BY
BECOMING WHO YOU REALLY ARE!

Divina

BALBOA
PRESS
A DIVISION OF HAY HOUSE

Balboa Press books may be ordered through booksellers or by contacting:

Balboa Press
A Division of Hay House
1663 Liberty Drive
Bloomington, IN 47403
www.balboapress.com
1 (877) 407-4847

Print information available on the last page.

ISBN: 978-1-5043-3716-8 (sc)
ISBN: 978-1-5043-3717-5 (e)

Balboa Press rev. date: 10/14/2015

FREE BONUS!
CLAIM 2 FREE TICKETS TO MY HALF-DAY EVENT AND A
FREE ONLINE TRAINING VIDEO SERIES:
"Awaken and Monetize Your Life Purpose"
YOU CAN WATCH ON MY WEBSITE BY OPTING IN ONLINE AT:

www.ReawakenYourAuthenticSelf.com

***

This book is dedicated to all the artistic souls and entrepreneurs who are hungry for answers on how to unblock their god given talents and attain the mindset needed to monetize their business abundantly.

***

"The sun casts shadows, but the sun does not have a shadow. To be free of shadows, one must embody the brilliance of the sun."
— Divina

Contents

Acknowledgments

I would like to thank all of the teachers who have touched my heart in so many ways.

I would like to thank Joshua Stone for affecting my life so deeply in my early years; your message was a life saver to me during so many of the troubles during my teenage years; wherever you are in heaven, thank you.

Thank you to Fabienne Fredrickson for loving me so deeply and growing my capacity to love in business and life. You helped me awaken to the most profound and important essence of my life, to love greatly.

To Steve and Lia, I love you both so much. You have given me my soul back literally. Thank you for opening your hearts and home to me and believing in and supporting me, even in the tough times I have gone through. I cannot thank you enough, and I also thank the community through which we are all connected; it has created a kind of nest for me in which to flourish and grow, spread my wings, and finally fly.

I would like to thank my parents for bringing me into this world. I thank you both. I know you both did the best you knew how to do, and for that, I am forever grateful.

And, finally, I would like to thank my sister, for rescuing me when times were tough. Thank you.

Love,

DIVINA

Introduction: Read This First!

"If realigning to your authentic self makes you unstoppable, and brings you everything you want—money, health, your dreams coming true, outstanding talent, and most importantly, true happiness—then the choices you make that enhance that realignment at every moment are what are most important. Focus on this very moment now to achieve the perfect joyful thoughts and actions that your heart can muster to build your unstoppable realignment to who you really are."
— *DIVINA*

I will never forget the night I had the most profound reawakening and transformation, not only in unblocking my artistic talents and life purpose, but also my authentic self. I felt the essence of my highest self reawaken in me, or rather, I reawoke to it. This same night, I had an immense pain where it seemed like all of my depression, holding on to a grudge, and not being able to forgive for years now accumulated into one giant nightmare that was torturing me and blocking most of my artistic creativity. The pain was excruciating and unbearable. I had accumulated so much bitterness against people who betrayed me, and I had lost so much joy and prosperity because I was too proud to let go and forgive. I was having the hardest time of my life, and I had the hardest battle of all in fighting the dark energies eating at me from the inside because I had chosen not to let go. Because of this choice, everything in my artistic and creative life seemed to go wrong. At the time, for example, I was taking acting classes and the negativity was manifesting in my performance piece and my teacher was not pleased.

Fortunately, I was being guided by Spirit to water fast every Sunday, to live permanently on blended, living, superfood soups with live juices, and to follow a powerful, Divine Diet physically, mentally, emotionally, and spiritually. What was so intriguing to me at the time was that my highest self told me that it was not a vibrational match to the density of my current physical body; therefore, more of my highest self could not enter completely if I did not change to the physical diet I was now specifically being given, nor could it enter completely without forgiveness. I knew that if I wanted to unblock my artistic creativity and life purpose, I needed to cleanse in this way and find my authentic self so that my god given talent could flow through easier.

After five or six months of excruciating discomfort, basically from all the detoxification and letting go of overeating, I finally lost all the unwanted weight and reached a size 4 (which I was told, through channeling my highest self, that it is a vibrational match in size to my soul). A few days after reaching size 4 (I had previously been a size 12), I attended a healing ceremony that would change me for the rest of my personal and professional life as an artist. My weight loss had opened up space to magnetize more of me into my body because I was cleaner, less dense, and higher in vibration. During this ceremony, I finally chose to forgive myself and forgive everyone who had hurt me. After thirty years—just about a month before my thirtieth birthday, I had the most profound spiritual awakening. On that day, once the foundation or essence of my soul was in me, I felt the most euphoric, intense, and alive feelings I have ever felt in my life and finally an abundant flow of creativity opened!

For a few years prior to this moment, I had been seeing in my dreams and inner clairvoyant vision a highest self part of me more and more often, which was hovering around me. The telepathic communication I received told me that my highest self was getting ready to and wanting to merge with me. A large part of my highest self merged with me during that life-changing ceremony. If I were to be viewed as a house, then my highest self was the foundation and the floors were installed that day.

Right before the moment of reunion with that basic essence of my authentic self, as I mentioned, I was suffering from not being able to forgive myself or others. That inability to forgive was letting a lot of dark energy cloud my mind and body. This situation was so unbearable that I had no choice but to forgive. In my third eye, I saw a very thin layer of darkness release itself, and all of a sudden, I felt what was like a burst of new abundant energy rushing through my body, and then I felt almost like another person was moving my body, and it was yelling in excitement, "Oh, my god! I'm in my body!" over and over again, nonstop, for about thirty minutes. I couldn't believe it! Was this me talking? It felt like a part of me, which had never before been in my body, was opening my mouth and speaking through me. The grateful energy speaking through me was somewhat familiar, but the part of me that incarnated in my physical body felt this new me as somewhat alien. That moment was the most perplexingly euphoric, ecstatic experience because, as I learned, the highest self is all happiness and joy—there is nothing else. When I finally let go of the last remnants of darkness and resistance to forgive, after four years of intense soul-cleansing in sacred healing ceremonies and soul-activation meditations, and I permanently adopted a divine sacred physical diet of living on blended liquid superfoods that I channeled from my highest self, I finally created a cleaner and higher vibrational body temple for the foundation of my highest self to expand itself into my body and express its joyful self!

Everything changed after that night; everything around me looked more alive and magical, and I experienced a more expanded level of joy. I won't say I was perfect after it; there is always another level to grow into no matter how high you go, but this experience was the very beginning of my hope for an abundant future. I was quite unstable and wobbly, like a newborn, hatched chick that had just pecked itself out of an egg's confinements and was now learning to walk. I began to notice a lot more presence and joy in the current moment— something I had never before been able to sustain for long periods of time.

Everything around me had a juicy energy to it. I was much more appreciative and able to enjoy everything that surrounded me. Nature seemed to give off an exquisite energy I could never sense before, and I could smile and realize there was no reason not to smile, even in the hard times. I realized that joy was who I was and who I was created to be, regardless of my outer situations and challenges. My heart still sang with joy quietly in the background of my emotional body in moments of discomfort.

Two months after I experienced this reawakening, my income increased! I understood now the power of anchoring the higher vibrations into my body and how they could attract more financial abundance. As a clothing designer, I could channel and receive inner clairvoyant guidance for my clothing designs much faster and better from the spiritual plane; I could see pictures of my art in my third eye come a lot faster; I increased my clairaudient abilities, and I could hear songs coming through me; I could sing with vibrato, which I couldn't do before; my dancing movements shifted into waves of new explosive movement, and I was a lot more talented artistically on all levels. I could not believe how much more talented I was and how my life purpose was finally blossoming just by a sudden shift in reawakening my authentic self.

After my transformation, I often thought of how many people are disconnected from their higher talents; some don't even know their life purposes or their powers to attract higher income for their life purposes. One thing I know for sure is that everyone is supposed to live his or her life purpose, but many are deprived from it, unfulfilled, stressed, and hate their jobs, which they really don't belong in, simply because they are out of alignment with their authentic selves.

I had a dream after this new alignment within myself, where I was walking in the middle of a large seminar I was teaching and had the word "teacher" written on my wrist. It was clear that I was being told by the Universe, my highest self, that it was time to manifest one of my life purposes, which was revealed to me to be a teacher. I was finally awakening to a hidden life purpose and talent that I had no idea existed within me. What I also understood from that dream, which was in accordance with what my inner guidance was telling me, was that there is a hunger among people for this new channeling of teachings that my highest self was offering me, and there is also a desire for a new perspective that brought light and love to teachings people already know but need to be enlightened to receive so they may grow their authentic selves and life purpose more completely. That revelation alone, along with the magnitudes of love that have been awakened in me for you, was a big enough reason for me to write this book and to create my seminars and academy so I can teach what I learned and accomplished, and, ultimately, inspire and nourish you to grow more authentically.

This book will help you grow more authentically into your life purpose and expand more fully your god given talents if you will let it. You can help the process by finding a journal to write in. Throughout this book, I will give you some activities to do, but I also encourage you to stop and write down any thoughts you have while reading, or to make a list of key concepts you discover or need to think about more after you finish each chapter. That way, it will be easy for you to go back to review what you have learned and focus on what you most need to work on in your journey. Writing will help you take action to make the changes needed. You wouldn't be reading this book if you weren't seeking some sort of change in your life. I'm here to help you make that change, but you also have to help yourself, and keeping a journal can be the first step to that.

First, though, let me explain to you the problem we are facing. We're at a time in our planet's history when many are awakening; however, many are not awakening more fully because of lack of clarity; a lot of people are struggling and hurting from this lack of clarity; they are resisting awakening, and they don't know how to get out of this state of resistance. Tremendous unhappiness and resistance to change exists in many people, who are confused about exactly how they have to change to make their lives grow more fully in all areas: financially, emotionally, socially, physically, spiritually, and mentally.

Those who are awakening spiritually are seeking to understand and learn more about their spiritual natures by attending spiritual retreats, seminars, and workshops, yet they are not in positions yet to fuel for themselves the divine unfoldment of prosperity or release the full power within their beings. They understand they need further spiritual development, but they still have a deep lack of clarity. Once a deeper clarity has been established for them, the breakthrough can happen. This breakthrough is a journey, and even this breakthrough can turn into another breakthrough. It is no accident that you are reading this book now; I know there is something here for you that will bring more clarity. I'm holding the candle for you brightly so the path to fulfillment will be clear and the missing links for you will be answered in this book.

I'm going to share with you now something important about how my teachings are shining their light to humanity, so please read with special attention. You can allow your dream life to be attracted to you at a far greater level by cultivating magnitudes of unspeakably delicious emotions; these emotions have uncontrollably explosive aliveness and ecstasy. I know because I am experiencing and allowing such emotions now to unfold through me! However, a tremendous disconnection exists to the authentic joyful aliveness that we are because of a lack of understanding about this sacred body temple we are gifted with and how it can nourish us. Without experiencing this explosively joyful aliveness, no one can be truly rich or attract and experience his or her authentic life with ease.

What I do see in abundance in humanity is a lack of integration and a disconnection to who we really are, to what we really came to do. Most people are disconnected from the inner guidance system that is supposed to be strongly guiding them in their journeys at every moment. Many people don't know what they want, or what their life purpose really is because they are disconnected and are asking for things that might not even be right for them. As a result, their lives are not abundant on all levels. Some people even attempt to manifest things with the application of universal laws, but they are still not getting them because of this strong disconnection to their abundant source energy and the understanding of who they really are.

Let me suggest to you that if this sounds like you, you're probably missing something and that something is the awakening of your authentic self to a higher level. You probably need more clarity about what is needed for it to be awakened. The more you grow spiritually, the more your divine essence will be anchored in your body; then your internal compass will be so strong that you can't help but move and manifest in the right direction. I've written this book to make you realize that what you are ultimately looking for is to awaken your authentic self; your real purpose and desire is not money or other outer material needs and wants, although we all know those things are really nice and sometimes even necessary, but even their existence in your life is only the outcome of how little or how much effort you make toward connecting to your authentic self! Oh, my goodness, was that last sentence good or what? Can I please get a hallelujah on that last sentence! That's worth reading again. Please go back and read it again. It's the epitome of the entire book!

Some people call this reawakening "enlightenment," but I don't want to intimidate you with that word because the meaning behind it might seem impossible to a lot of people. To tell you the truth, it's quite simple to reawaken when you don't have the ego trying to complicate things. If you think it's simple, it will be. I have made the process of reawakening to your authentic self as simple and as clear as possible in this book; all you have to do is follow the directions just like you were taking direction from your car's GPS to get from point A to point B. You might have mountains of ego and dark energy to clear before you get there, but you know what? I did, too. You would not believe how bad it was for me. I mean it was so bad; I experienced scattered energy, bitter anger and depression, and a tremendous lack of presence with dormant talents. I do not wish that on anyone, so even if you're in the same boat I was, I know it's definitely possible for you to move beyond it. Don't get me wrong; I still have more negative energy to clear so I can completely awaken, but the truth is, spiritual work never ends; it just eventually begins to turn into joyful play. You can begin to awaken your authentic self and create absolute abundance in all areas of your life by applying the principles in this book as I did.

When you awaken your authentic self to a higher abundant level, miracles start to happen in your life! God/ Universe starts to pour out to you everything you need and want so fast that you start to realize how important it is to be authentically you. Before you finish this book, be sure to read the story in the last chapter titled "The Story of Reawakening." I wrote this story about a man whose true highest self came to him. When it took over his body and merged with his "smaller" self, everything changed for him. After years of struggle in his life, he cleansed his body and merged back to become who he really was.

This story was almost like a mirror of what happened and is continuing to happen to me. I'm here to tell you that to reawaken is why all of us are incarnated on this planet. We each have small aspects of our soul incarnated here, but because of our uncleanliness, poor choices, and family karma passed down from thousands of generations to our parents and then to us, our highest self cannot live in a body that does not vibrate at its maximum level, and so it hovers above the body for many of us!

My friend, when you have more completely merged with it, your highest self is your ultimate prosperity, happiness generator, and fun factory. Then your body feels alive and euphoric, you have infinite creativity, and your personal mission, which you came to this planet to fulfill, will no doubt channel very easily from within you, and it will be coming out of you like crazy! You will become like a kid again, vibrantly wanting to play and enjoy life; enthusiasm will come to you easily, and your ability to communicate what you came here to do will be easy! All your "sleeping" talent will become activated like you never thought possible! I believe my message can help you get there, so please do read on!

What will it be like to be more fully reawakened to your authentic self and god given talents? Some examples are people like John of God, Esther Hicks, and Michael Jackson. These people are highly magnetic; they aren't necessarily fully integrated completely with their highest selves, but to attract the talents and abundance they have or have had in their lives, they have a substantial amount of integration with their authentic selves.

I cannot emphasize enough that being who you really are brings you everything you want as well as miracles you didn't even expect in your life. And also, don't beat yourself up because you're not perfect. I'm definitely not, but I am proud of the level of integration I have achieved with my authentic self. You definitely don't have to be perfect to achieve a high level of abundance and wellbeing, you only have to perfectly do your best. I certainly have, and the above-mentioned people certainly have, but I guarantee you they are not all perfect, so please keep that in mind. With that said, let's move on.

So let's talk about the planet, and where we are. There is an enormous transition happening on the planet today. The masses are starting to wake up and take control of what is really possible in their lives. Movies like *The Secret* have made people start to realize that they are the creators of their own reality. Although this book will not be directly talking about the Law of Attraction, reawakening to your authentic self definitely includes attracting what you really want, and I will certainly address some key points that will be valuable in getting the things you truly want, and which may not have been addressed in many of the other books and sources of information coming out today.

We are starting to understand on a more massive scale now that the outer world is a reflection of the inner world. If your outer world is not where you want it to be, chances are you have something that needs to be cleansed or resolved in your internal world. I have spent over a decade dedicating myself to growth, going to retreats and seminars, reading books, listening to tapes, and attending spiritual events to figure out how to become financially free, be emotionally abundant, maximize my talent, be physically abundant, and attract abundant people into my life. And I can say that this book is a collection of all of my treasured spiritual practices. This book and all of the programs and services I offer in my academy offer a new model to reawaken in the easiest, most comprehensive way for the majority of people.

So here is the concept of this book. Think of it as offering you four Divine Diets for your mental, emotional, physical, and spiritual body to awaken your authentic self. If those four bodies were perfectly clean, wouldn't you be channeling all your god given talents and perfectly embody who you really are? If someone gave you the exact techniques for how to do that, wouldn't you think your entire soul would enter and fill the place that was previously filled with toxic dark energy? That's exactly what this book is meant to do for you. Wherever an unclean space is in your being, your higher or authentic self cannot anchor to your being, so instead, it is hovering above your body; it can't vibrate and merge at a level that is unclean.

I'm speaking from personal experience. Millions of us on this planet are disconnected from our talents and can't share their abundance or benefits because we aren't even in our bodies completely and powerfully. We must cleanse our four bodies because cleanliness equals godliness! It truly does. I never fully understood that concept until the night I reawakened to the essential foundation of my authentic self. Have you ever walked into a messy room and suddenly felt uncomfortable or less able to concentrate? Imagine what a clean inner body could do for you. You must follow a Divine Diet not just for the physical body, as taught in this book, but also a diet for the mental, emotional, and spiritual bodies.

This book will give you the missing links and the Divine Diet to follow to clear and transform your four bodies (mental, emotional, physical, spiritual) so the divine, authentic you can merge with your present being in ways you never would have expected! You may learn about things you never heard of or find tools you never used before that will revolutionize your being at levels you never thought possible.

I have grown massively in consciousness during the last few years, which has given me great success and abundance in my life. To see myself skyrocket, become brilliant in my being, and so much more integrated has been a delight to watch. I went from living in a dysfunctional family, being broke, having negative people in my life, and being depressed, bitter, angry, closed down, and overweight to having explosive unbelievable amounts of energy to get things done and create so much abundance in my personal and professional life! My current sense of presence and focus compared to my past is like night and day.

I now know very clearly that I am being intuitively fed and internally guided at every moment, but I never would have known my spiritual mission if I hadn't followed the guidance you're about to read. I gratefully have given birth to a new awakening, and I still am awakening to more refined levels of my artistic talents that are abundant and limitless.

There is so much more joy and love in me now that it's ridiculous how overwhelming it can get. It's unbelievable what I have accomplished in the few years that have gone by. I am a certified Law of Attraction coach, but that really doesn't mean anything in terms of my credibility compared to the results I have accomplished! People I know look at me in awe and ask, "What happened? You look one thousand times better than you did two years ago." It is important to understand that this book has a clear understanding of every aspect of your being and that divine guidance is here to assist you. There are a lot of self-help books out there and a lot of diet books. This one in particular might be "too hard" for certain people, but I tell you this: raise your standards; spend time around people who make you want to be better and do better.

Reawakening your authentic self is the same as enlightenment, or what is also known as "ascension" in the spiritual movement. (I would like to suggest, however, that it's really descension of your soul.) On that note, I would also like to add that you are very lucky to have a body and the opportunity to work toward reawakening your authentic self. Without a body, your evolution is very slow, so take advantage of the body you possess and use this book to activate your growth faster! Remember that before you die, all you can take with you is who you have become. I dare you to become something extraordinary!

Being extraordinary is possible, and any amount of discomfort that you have to go through is well-worth the price of having your soul completely activated and integrated into your physical being so you can experience happiness, endless prosperity, abundance, euphoria, and the most amazing emotional feelings and lifestyle. If you just trust that you are a powerful soul capable of great things, you will see yourself transform, and people will look at you differently. You will have opportunities, which seem out of reach to the masses, come to you because of the level of awakening you have accomplished; believe me, it's well-worth your time. *Yes, you can do it, and it's your time to reawaken.*

    Reading this book is truly going to transform your life if you open yourself to it! Even for those who have already greatly awakened much, something deeper can be found here. I hope you will read this book many times. I know it is going to change the paradigm for you because it changed it for me, and that change is still happening. I promise you the level of happiness you will feel is far greater and worth far more than any challenges along the way. Don't kid yourself and trap yourself into a long life of misery. Be bold. Live the courage to reawaken your authentic self. The time to act is now!

With love,

Divina

P.S.
Please feel free after you have absorbed this book to check out the FREE bonus webinar! Free training videos and half-day event tickets are available when you opt in with your name and email at:
www.ReawakenYourAuthenticSelf.com

They are my way of saying, "Thank you for reading my book!"

Chapter One
Reawakening Your Authentic Self

"The spiritual path is not about getting anywhere;
it's about reawakening to who you are."
— Dr. Joshua David Stone

THE CURRENT STATE OF WORLD CONSCIOUSNESS

Literally, thousands of people on the planet are currently awakening to their highest selves and embracing their life purposes in service to humanity. There has been a popular rise in yoga, spiritual practices, books, and tapes, and many people have been successful in giving back to society once they have awakened their consciousness enough to be leaders and teachers in their fields. And I am very happy about that; it's great! It really is exciting to see great, wise souls and spiritual teachers in the media. Their work is truly inspirational and transformational, and it has helped me and countless others so much in our personal journeys. So much good is coming from mainstream media embracing spiritual subjects. Oprah Winfrey and her many guests on the subject of spirituality is just one example. More movies are coming out that have deep spiritual messages, like the film *Avatar*. That movie attracted so many viewers that it's very obvious how the world is hungry for a sense of spiritual connection and an awakening to their own consciousnesses and a higher purpose in living.

However, while there has been great improvement, a great many are also being left behind and still feeling challenged to grow because they haven't been introduced to the right strategies. Sure, many have read tons of spiritual books and gone to lots of seminars, but then why hasn't a spiritual reawakening happened for them yet? Why aren't they playing the game at a higher level? Why aren't many of us flowing in the knowledge of success? Of course, things take time to reach a considerable level of awakening, but it also takes the right action and understanding, and a lot of people are disconnected from that; they are still missing the key to unlock their own awakening. And sometimes that awakening is very difficult to unlock, but having it is really the only way for many of us to thrive in the this fast-paced, changing world that otherwise can pull us down.

After I reached a certain level of awakening, I was asked by Spirit in a dream to become a teacher. I am here to offer you an entire new way of looking at things in order for the deeper awakening in your life to happen. I want to shine light to clarify at a deeper level what you need. I have pieced together this unique perspective in this book, along with my academy program, to create a clear, simple, and understandable path to your authentic self. Along the way, I will offer you wisdom based on my own experiences on this journey so you can easily follow my footprints. I can tell you right now that one of the big issues I see is an unknown hunger for tremendous light and love that needs to be magnified in order for people's consciousnesses to follow through into their higher abundances in all areas of their lives. Simply learning without magnitudes of this nourishing energy is not enough, which is why I have created year-long programs to give you enough time to nourish your consciousness into a deeper level of experience and expression. When I first started to apply this information for myself, it was like magic! Books I reread I now understood differently; I implemented old information in new ways; the courses I attended were understood differently, and I started to attract the divine unfoldment of my abundance in a far more complete way.

Also, I want to say here that the people who will win in this fast-changing world are the ones determined to change their lives, no matter what! The people who will win are the ones willing to demand more from themselves than ever before and who will joyfully go the extra mile despite the discomfort! Mediocrity is the norm, but you are being called to excellence, which is part of your authentic makeup. The people who will win are the people who choose and decide to use the principles in this book and commit to practicing them as a long-term lifestyle, not as a temporary process.

The people who don't progress are the ones resistant to change because of their mindsets—I provide the solution to this problem in my programs. The people who lose are the ones who are not open to the new ideas and concepts of spirituality, who think they already know it all, and who are holding on to their egos and constantly making excuses to avoid looking at or dealing with the uncomfortable healing journey. Everything we want is outside of our comfort zones. These people are going to continue to suffer until life gets too unbearable, and then, maybe, they will budge for a change.

I am not pointing fingers here; quite frankly, I have been both a winner and a loser in certain areas of my life. On one hand, I was changing massively in one area of my life, but on the other hand, I was resistant to forgive until the Universe presented me with karma that cost me a lot in terms of my career and life in general. My journey was long and hard, and for years, I was on a quest to figure out the complete integration of what it takes to awaken my authentic self. Much of it was from following my heart in what to do and where to go, but mostly, the answers came from the spiritual practices that awakened the light and love within to channel wisdom from the Divine.

THE CHALLENGES I FACED AND MY WAY OUT

I can tell you that my life story wasn't easy. I dealt with tremendous challenges while I was growing up. In high school, I was depressed, lost, and didn't know exactly what to do in life or what the meaning of it all was. I felt so different from everybody else. I felt I couldn't mingle with many of my classmates so I kept to myself a lot. I carried so much negative density in my energy field that my energy level was a lot slower, my studies took longer than for most people, I needed to sleep a lot more, and I couldn't understand why I had such a scattered energy that made me unable to focus for long periods of time. I attracted negative people all the time, and when I graduated and left school, life on my own got even worse. I was so disoriented that I didn't even know what I wanted to do with my life, and I ended up living in a small studio after struggling to make ends meet while moving from living with one friend to another.

I always wanted to be financially successful, and I worked for numerous businesses in pursuit of such success. I always admired the success stories present in many companies, but I never really understood why it was so difficult for my own financial success to take off, so in very little time, I quit every single job. It felt as if I had no sense of direction for where to go or what my life purpose was. I felt an energy of desperation and loneliness, and all I had was my hunger for more, a willingness to move forward with strength, and a growing intuition that I listened to and cultivated further whenever I did listen to it.

As I applied the principles that you will read in this book, things slowly but surely got better. It is like that snowball analogy. You start with a small snowball, but as you roll it down a mountain, it gets bigger and bigger. Like a snowball, my success slowly but surely gained momentum as I aligned more fully to my authentic self.

But as you get bigger and stronger, life sometimes throws you bigger challenges and tests. I was faced with people around me trying to take advantage of me, and most challenging of all for me was that I had to become willing to forgive and let go of the anger that was eating me from within.

I don't know what your biggest challenge is, but you should ask yourself what it is because it is what is mainly blocking you from your authentic self. For me, as I said, it was the inability to forgive all the people taking advantage of me on all levels. I was holding a grudge and full of anger, bitterness, and thoughts of revenge. Although I frequently reminded myself of Jesus' ability to forgive even when he was being crucified, and Nelson Mandela's ability to forgive the people who imprisoned him for so many years, for some reason, those reminders were not enough to make me shift, so I had to learn the hard way.

I had to go through hell and back to be able to forgive. My anger was causing so many blockages in my life, including scattered energy, that made it hard to stay focused and present. I finally realized the damage I was causing in my own life, including the financial drain, the lack of presence, my closed off energy, and my disconnection to my inner channeling of my artistic talents. This situation became so painful that I was cornered; I had no choice but to forgive to release all this negativity and reconnect back to my power. Unfortunately, my way out meant first torturing myself deeply into trouble. I share this because I don't want you to do the same; you can, in this moment, give yourself a shortcut: you can forgive now; you can fix every single lesson now, and you don't have to dig yourself into deep trouble and suffering.

But most importantly, out of my tremendous struggle growing up, my intuition never left me, even though I didn't listen to it 100 percent of the time. Sometimes, I doubted it, but I'll tell you one thing: your intuition really is your way out and toward a deeper level of your authentic self. I invite you to let my message help you cultivate it; follow your intuitive heart always.

MY AND MY STUDENTS' SUCCESS STORIES

After the life-changing night I talked about in this book's introduction, where I held a ceremony to birth myself into the beginning of finding my authentic self, I felt a new rebirth in every single aspect of my life. Everything changed so drastically that I couldn't believe it. In a matter of a few short weeks, I saw my income increase just by having released certain energetic blocks within myself. I attracted into my life people who were so much more energetically-compatible to me, and I could discern better which people were not good for me and which were going to transform my level of success.

I couldn't believe my mental clarity. I was more telepathic; I could read the energies and thoughts of people around me, and I could channel my god given talents more fully and easily. I could focus clearly and stay present like I never was able to before. My friends noticed the difference within a few days after my transformation; it was the most amazing compliment I had ever received in my life. I was so proud of myself.

Emotionally, I could feel love for the entire planet and my love for myself was overwhelming. Sometimes, I find myself waking up at night with overwhelming loving feelings, and I experience bursts of love as well throughout the day, as if the Universe is making love to me and orgasmically expanding the love within my heart. My love and wanting to help the planet is so emotionally touching that it would, and still does, influence me to work for hours on end with a passionate joy and mission to share my love and talents with this world. It's an unbelievably fulfilling gift to awaken to that!

I channeled a diet from my highest self that physically transformed me from a size 12 to a size 4, which is considered tiny in this plus-sized society and especially for a 5'11" girl. Most girls have to starve themselves to stay that size, but I didn't. I still got my normal periods, my hair grew thicker, my skin looked more supple and vibrant, and I couldn't believe the amount of energy I was channeling into my body with this sacred spiritual diet. Most of my friends now say I look much younger. I'm currently thirty-three, but I could easily pass for twenty-three. I was able to concentrate better on what I was doing because I wasn't expending all my energy on digesting heavy meals. I was able to become more stable to serve others on a daily basis because of the extra energy I was able to channel and harness with a diet divinely revealed to me by my highest self.

Spiritually, I have a deeper connection with God and my highest self than I ever felt before. I can't believe how I have been given such a number of artistic talents as a spiritual being, plus clairvoyant abilities to tap into the spirit world, or the ability to channel from the spiritual, unseen plane. As a spiritually-expanded and more awakened being, I have the grace to transmit my artistic and creative abilities into teaching in my academy, artwork, costumes, clothing designs, singing, dancing, and performing—none of which were present when I started my spiritual journey at a very young age.

And I am not alone. Some of my friends and clients have embarked on the same journey and had tremendous success. Many students who have applied the strategies shared in this book and in my academy have achieved such a profound level of healing that it is like the difference between night and day to watch them. I have been so touched by their stories, and I am thrilled to say I am not alone in my success. They had such tremendous levels of transformation that I couldn't believe it when I saw them; they not only looked amazing from a physical standpoint, but they looked so much happier, their sense of confidence within themselves was so expanded that I couldn't even recognize them. All I could think was that these principles work, no matter who you are; all you have to do is decide to have the courage to apply them and learn to find enjoyment in the comfort and discomfort of the spiritual practices offered here.

My intention for you with my academy program is that you find greater fulfillment with your life purpose and be able to monetize it abundantly through reawakening your four bodies and changing your mindset around marketing and business. Please do check out my one-year and two-year programs to enhance these areas of your life on my website.

THE BIG PICTURE: THE INTRODUCTION OF THE FRAMEWORK

What is the meaning of the word "diet"? The word originally referred to a way of living, or thinking, or a day's journey. Although the word "diet" is often associated with food and painful failures to lose weight, and although this book does address food in the fourth chapter, dieting can be applied in all areas of your life, including the ones listed below. Please remember that dieting doesn't have to be the joyless journey often associated with it:

THE FOUR DIVINE DIETS:

- MENTAL DIET
- EMOTIONAL DIET
- PHYSICAL DIET
- SPIRITUAL DIET

Think of your authentic self as being like a tabletop. That tabletop cannot be sustained firmly or used for its purpose without a strong foundation—its four legs. The four legs holding up your authentic self are the four Divine Diets: mental, emotional, physical, and spiritual.

The Mental Diet is probably the most important aspect of your diet. It's the foundation to your success. Without thinking the right thoughts and beliefs, you cannot unlock the pathway to the right emotions. Without the right emotions, you cannot fully attract abundance to you or unlock the pathway to right action. Without right action, you cannot unlock the pathway to an energetic physical body, and without the right clean conditions in your physical body, you cannot completely integrate your spiritual body into the physical to awaken your authentic spiritual self fully. It all starts with the mind and a successful mindset. First, with the absence of thought through meditation so the right thoughts can come in; also, with divine thoughts that are positively inspired from within, and with great thoughts from people who have already traveled down their paths to success.

The Emotional Diet is the key to real success—not money. As Abraham, as channeled by Esther Hicks, says, the greatest gift you can give to the planet is your emotional wellbeing. The most successful people are the happiest people, not the monetarily richest people. When you're emotionally grateful, ecstatic, joyful, happy, and, overall, feeling all the good feelings that God has given you to feel, and you have developed those feelings to a point where they are sustained despite whatever is going on around you, you can be sure that things are going to prosper in your life even more because like attracts like. The three other bodies really are tools to make this most sacred emotional body, which attracts all abundance, to feel really, really good so this good feeling can attract everything you want! In this chapter, I am so excited to share with you how to become abundant emotionally in your life.

The Physical Diet is overlooked by many, and it's underestimated how powerfully it affects consciousness and your sense of aliveness in your body, and especially, how ecstatically good the emotional body can feel! You have no idea how good you can really feel if you are not in complete alignment with your Divine Physical Diet, which I will explain in this book, and in more detail, in my other events and yearly programs. What you put into your body directly affects your emotional feeling body because what you eat can either slowly numb your five senses or strengthen them. Without knowing it, as we age, we lose our five senses very slowly and gradually if we are not following a diet that strengthens them and our nervous system. Again, I want to stress that most people have no idea of the immense joy to be experienced in feeling alive and experiencing the full vibrancy of their five senses because they are feeding their bodies with dead food. This Divine Diet, the complete advanced version I teach in my seminars and programs, is nothing like anything you have heard before. I have channeled this diet from my highest self, and it is one of the most essential reasons I have been able to attract such emotional abundance into my life, which in turn attracts more prosperity to me in my business. Life is meant to be a sensuous experience; your senses and joy with everything in life will be enhanced! You will see, smell, touch, taste, and feel better!

I know that many people don't do anything to change their physical diets because the change is so gradual that they can't tell the difference after decades of slowly numbing their bodies and robbing themselves of the joy of vibrantly feeling their five senses, which is key to attracting more prosperity. In this chapter, I will delve into the Divine Diet that I truly know was given us to follow by Spirit so we could have perfect, radiant, ageless bodies filled with an alive feeling, fully-awakened five senses, good energy, and overall wellbeing.

The Spiritual Diet is a powerful technique I believe works the best when all the other three diets have been activated at a high level. In this area, we will explore the concepts of fasting, spiritual body activation meditations, sacred plant medicines or entheogens, and how they can call higher aspects of your soul into your physical being for true authentic self-awakening. These techniques will give you more presence and aliveness within your body than you have ever experienced before.

So there it is: a quick overview of this book. I am so excited to share with you how these four major body diet changes can be applied, how you can quickly and simply start to take action, and how you can finally transform your life!

OVERCOMING OUR BIGGEST OBSTACLES

So, now that you have gotten an idea of what this book is about, you're probably having many thoughts that are already blocking you from wanting to read on. So I wanted to address some thoughts that are either coming up for you right now, or will come up while you read.

THE VOICES IN YOUR HEAD:

"I DON'T HAVE THE MONEY"
Listen; we all have our budgets, but that doesn't mean you can't apply at least a small portion of what I am talking about with the money you've got. The hardest chapter will

probably be the diet chapter, and I can tell you that to start being healthy won't cost you very much. You can start with what you can afford and thank yourself for that. If you try long and hard enough, you will always find a way, and don't forget to ask people for help. Many people out there are willing to help, so don't be afraid to ask. Please also ask yourself, "How can I creatively buy these healthy foods or products with my budget?" Then watch your mind come up with an array of ways to get around your budget or financial situation. Finally, doing what is necessary for good health now will save you a ton of money in healthcare costs later; invest in your good health and it will pay off.

"IT SOUNDS SO UNCOMFORTABLE"

You know what? It's probably more uncomfortable to be in the situation you're in, but you're probably so used to it that you don't even feel it. The truth is that success comes with massive transformation and action, and if you're not feeling uncomfortable, you're not growing. The more discomfort you feel, the less it will eventually bother you, so embrace it and you will start loving it. Embrace the positive discomfort of growth and love what is; it makes everything easier. Learn to change your mindset to love the discomfort. Everything you want is just outside your comfort zone, and there is no reason why you can't enjoy it. You create your own reality within your mind. If you start to believe in statements such as "I love the discomfort of growth," "It's enjoyable to change," and "I love growing," it will make things easier because you're activating your mind to find ways to follow through. Remember the wise saying from Henry Ford, "Whether you think you can, or you think you can't—you're right."

"YOU CAN DO IT, BUT I CAN'T"

Yes, you can! You are a magnificent creation capable of great things. Start believing in yourself. I believe in you. Your beliefs have tremendous power and define your outcome. I can tell you that I have been where you are now. I remember my lack of self-worth and self-love, looking at so many successful people, going to their seminars, workshops, or concerts, and thinking that I would never be able to be like them; I believed I was not good enough to get on stage and speak, so I didn't bother, but the only reason they were successful was because they believed they could do it. I can tell you one thing, you are a creation of God who is loving and supporting you, and that is a very powerful thing; you are capable of immense amounts of success. You are capable of so much. Just do it anyway. Don't let thoughts like these slow you down. Just begin to state that you can, have faith, and trust in yourself and your creator. When you have non-supportive thoughts, observe them, but do it anyway.

"IT'S TOO COMPLICATED"

We all like complicating things and saying to ourselves that because something is too complicated, we won't try it, but I can tell you that things are simple if you simply state, "It's simple." Everything is simple if you believe it is. "Easy" and "simple" are states of mind. Just take it one step at a time and stop looking at the entire picture or you will be overwhelmed by thinking it's too complicated. What is it that you need to focus on now? It's baby steps; do one thing at a time. If you're still saying, "Yeah, but..." ask yourself, "Why is it that I'm making excuses?" Is it fear of the unknown? Lack of self-esteem, self-love, or self-worth? Find the root cause of it; start stating, "It's simple" anyway. Don't listen to your mind, and start doing it anyway; you will gain momentum.

"I DON'T HAVE THE WILL"

The only thing stopping you is this statement. You are a creation of the most powerful creator. Say you can and you will. Grow into it by developing a strong enough why.

What big enough reasons in your life can you think of that trigger you to have the will? You have some will to start with. Everybody does, so tap into it, and expand it with habit and focusing on your big enough why. Write down all of the things you really want in your life—the things that motivate you and move you. Do your children, spouse, family, or friends make you want to have more will to grow? Write down everything that gives you that will and motivation. Then read your list every morning and go about your day making those things happen! Yes, you can; don't forget that. Let me also give you a good hint to give you the will: learning to enjoy the journey now instead of waiting for your goals to happen is always an enhancement to your will!

As for anything else I might have not covered that is stopping you from continuing, all I can say is this: Yes, you can; you can create enjoyment in the journey, so don't let a silly thing like a negative thought stop you; you are a powerful creation of God, the universal force (or whatever you want to call it). Even if you don't feel like you are powerful, I can tell you that I have accomplished many things of which I thought I wasn't capable. Believe in yourself always. I believe in you, and your creator definitely does. We both want to see you succeed, so go for it, despite any fears or disempowering thoughts. You will then see that you really can do it.

Here is the difference between successful and unsuccessful people: Successful people go for it anyway; they generate as much joy in the moment as they can, despite any fear or thoughts, and they choose to have faith and affirm empowering beliefs!

Chapter Two
The Divine Diet for the Mental Body

"The mind creates bondage, or the mind creates liberation."
— Sai Baba

THE FOUNDATION OF YOUR SUCCESS

This chapter is by far the most important chapter in this book because everything starts with a thought, and that thought is the foundation that catapults you to your success in all areas of your life. Thoughts will help you access and cultivate your authentic self, which is your true and limitless power and potential, and which is waiting to awaken because you already have it inside yourself! This chapter is about activating a mental body that serves you and empowers you from the inside out to achieve every goal in the most effortless manner. I don't mean that no effort will be required, but this information is the shortcut to relieve you from wasted energy and suffering, so you can achieve your goals in the most effortless and most enjoyable way.

The opening quote of this chapter by Sai Baba is a very profound statement. You can either be the master of your mind or the mind can be the master of you. Only with a mind subservient to your authentic self can success be accomplished. The mind creates thoughts, and through positive or negative thoughts, positive or negative emotions are created. These "e-motions" create the motion or physical action to manifest as well as attracting positive or negative experiences. So a liberated mind is one that thinks empowering thoughts, and those thoughts influence the emotional body to experience the necessary blissful emotion that fuels you to take action more effortlessly as well as attract more abundance to you. A mind in bondage is one that thinks of fearful thoughts and disempowering beliefs, which in turn create an unhealthy emotional body full of fear and limits the amount of energy to take divine action, think, and channel clearly for your divine unfoldment, and attract the abundance you deserve.

So before I continue, what is your authentic self? In essence, it is the space, the nothingness, and the stillness within you; it is the observer that has no content, no thought. It is where everything comes from, and it is your true power. So if you're wondering why your life is a mess or why you keep repeating the same mistakes, I would suggest you learn to strengthen the connection to your true power; begin by choosing positive thoughts that come from your loving authentic self to create liberation; then you will start to see a true and lasting transformation in your life.

Everything in your life, good or bad, is the result of a mind either controlled by ego thoughts or thoughts of the Divine, or a combination of both. Most people are operating from a place of disconnection with their authentic selves/sources of power. That's why it is so important to adopt the lifestyle that reconnects you back to your authentic self or source of true power. So ask yourself, "Which part of myself am I creating from? Am I creating from my fake self, which is limited consciousness and perception that sees itself as limited, as something to fear, not worthy enough, and separate from the universal flow? Or am I operating from fear of things not working out?"

When you are creating from a perspective of fear, you are operating from a thought world in your mind of old negative thought patterns, stories from your past that you haven't let go of, and negative social programming that keeps looping in your mind to sabotage you and keep you disconnected from this limitless source of possibility! This perspective truly is blocking you from creating and being a clear channel for powerful manifestation of your mission here on earth. These thoughts of limitation—sometimes, we are not even aware that they are negative thoughts—are making us operate from a place that is not even real, and it comes from your mind's addictive need always to be thinking and processing things. This negativity is very dangerous because it will create a reality in your outside world that you do not wish to have. So, that said, I want you to come from that awareness and take a step back from this world to realize these negative thoughts are not you, but they are thoughts you have subconsciously chosen that have been living there a long time. You can transform them into joyful empowering thoughts, and then you will see how they were previously affecting your results by comparison.

Every single moment of your life, it truly is your choice whether to create from a place of limitless power and the authenticity of who you really are. You are the infinite potential of your life; you have no limits; you are fully resourceful in creating what you want, and creating from this knowingness and awareness is where the source of your power really is.

It's important to understand that the Universe is always lovingly supporting you and talking to you through your intuition and inner knowing. Your inner wisdom is always guiding you, but if you have loud and negative mental chatter, you cannot allow this wisdom to guide you at a deeper level because it's being blocked some or most of the time. Let me give you a metaphor to explain this. Think of your authentic self and your power as a pond. You can see instructions written in the bottom of a pond for your life to succeed, but because the pond ripples (representing mental chatter), you can't really read the instructions. Only when the surface is calm do you realize you have access to your authentic self or true power. Therefore, it's important to calm the mind to observe your life from a greater awareness and perspective, instead of being consumed by the waves and storms of old thought patterns. It's all about being aware of your thoughts and cultivating this awareness through meditation instead of identifying with the thoughts.

Through awareness, you are able to make a more empowered choice; you are able to have a higher perception of how things are and to listen to your inner wisdom and your creator's guidance, just like if you were tuning a radio station; you can then "download" information such as books that have already been written within you, as well as songs, art pieces already within you, or whatever reflects the talent you have, and at a higher and more polished level. All you have to do is carve them out, just like Michelangelo talked about with his sculptures. He said the piece of art was already there; all he had to do was carve it out of the marble. So, in essence, your life becomes more effortless because you don't have to think about your life running around in circles, confused or concerned about whether you are doing the right thing or not; when you're not blocked with ego or dark heavy energy, the flow of your life purpose just effortlessly comes through you, so you then become a clear channel for the Divine to unfold through you.

The question now is: How do you get yourself to the point where you are not at the mercy of negative thoughts, the unhappy story, the drama, or being overwhelmed by limiting beliefs and thoughts that tell you you're not good enough, which emotionally drain you and make you manifest unwanted negative emotion and then, eventually, block you from taking actions toward a successful life? How do you get greater access to your authentic self or true power?

In this chapter, we will explore the following major components of the Divine Diet for your mental body:

1. Life Purpose
2. Faith

3. Goal Setting
4. Personal Power
5. Habit
6. Meditation
7. Affirmation and Visualization
8. Prayer
9. Association with Positive People
10. Joyous Presence

LIFE PURPOSE

People whose minds are firmly focused on their life purposes are aiming their lives toward authentic awakenings. Such people know deep down that they have sacred divine missions to accomplish. Many don't know what their life purposes are yet, or they do know their life purposes, but those purposes have not fully been expressed yet due to lack of integration of all four bodies. If you're one of those people, my message will help you awaken deeper to it. Your life purpose is the most important component to be crystal clear on before you take any action or even set your goals because it is the essence of why you were born. A life purpose not manifested is truly a wasted life. What is the point of going through your entire life working at a job you don't love? For most of us, our job is where we spend the majority of our life, so why not spend that time doing what we love and are meant to do in life?

Having a proper mindset to fulfill your life purpose should be your starting point so that everything else can manifest to the best of its ability. If you want to manifest faster, if you want to be prosperous in every sense of the word, then having a compelling life purpose and meaning in your life is everything.

To acquire the right mindset, create a purposeful, meaningful statement of why you are here so when you wake up in the morning, you live life with a focused goal and you live to the fullest. Then you can give it your all at every moment until the moment you fall asleep.

For me, personally, discovering my life purpose was an evolution. I really didn't know why I was here on the planet or what I truly came to do. I knew I was an artist of some sort because I could draw and was interested in the performing arts, but I really didn't express it fully; most of my talent was dormant, and I didn't make any sort of profound connection in terms of what I was meant to do with it. I also didn't think I was talented enough to change lives or inspire people with my art, so I didn't think my life purpose was serving others.

If, at this point, you don't know your life purpose, that's okay. If you don't know what you want to do with your life, it's okay to do the best you can in writing down your life purpose, even without the career aspect in mind. For now, your life purpose could be to reawaken to your life purpose through reading this book and being kind to people the best way that you can. As you activate your authentic self more and as you reawaken to your god given talents more, you will notice your life purpose evolve and change as it did for me.

I'm going to ask you to pay really close attention to this section of this book, and read it over and over until it just drives you. Post sticky notes all over your house with the essence of it; frame it and hang it up on a wall; post it on your Facebook page, to Twitter, or whatever. Just pay attention because your success starts with this deep passion for your life purpose and meaning that I'm about to talk to you about. Unbelievable success starts with the psychology of your emotionally compelling life purpose and meaning, which create a deep drive in you to achieve what you were assigned to do here on this planet. Many different beautiful life purposes and meanings exist for different people who are connected to their god given talents. Know that the primary life purpose beneath all of that for everyone is the same: to awaken and be authentically you so you can express that uniqueness with your god given talents and be of service to the planet.

Also, be aware of disempowering life purposes. To explain these, let me begin by telling you that you first need to accept that your problems are never going to go away. If the purpose of your life is to achieve comfort, your million dollars instantly, and a house on the beach, you're not going to find yourself authentically happy. Remember, happily achieve, not achieve for happiness. I'm not saying there is anything wrong with wanting to be comfortable, but if you're trying to escape your problems, authentic joy is never going to happen, and that desire is not coming from your authentic self in the first place. Problems are to be embraced and loved because they are here to stay so you can learn and grow. Problems become not a problem at all with the right perspective. They are to be enjoyed, blessed, and something to be grateful for, not dreaded. For example, excellent health requires some level of discomfort, like working out six times a week in the gym. Okay, then accept that that's what it's going to be for the rest of your life. (Don't panic; you'll grow into it, and through habit and by creating liberating thoughts in your mind that come from your authentic self, you'll start to enjoy it!)

Here are other examples: you crashed your car, you need to fly twelve long hours to a wealth seminar, you lost your arm, you're sick, you're broke. Be okay with whatever it is; don't be attached to how things are supposed to be. Why should you let whatever it is stop you from moving forward?

23

Is it really stopping you? Or did you just decide to stop? Why not make the decision to act from the courageous aspect of your authentic self to overcome anything, instead of having that lazy "I want to be in my comfort zone" attitude.

The truth is that it's not the problem that's the problem. The problem is who you are being. The authentic you is bigger than any problem. You can have a ton of problems, but you decide whether you will let them paralyze you. Are you letting them stop you from being an authentic great human being who cares for others and works joyfully and diligently in service to humanity with your own gifts and talents? How are you handling these so called problems that are showing up in your life? Are you deciding to let them handle you?

If you're going through something really tough in your life, I can tell you that it's a gift because it's cornering you to face *you* and bring out what you're really made of. You can create joy instead of fear by focusing on positive thoughts, so have the courage to enjoy the challenge! Not with just one foot in, but all the way—throw yourself in it forever and completely; I guarantee you that is where the joy is. You know we didn't incarnate on this planet to accumulate things and be comfortable; things are great, and sometimes comfort is great, but the greatest gift is you and the full demonstration of you. The purpose and meaning of your life is to demonstrate being a person of joyful excellence every single moment of your life. Your life purpose can involve being the best singer, actress, painter, speaker, etc., but it ultimately comes down to being the best authentic you.

What does the best authentic you look like? What does a person who rises above mediocrity and is made of over-the-top excellence look like? It's a person who is not afraid to be who he or she really is in front of people. It's a person who is not afraid to love and enjoy life fully, no matter what. It's a person who puts serving others first and puts aside the fear of not being good enough to say what he has to say. It's a person who is no longer afraid of public speaking, leadership, or community service, a person who is fully present and focused in teaching others through her talents and abilities. It's a person who gets up really early in the morning and goes to bed late at night and spends all day giving her all with all her heart, mind, and soul 100 percent of the time without wanting to stop, without giving much focus and attention to a body that wants to sleep or take a nap or that's aching. It's a person who has made the decision to be fully focused and present in this moment as best he can for the love and sake of service to others. It's a person who cares enough to be determined to find a way to smile and be enthusiastic even when problems seem so dark and gloomy. It's a person who is willing to be the giver, the lover, the consoler, the teacher, and the leader because she understands that it's in giving that we receive. It's the person who is not afraid of creating products and services for people and is willing to figure out how to make things happen even if he doesn't know how to go about it. It's the person who is not afraid to ask questions when she doesn't understand things. It's the person who is fully immersed in a subject he is passionate about without giving in to distraction. It's a person who is courageous enough to admit when her head is starting to talk nonsense to her to try to make excuses not to do something. It's a person who is so fed up with all the excuses, all the laziness, all the "I could haves" and "should haves" and makes them into "musts" instead. It's a person who engages his emotional fire and passion to fight joyfully for the light of God within himself. And you know what? Becoming such a person is as simple as deciding to act and behave that way, until it becomes a habit.

God and the Universe are just waiting for you to wake up, to have had enough of living a mediocre life. Because you deep down know who you are—unbelievably magnificent, beyond excellent, outstanding—your ability to accomplish whatever you set out to accomplish can be grand, you can take on much bigger things than you have so far, and your ability to develop further who you really are can be done in a prosperous way.

I want to remind you of the incredibly amazing soul that you are. I know your amazing spirit is there and your potential is there, and I know you can do it; you're bigger than you think, and it's always easier than you think. What are you afraid of? Is it speaking up when you know someone is talking nonsense? Is it getting in front of people? Is it writing a book? Is it choosing to enjoy your life no matter what? What is it? You can give your all despite the discomfort because you're an amazing creation of God/the Universe! Be bold and dominate your discomfort; enjoy yourself in it! You can enjoy it because you can create whatever experience you want within your mind. Is it the gym that's not been seeing you lately? Are you not accepting the discomfort of it? Okay, then try it; visualize yourself effortlessly doing it and enjoying it. With all the emotional intensity you can, say, "I will enjoy this experience!" Yeah, that's right; you will enjoy it, with the challenges and all. Imagine yourself accomplishing it. How does that feel in your mind? Doesn't it feel good to be free, to enjoy things you once thought you couldn't? I can tell you that when you're in your mission and you've decided to dive in completely without holding back, and when you're fully focused to complete your mission or whatever you came to do on this planet, that's the greatest feeling in the world. I don't care how much pain surrounds you; you're in it, you're free, and the emotion that comes with being authentically you is the greatest gift. It doesn't matter whatever problems you have, what family member you lost, or whatever other circumstances exist; you've got the only thing you can truly hang on to, and that's giving joyfully through your life purpose; it's being yourself and not letting anyone stop you from your mission because you're fully present, you're immersed, and your doubt and fear is replaced with your faith that everything is going to be all right. And yeah, you can have fun and enjoy the moment, even when there is discomfort present. That's the true purpose, meaning, and deep drive that you need to adopt in your life. That's your authentic self.

So take a moment here and perhaps take out your journal to write, but before you write anything, take five or ten minutes to be silent and listen in on what's going on within yourself. Where do you feel the pain in your life? Are you happy? Are you sad? Maybe angry? Are you frustrated? On a scale of 1-10, how productive are you, and are you giving it your all? Are you afraid to be really you when you walk down the street or when you are around people? Do you walk tall and proud and sit up straight with confidence? Are you confident that the Universe supports your dreams and you can achieve whatever it is you want? Write what comes to your mind and see where you're at and where you're wanting to be. Remember that when you are authentically you, this goal is instant because you're giving it your all, your focus, your presence, and all your love and sweat at every moment of your life. You continue to make that decision at every moment for the rest of your life. You've already won; everything else will come and go, but if you have you, the authentic you, you have everything.

I want to share a profound and important dream I had with you that perhaps will spark a deeper understanding. In this dream, I was being attacked by dark forces. I couldn't understand why I couldn't shake them off, why they had power over me, or how they were able to steal light from me. I finally got fed up and intuitively called all of my presence and focus into the moment; then I said, "No. That's enough!" I said it with all the emotional strength I had, and I didn't feel mentally scattered or idle anymore. I simply chose to let that go. I chose to be intensely and fully focused and present in the now with all the energy and strength I had and commanded the dark force to leave. Then, finally, I felt my entire soul get in my body, and so much light was beaming off of me that the dark forces just left. The energy made me feel like I was a bull charging against dark forces—like I was a bull that was fed up, so no one was going to get in my way because the energy that I was carrying was so strong, courageous, bold, and full of light and full of the everything that I was that there was no way anything could stop me.

I share this dream with you because I believe it's a powerful metaphor for being authentically you, when you're fully present, fully focused, passionate, enthusiastic, determined, and immersed in your mission and not distracted, idle, or lazy. When you're authentically you, you're really calling your entire being into your body to fulfill your life purpose more completely. It's like building a muscle, the muscle of growing into your authentic self. It takes effort to call in whom you really are if you haven't done it and you are used to being slightly asleep under the wheel or idle, but you can do this! What this dream taught me was that by doing this, you are activating so much light within your being that it protects you from the dark energies that unfortunately surround this planet.

I'm also reminded of the Michael Jackson video "Bad." If you haven't watched it in a long time, go watch it again on YouTube. In that video, Michael Jackson expressed so much of his talent and was clearly in alignment with his life purpose; you can see how he was calling upon so much energy and his presence and focus in every single moment of that video. It is with that kind of intensity, power, and focus that we should approach our journey in life and whatever problems are thrown at us. We really can build our presence, vibration, and intensity to that level of passion and expression. And really, like the music video suggests, if you do that, then who is the badass?

Your life purpose, awakened or not, is meant to be fully expressed, to shine so brightly that it takes people's breaths away to watch you express it. A fully expressed life purpose, mission, and god given talents comes from a soul that has chosen to give its all and rise above mediocrity. It's time for you to take your life purpose to another level, by either committing to find it or committing to enhance it. Write out your life purpose and put it somewhere you can read it daily.

FAITH

Before I introduce any other concept or any other technique that will help manifest more of who you are into your life or your dreams and goals, the single most important mindset to have is faith and trust that we are living in a supportive and loving Universe and that the abundance of the Universe is yours to claim. I just talked about the power of knowing your life purpose. If you resonate with what I wrote about it, you must know somewhere deep inside that your life purpose was given to you by your creator. That said, you must also develop a belief and trust in your creator, a deep knowing that your creator—God, the Universe, or whatever you want to call it—has big dreams for your life, has 100 percent backup support for you, and doesn't want you to limit yourself from going for big ambitious goals to make your mark on this planet. Your bright future is yours to claim, affirm, and visualize because you have faith and trust that the Universe is 100 percent behind you to deliver what you want. If you don't embrace or believe that the Universe will deliver to you the dreams that are divinely aligned with your life purpose, then that is exactly what you will attract—nothing. If you hold a vibration of faith that things will work out, then that is what the Universe will give you—what you want. Like attracts like, so it is time to hold your faith in the unfolding of your life purpose with total and complete firmness.

Now please listen carefully because here is where most people fall into the lack of faith trap. They don't realize that by being afraid, they are blocking what they want either partially or entirely. Many are afraid that they never will get what they want or afraid because they think they are going to fail; that belief is what blocks them and attracts failure to them. That distinction is very important to understand. Faithful people, however, have no fear—only love and excitement in their hearts because they know they are living in a supportive, loving Universe, and they know that having faith within their hearts will open the doors for them to access that loving abundance being offered to them. Remember not to put a lid on that abundance with fear and doubt; simply let go and trust that your goals and visions are heard by your creator and your highest self and they are in the process of being manifested. You then need to take lots of faithful action, keep visualizing and affirming your outcome, and continue to have faith in yourself and God. Be in a state of love and loving every minute of your life in your heart so your desired outcome can flow in much faster. Faith and love are such highly vibrational energetic states that they act like magnets to attract what you want faster into your life.

Believing that things will go well activates God's power, while fear activates the enemy's power or negative energy. It's up to you to choose which one you want. It takes the same amount of energy to believe as it does to fear. Why not believe that the Universe only wants to give you a flood of overwhelming success and abundance for all eternity? It really does! When you believe it, you will see it!

The problem I see when most people do affirmations and visualizations is that they do them without any faith! They are affirming and they are visualizing, but they are not trusting that these tools are activating powerful attractions to them. For example, a person may affirm "I am overflowing with energy and abundance. I am a millionaire." But a voice in her head says, "No, I'm not" and cancels out or weakens the affirmation activation. The way around this situation is to understand consciously that using affirmations or visualizations is not lying to yourself. You are activating and opening doors to an aspect of yourself that already exists! You must trust and have faith while you activate through affirmation and visualization. Once it becomes an active part of your consistent lifestyle to affirm and visualize daily, you will see the energetic difference within and without. Faith not only applies to your affirmations and visualizations, but to every other technique or action you take toward your goals. Be aware of your fears because where there is fear, there is a lack of faith, gratitude, and love.

Fear and faith have something in common. They both ask you to believe in something you cannot see yet. Whichever you choose to activate will show you its faithful or fearful outcome. Have the courage to believe in yourself and to have faith that your brighter future is on its way!

GOAL SETTING

After you have written your life purpose, you are aware that you are here to fulfill a specific mission on this planet, and you have deeply embraced your faith in your creator's support in manifesting your mission, it is time for you to set some big goals to achieve that mission. Think big and expect a miracle as a demonstration of your faith. A life without big goals and a strong foundation of faith is a life that will never prosper. Those who end up broke and unsuccessful usually never had clear goals, never focused on their goals daily, and lacked faith.

Those who set goals tend to make more money and are far more successful than those who don't. Why is this? Because we have built-in focusing mechanisms that attract what we focus on. This fact is very much related to the Law of Attraction. When you set goals, you have something very clear to focus on. If you have no goals, you have nothing to focus on and you will get nothing. Obviously, your goals should stem from your life purpose. Make it a point to set yearly goals and focus on them daily. Yearly goals break down the time long enough, yet short enough, for you to accomplish enough tasks to move you on to the next level of goals for the next year. Writing down your goals is important; it makes them more real. Write them in your journal or on an index card and read them daily, morning and night. Your subconscious is more receptive in the morning and at night, so reading them at those times will make them more powerful. Also, note that your goals may change from time to time, so give yourself permission to change and rewrite them as needed.

Now that you know and have written down your goals, it's time to focus on why you want these goals. Goal setting without having a strong enough "Why?" behind doing them is not as effective. People who achieve their goals quickly and effectively have a strong enough "Why do it?" to motivate their actions. What moves you to action? Is it your family, your friends, or your sense of self-worth? Are you fed up with life's injustices? Write down a list of why you want to achieve your goals. Circle the top three strong enough "whys," and then write them below your goals to remind you why you are taking action to achieve them.

PERSONAL POWER

After you have embraced the power of goal setting and a big enough "why" to accomplish those goals, it's important to be aware of the incredible power you have within you called your "personal power" or "will." Your big enough "why" is already activating your personal power at a higher level. But when you fully embrace and have an understanding that you have personal power within you to achieve all you want in your life, despite the challenges, the sky is the limit.

So what is personal power? Personal power is nothing more than using your conscious mind to direct energy into your physical body to move toward your desired goals. Personal power involves an attitude of strength to keep doing your conscious action despite negative, old habitual patterns or uncomfortable circumstances. To be truly authentic in the expression of your highest self is to own your power at all times. All enlightened beings hold their power. It is the nature of a sound and healthy person.

Part of owning your power is understanding that you already possess it because you are a divine creation of God, capable of accomplishing greatness. It is also about understanding that you have three minds: 1) the subconscious or non-reasoning mind, which will habitually do good or bad and is the subservient mind that develops habit, 2) the conscious mind, which decides on what action to take, and 3) the superconscious or all knowing mind, which divinely gives messages through dreams or channeling to the conscious mind.

In order to master the subconscious mind, so you can program positive habits that move you toward your desired goals, you must be able to own your personal power through your conscious mind. Most people let their subconscious minds run their lives, either because they don't have a clear goal in front of them, don't own their personal power or even know they have it, don't have a big enough why to do things, or simply don't have faith or enough belief that they can manifest their dreams through positive thought and visualizing what they want in life.

It's important to emphasize here that personal power first comes from having a strong enough "why" for why you want to achieve your goals, and then from making a decision and taking action. Decision is key. Once you decide to do something with enough emotional power behind it because why you want to do it is strong enough that you will take action, then that decision will lead you to own your personal power. Decision allows you to have more power over your life instead of letting others have power over you. If you haven't decided what you want, then others will do it for you.

It is equally as important to mention here the nature of life and how it applies to personal power. Personal power has a warrior spirit attached to it. Warriors engage in battles, so if that's the case, then what is the battle about? Life has two opposing forces: 1) God, the Universe, goodness, and light, and 2) darkness, ego, and negative forces. Life is a battle of light vs. darkness. Owning your power allows you to grow into more positive energy, and it allows your authentic self to reflect more of your creator within your being. Personal power is the number one force that allows you to bridge the gap more effectively so you can reach where you want to be. It's your sword as a warrior of light to fight the negative and awaken more of the positive. I also want to clarify, so as to not confuse you, that although terms like "warrior" and "battle" can sound very serious, your "sword" could very well be "fun," "joy," "enthusiasm," "excitement," or "love," which lightens the path to owning your personal power and allows that power's energy to be even more explosively effective.

Owning your power doesn't have to be complicated. Know your goals, your big enough why; read them every day, and then after you know where you're going, simply state and re-declare your decision that you will own your personal power no matter what. You can say something like, "I own my power 100 percent. My will and God's will stand as one, so nothing will stop me." Another saying might be, "I am surrounded by the power of God, and His celestial beings protect me now, so nothing can stop me from achieving what I set out to do today." You get the idea; make up your own saying that works for you, or use these statements if you like them. Affirmations have tremendous power when said out loud with emotional intensity. Make sure that they are enveloped in faith, and believe that you do possess your personal power and see yourself accomplishing your goals. It is time to quit letting anything in this Universe stop you from expanding the light that you so richly deserve in your life.

HABIT

After you develop your personal power, you will develop what is called discipline. Conscious action toward your goals develops habit over time, which makes things easier for you to follow through with. It takes twenty-one days to form a soft habit, and, of course, the longer you do it, the easier it gets. "Yes, okay, Divina; tell me something I don't know already!" Yes, you might be saying that, and you have probably heard that you need to set good habits a million times, but boy, I hope to shed new light on the subject and, hopefully, encourage you to set new habits. By the end of this section, I challenge you to decide to change a limiting habit into a more supportive one!

Gosh, if there is anything more important than habit, let me know because I believe this baby is everything, and it plays a big role in activating your mental body for success. As discussed earlier, habit is directly connected to the subconscious mind of the mental body. (We have a subconscious, conscious, and superconscious mind.) Some of us have so many old habits that we start to identify them as part of us. This kind of identity with habit can make or break us, depending on the habit. This section on habit is going to set up a powerful understanding in your mind and set you up for the following chapters on meditation, affirmation, and visualization.

So, first of all, what is habit? As the dictionary states, it's a recurrent pattern of behavior that is acquired through frequent repetition. Habit is related to the subconscious mind, and the subconscious mind's ability to program the body to repeat behavior in an effortless way is astoundingly powerful. It is so important for you to understand that if you want to be successful with the mental diet, you must build some major daily habits in order to activate your authentic power. Some of these habits are: always doing your best, positive thinking, having faith and trust in the Universe, enthusiasm, courage, meditation, affirmation, and visualization. I can tell you that daily practice is key. Your habits will gain so much momentum that within six months' time, they will be such easy tasks that you won't even think about them and they will be as second nature as breathing. The energy of these practices will be so ingrained in you that the suggestions of them will automatically overflow into your daily life. In fact, if you stop doing them, it will feel very awkward to you and you will crave returning to them.

The hardest part is to start. Most people quit before they are able to create a habit, but I will share with you the secret, even if you can't find a strong enough why to do it, for getting beyond that point: JUST DO IT! It's usually easier than you think. I cannot tell you how many ceremonies and rituals I have done in which I said, "This is the special day when I will start doing this habit every single day," or "I will start on my birthday," (or New Year's or the first of the month). I can tell you that none of that really works. You don't need a special day like New Year's to start. When you say such things, you're just creating the habit of putting it off for a special date, and that special date will never come because you'll keep putting it off.

The habit starts now. Don't let your negative thoughts stop you. Don't leave it till tomorrow. I can tell you that when you start now, that is where the true power lies. You don't need to put it off until you're ready because you will never be ready. If you think you don't have a strong enough will to keep you going, remember that you will always have the power of this moment to just do it. Don't think about it too much, and just remember the massive benefits you will get and all of the things that will get better in your life when you commit to your new habit.

Let me tell you my own personal discovery story about habit and how it changed my life. Probably the most difficult habit I had to form was doing the original hot yoga six times a week. The original hot yoga is one of the most challenging exercise programs, and it is performed in a hot room. It's quite uncomfortable when you begin to practice it because you're not use to it. Personally, I went back and forth, quitting and starting it again for about six months. When I finally decided to just do it and not pay attention to my distracting thoughts of why it was boring to go or that I was too tired to get out of bed, things started to change. I realized that all I had to do was make the decision that I was going to get up every morning, observe the moment, and not get caught up in my negative thoughts but stay in love and peace. They were just thoughts and not the real me. I also finally accepted the positive pain and discomfort and decided I was just going to observe them. Pretty soon, I was doing the original hot yoga six times a week, and now it's been over three years that I've been doing it. Today, I cannot believe how I just automatically wake up and go; it's a no brainer and it's so amazing how easy it feels to do it because the habit is so strong.

Later on, I added the habit of saying, "I love yoga," and what I appreciated about it every morning I went to do it. I also created a habit of smiling when I did yoga and thinking about how it was nurturing me. I created a habit of it being fun. The more I reinforced the pattern, the stronger and more effortless the habit became of enjoying such an intense workout. Creating a habit of making things fun in your mind is crucial to becoming unstoppable in your career and personal life.

I find it so unfortunate when I explain all this to people, but they don't take action to change their negative habits of creating a suffering reality by not enjoying their jobs or lives. Life can be enjoyed simply by a change of attitude and deciding to explore within how you can make it fun. People often identify their negative thoughts and lack of enjoyment so closely to their personalities that they mistake their bad habits for their identities. You really can change your habits one step at a time.

I really want to say here that once you begin a habit, it gets easier, and no matter how difficult it feels at first, it will feel easier very soon. Don't give up until your habit has been set in place. That said, now that you understand the importance of habit, please read on and explore the deep importance of making meditation, affirmation, and visualization part of your daily habits.

THE SUNFLOWER OF POSITIVE EMOTIONS MEDITATION

What is meditation exactly, and what can it do for you? Meditation is the experience of having communion with the Divine when the mind ceases to be dominated by its usual mental chatter. Think again for a moment about a pond; when the pond ripples, it is difficult to see through the pond, but when the pond is still, you can see clearly through it. This is what meditation does; it stills the mind of its usual chatter so you are able to have more clarity.

"The Sunflower of Positive Emotions Meditation" is my own personal twist on basic meditation itself. I find it to be more powerful than just meditation itself, and I am so excited to share this technique with you, but before I dive into what it is, I want to mention some important information about meditation.

The number one practice I recommend you do so you can have a balanced mental body is to meditate daily for twenty to thirty minutes once or twice a day. I personally enjoy twice a day. Meditation is a fundamental key for some of the most successful people in the world and is mentioned as a key component to success in almost every self-help book worth reading.

Meditation is not the latest fad; it has stood the test of time, and it has been around for thousands of years, if not since the early beginnings of humanity. Even if you don't believe in God, or the Universe, or you have some other belief system, meditation is an important practice to enlightenment, and without question, it will surely awaken your authentic self and expand your inner intuition to knowing the exact thing you are meant to be doing in this very moment. What meditation does is keep us in touch with the teacher or God/Universe within. It opens up higher energy sources and recharges us. The popular book *A Course in Miracles* talks about how we have limited perception and perception depends on our energy level or vibration. Meditation is the way to keep our energy at its highest. It really awakens the ability to hear that small inner voice that is constantly trying to guide us through our loud ego thoughts that can distract us from truth.

Also, please note that meditation is highly recommended as a lifestyle; it's not something you just do once for an hour and then automatically you're enlightened. Be patient with it; expect a miracle from it, even if it takes several years. As you do it slowly, your true power—which comes from awakening your authentic self—will build substantially to a level where it's so easy for you to flow into the knowingness of what to do at every moment to direct you to a higher level of success in your life.

The beauty of meditation is that as you observe your thoughts flowing by in your mind, instead of identifying with those thoughts, you start to strengthen your authentic self, which is the observer. In other words, your higher consciousness becomes more awakened and starts to see that you are not your thoughts; you are far deeper than them, and your thought processes are only but a part of the totality of who you are.

I truly know from experience that meditation is one of the strongest foundations to activate your authentic self, and although many books have been written on the subject, I will stick to the essence of what has helped me the most and offer you simple exercises you can use to start making meditation part of your life today. It is probably one of the most profound practices you can do for yourself, yet at the same time, it's something that you have to be patient with; don't expect to be perfect at it or to be completely able to terminate your thoughts in one sitting when you start. Make meditation a vital part of your daily lifestyle, even if it's only fifteen minutes a day. Reminder: Irregular practices often don't build momentum or give you the more permanent transformation that regular practice does.

Meditation will increase your intuition and your ability to make the right decisions. It really is like an inner knowing sharpener that refreshes you, and once you begin it, you will be able to perform at deeper levels than if you don't practice it on a regular basis. It also allows Spirit to enter through you and give you divine ideas through channeling. Where empty space exists, so does the opportunity for Spirit to give you divine suggestions. Esther Hicks, who channels Abraham, which is a collective consciousness of beings, talks in her book *Ask and It Is Given* about how daily meditation for nine months straight opened her ability to channel! I was impressed and really hooked on meditation after that because it really allowed me to understand its true power.

Everyone with tremendous talent really has open channels to channel from the Divine. If you are looking to live the life you are truly meant to live, then daily meditation is a given. A life without a lifestyle of meditation is really a poor life that is not awakening to higher levels of channeling the Divine for the purpose of expressing your life purpose and talents at a higher level for humanity.

Another aspect of meditation I have found to be quite powerful is that it provides an opportunity to center yourself with the energy of peace. Peace is the foundation of happiness and wellbeing. When you're at peace, no matter what, and you're taking the time to cultivate it through meditation, you will allow the abundance of the Universe to come to you because you are not blocking it with worry or stress. Take the time to find peace in your meditations and you will find joy well up easily.

So now let me address what I mean by "The Sunflower of Positive Emotions Meditation." I wanted to share with you a meditation I created that has changed my life and really enhanced my vibration immensely. Most basic meditations that are taught focus on turning your attention to one point of focus, usually your breath, and when you're distracted by thoughts, to go back simply to observing your breath. In this very simple meditation technique, you're in a chair, sitting straight up, and wearing comfortable clothing. This technique is what Esther Hicks did to open up to channel her spiritual guide Abraham.

What I have noticed, however, is that by using the "Sunflower of Positive Emotions Meditation" during the first five minutes that I am meditating, my emotional frequency and vibration become a lot higher than if I just focus on my breath alone without this visualization. Because the energy of good emotions well up—in particular, love—the tendency is to focus more on the meditation because of the enjoyable emotions, so the meditation experience is enhanced.

My inspiration to create this meditation first came from reading the book *Ask and It Is Given* by Esther Hicks. In the beginning of the book, Esther asked Abraham, "How can we most effectively achieve our goals?" Abraham responded (I'm paraphrasing here), "Meditation and affirmation; if you do it with your partner, it will be more powerful." When I read this, it struck a chord with me. My inner highest self was speaking to me loud and clear about what I had read. Esther Hicks meditated with her husband, Jerry. I now heard my internal guide speaking to me, saying, "Start meditating with a partner or group of people." I cannot tell you what a difference it makes when you do this; the meditations are more powerful; there is accountability to do it on a daily basis, and my level of presence increased simply by having a meditation partner there. Secondly, Esther mentioned that she never skipped a day of her fifteen- to thirty-minute meditation, and again, I heard my internal guide speak to me and say, "Persistence is power." Of course, persistence is power! Esther Hicks raised her vibration high enough after nine months or so to be able to channel her spiritual guide Abraham! Do you understand what that means for you? You are opening the gateways to the spiritual word for higher and more brilliant divine guidance expressed through your life purpose, your god given talents, and your intuition so your life may unfold with more prosperity! If that doesn't excite you to do "The Sunflower of Positive Emotions Meditation" every day with a partner or group of people, then I don't know what will. Don't let your ego get in the way with its "Yeah, but it's too much work; yeah, but nothing is going to happen; yeah, but I can't do it," etc. If you fall for those thoughts that stop you, you will not grow. "The Sunflower of Positive Emotions Meditation" needs to be done with expectation that if you adopt it as a permanent lifestyle, it will help you immensely to progress on your spiritual path.

After I began meditating, before I went to sleep one night, I heard my inner self speak to me. It said, "Your meditation will be enhanced if you generate love in your meditations." "The Sunflower of Positive Emotions Meditation" is all about generating love by having a loving relationship with the earth, the Heavenly Father, your partner or your group that you are meditating with, and any angel, archangel, or enlightened being of the spiritual realms of the light you choose to call in. After five minutes of visualization and raising the love frequencies, you start your breathing meditation for twenty to thirty minutes. When I first started it, I couldn't believe the difference it made! I was in bliss, and my feeling good energy was very much apparent compared to when I meditated by just focusing on my breath rather than using the "The Sunflower of Positive Emotions Meditation."

So I know you're still in the dark about what "The Sunflower of Positive Emotions Meditation" entails, so I am going to give you the visualization aspect and walk you through it, so you can practice at home with a partner or in my academy's first and second year programs if you choose. Here it is:

Start by sitting straight up in a chair with comfortable clothing and close your eyes. Imagine roots coming down from your feet and enveloping the earth. Feel these roots nourishing themselves with love of the Earth Mother as she sends that love up your roots, up through the green stem of your sunflower that goes all the way up to your heart. Now see your heart as the center of your sunflower. See the petals of your sunflower surrounding your heart. Know that we are using the sunflower as a metaphor for the sun. The heart is really like the sun center for the galaxy, which is your body. Everything is really centered in the heart. Heart-centered individuals who generate and lead with love are always individuals who manifest authentic prosperity. Feel as the Earth Mother nourishes your sunflower heart of love. Know that the Heavenly Father wants to connect and nourish you as well. See a vertical golden tube of sunlight from the Heavenly Father loving you and surrounding you now that's connected to a golden sun above you. The golden tube is entering you through your crown chakra and meeting the sunflower of your heart. Feel as the love of the Earth Mother and the love of the Heavenly Father meet at the heart with peace and love, and make love to each other, and generate even more love. Feel and send your love both to the Earthly Mother and the Heavenly Father, and as you do this, feel their love bounce back to you and intensify.

Become fully engaged now in connecting with your meditation partner or group with a horizontal tube of light from your heart to theirs. Know that you are sending and receiving love and magnifying your love as you do this. Call for all of the spiritual and cosmic hierarchy and those spiritual guides and angels whom you would like to call forth at this time to connect with you, heart to heart, in this meditation. As this visualization completes with a loving relationship that is nourishing you now, know that love grows by loving each other, as we are doing now in this meditation. As you love each other, start to breathe in deeply and focus on your breath. When you breathe in, feel this breath intensify the fire of love in your sunflower heart as if you're adding fuel to a fiery love. Breathe out and let go of anything that does not belong. As you do this, make sure that you focus on your breath like this for twenty to thirty minutes or however long you want to continue.

That is the basic foundation of "The Sunflower of Positive Emotions Meditation." Another aspect of the meditation I want to mention is the positive emotions you are creating. There is a term Esther Hicks talks about that really hit home for me so I hope you are paying attention. The better you feel, the higher the vibration, and the more it allows you to manifest your goals and dreams. She calls this state "The Vortex," that place where you can summon in anything you want by the art of feeling good. You get into the vortex by feeling good. When I read this, I thought, "What a great concept! Isn't this what I'm doing with 'The Sunflower of Positive Emotions Meditation'?" You can feel good through thoughts, but I have never seen anything more powerful than having a long relationship with people and beings who create such a high vortex of energy. This meditation might as well be called "The Vortex Sunflower of Positive Emotions Meditation." Other words have been used as well to refer to this positive emotion, good feeling state, such as "State." When you get into a good state of positive emotion, you are more able to follow through. "The Sunflower of Positive Emotions Meditation" creates a positive state among the meditation group or partner; you're basically helping each other raise such a high frequency that you just attract better things unexpectedly into your life. I have had unexpected blessings come my way since I started applying this concept to my life. If you are looking for a high vibrational group energy to enhance your life purpose as a full time career, I highly encourage you to join us at the first year of our academy program, and if you love it, to go on to the second year of our program.

Other forms of meditation exist that include subliminal messages to activate whatever you want to achieve. Some hypnosis meditations on achieving wealth will program your subconscious mind, and there are others on health, energy, or you name it. Any of these meditations can help you transform yourself to the next level. You can either try my meditation products or do research on Google if you have not explored the subject of subliminal meditation or hypnosis meditation to reprogram your subconscious mind. Although I do recommend silent meditations as a daily foundation, these other types of meditation offer a very powerful dynamic element to your success in whatever you are trying to accomplish.

Finally, I wanted to mention vipassana meditation. It's a retreat where you get to meditate on average anywhere from seven to thirty days or more. During this extended period of meditation within a retreat, you have the opportunity to leave your busy life, if you have the time and money, and let your mind and body take a vacation. It can be very difficult during the first few days since your mind will be uncomfortable with its chatter and its unwillingness to let you sit still and concentrate. After a few days, however, you will notice your thoughts subside and you will have an easier time as you move along. But what you will notice is a profound transformation within a few days. I really recommend doing vipassana meditation at least once in your life, and then keep up a thirty to sixty minute daily routine to maintain it once you return home. As a result, you will notice you are sharper, recharged, and better able to deal with life. Visit http://www. dhamma.org/ or Google "vipassana" for other organizations. As I am writing this book, I am planning a retreat of my own that follows along the lines of a silent retreat, so stay tuned for that. I will notify anyone who opts in at my website. You can also Google other programs that may be taught in your area.

Having meditation as the foundation of your mental diet will transform your daily life, and if done during the morning, it may give you a more fulfilling day. If done for thirty minutes in the daytime and thirty minutes before bed, then you may have a more fulfilling sleep and life as well. The more presence you have during your meditations, the more presence you will have in the present moment because meditation will quiet your mind, allowing you to be more focused on the now. That said, please remember your goal: to be fully in the present moment.

AFFIRMATIONS AND VISUALIZATIONS AND THE SUCCESS MINDSET OF ACHIEVING YOUR GOALS

Before I tell you about affirmation and visualization, I want to mention here that allowing yourself to be in a state of peace, love, joy, and calm from meditation will make these practices more effective because you are allowing your authentic self to flow more fully. Practicing "The Sunflower of Positive Emotions Meditation" is a powerful way to raise your positive emotions so you are in the state or vortex of allowing all that you want to manifest faster. Remember: the more positive your emotions, the higher your frequency to attract what you want and the stronger your inner guidance on how to manifest it. If you haven't read the section above on "The Sunflower of Positive Emotions Meditation," I highly recommend you read it because affirmation and visualization alone with negative or not extremely positive emotions are less effective than if you are coming through a state of positive emotions.

The more you allow these positive emotions, the more effective your affirmations and visualizations will be. You must also understand that being conscious about the fact that you are not your negative thoughts is key. The majority of us are so identified with our mind chatter that we start to believe its nonsense without realizing we are living in a mental world that is not real and very disconnected from the true reality of that joyous state of what we really are. Be aware and have faith that positive emotions will work. Allow their magic to happen; fear that it won't work blocks the manifestation of your goal. Have faith and trust as I discussed earlier.

When the mind is not thinking or affirming the right thoughts, visualizing the right images, and believing the correct beliefs, it can break a healthy body and the healthy soul inhabiting that body. With the mind, you are able to picture or visualize for yourself the size you want to wear, the money you want to make, or the lifestyle you want to create. For example, you can program your subconscious to help you reduce your dress size. Your mind can also help you do and focus on affirmations, declarations, invocations, and incantations in order to say the word or think the thought that magnetically attracts what you want in your life. Remember, your inner world will eventually reflect your outer world, so make sure your visualizations and affirmations in your internal world reflect what you want to see in your outer world, and that you are connected not only mentally, but emotionally with your positive emotions.

I now want to talk a little about people taking action toward their goals and how that connects to visualization and affirmation. How many people have bought programs and books and attended seminars to change their lives, but once they purchased them, they never use the products? How many have not followed through in their goals? I know

I have done this. Wouldn't it be awesome if every single product you bought to transform your life, you actually read in its entirety, and you actually took full action to change your life with it? How about if you followed through on your goals? So what is stopping you and all of us? The answer is complex, but in simple terms, let's just say, "Fear and lack of faith!" People who don't follow through are not seeing themselves succeeding in their mind's eyes; instead, they are subconsciously picturing themselves not succeeding, and they are affirming negative thoughts that induce lack of belief and faith, which leads to inaction toward their goals and dreams.

Here is the foundation for understanding how to take action and achieve your goals; it is the difference between people who follow through and those who don't. Let me add that it doesn't matter how many times you have failed to change any aspect of your life; this chapter is the solution to this problem if you choose to pay attention to it. (I also will note that this information will help you follow through with the practices in the other chapters, particularly in Chapter Four: The Divine Diet for the Physical Body.) You could have decades of being stuck with the same problem, but by applying these principles, you can finally break through!

So what is the formula that successful people follow? One, if not the most important, key for success is belief in your self-worth. It's important to understand how important it is to have a strong foundation of self-worth. If you don't, then learn to affirm that you do for at least five minutes daily. Again, think of a table; if you don't have four strong legs, the table will fall. Think of your self-worth as one of the table legs that gives you a strong foundation in whatever you want to achieve in your life, especially in terms of your business or career. Self-worth is believing in yourself; it's having faith in yourself and knowing that you are created worthy by your creator and you are loved deeply. If you believe and have faith in yourself and you feel worthy enough to share your talents with the world, chances are you will go for it in your business or career. Self-worth breeds positive emotions, such as confidence, which raises your vibration enough to allow faster manifestation of your dreams.

We live in a world where we are taught that our sense of worth is outside of ourselves, so we look for it outside in other people, relationships, success, money, fame, and material things, all to fill the void we feel of lack of self-worth; this void is caused by the ego and its feeling of not having enough so it constantly seeks more. Nothing outside of ourselves can ever truly fill it. If we become addicted to finding it outside of ourselves, then we just get stuck going in loops. We also get caught in the trap of the need to prove ourselves—prove our worthiness—because deep down inside, we have a weak unhealthy foundation of lack of self-worth. And with a weak foundation of lack of self-worth, which is essentially unstable, anything that you build on top of it can be knocked down easily anytime something goes wrong. The good news is that it's possible to fill this void, but the only place we will be able to find what is needed to fill it is within ourselves. It is very important to do this because every time you're faced with your own insecurities or limiting beliefs, criticisms, or judgment, which you're bound to have, you're not going to be able to stand your ground and stay on top of your game to keep your commitment toward your goals. If it's difficult for you to allow yourself to embrace your worthiness, I shall bestow it upon you now. Know this: you are worthy, you are an amazing unbelievable creation of God, the Universe, the Creator. I give you permission to stand in confidence with the self-worth that is your birthright. You have unique talents meant for this world, and you have something special to say. There, it's done; you have been blessed and given permission to stand in your own self-worth with confidence.

Nobody else can accept this blessing for you; you're the only one who can truly change yourself! So take it; it's yours! If you want further help with affirming your self-worth, I have a guided meditation available in my transformational meditation CD package. It's the last one in the package and titled "Self-Empowerment, Confidence, and Courage Meditation." You can also vocally affirm your own self-worth daily. The irony is that your self-worth is already there; you really don't have to do anything to create it; you just have to awaken to the understanding that simply because you exist, you are worthy. Once you understand that, you will be able to cultivate it by affirming it every day and bringing it to your everyday life journey.

To activate your self-worth, it would also help to understand more about who you really are. We really are, on a subatomic level, quantum fields of energy with infinite possibility and potential. We have the ability to tap into and awaken the superb energetic field within us to help empower our lives. We are incredibly powerful creators to be able to do that.

The Universe really just wants to give birth to itself through you. It wants to expand within you, so it's up to us to learn how to get out of its way. Becoming firmly grounded in who you really are takes daily practice, and when you do practice, you will be able to cultivate your infinite potential into your life. You will start to uncover talents and abilities that you didn't even know you had.

So your daily practice is to be in the present moment joyfully because when you are in the present moment, you are not focused on past thoughts or worries; instead, you focus and give yourself the access point to your true power. So basically what you're doing is living in actual reality in the present moment and not in a fake mind world with negative thoughts that are limiting your success. Being present is so important because then an effortless energy takes over to do what is meant to be done in the now. It allows the limitless power of the Universe to flow through you, and in knowing this, you can have the confidence to move forward. But when you are coming from just a conscious place of mind chatter where you're thinking about what you're saying or doing, you are really coming from a less powerful perspective.

As I mentioned earlier in this chapter, successful people also make it a point to write their goals down and review them on a regular basis. Do this twice a day, morning and night, for just a few minutes a day to reorient your subconscious in which direction you're going. I personally review the goals I have for the next twelve months twice a day, morning and night, so my subconscious mind can redirect me toward where I'm going. I would like to point out here that twelve months is the perfect amount of time to focus on as opposed to focusing on your goals for the next five or ten years. A twelve-month time limit allows you enough space to work on what's most important now.

Writing your goals down is the first step toward materializing anything. It comes before creating your affirmations and visualization techniques because when you write your goals, you have a better understanding of what affirmations and visualizations will best serve you to meet them. The actual writing of them gives your subconscious mind something more tangible to grab onto to bring them forth. After you write them down—here is the important part—ask yourself, "Who do I have to become to achieve my goals?" Then set your affirmations and visualizations to reflect the person you want to become. Again, as I said, reading your goals on a regular basis gives your mind the focus and energy to bring them to fruition. I won't write too much on goal setting for this section because the theme is affirmations and visualization, but I will mention one more time this powerful message that will get you to see the importance of goal setting: You will accomplish a lot more and make a lot more money than those who don't write their goals down. That's the power of goal setting and writing your goals, so write them down and keep them visible where you can look at them daily.

Goals can be thought of as a form of affirmation. The act of writing your goals is like carving out exactly what you want and asking the Universe to help you get it. Also daily goal setting and writing down goals is so powerful. I have my daily planner sheet ready, and I set my goals for the day, instead of going through the day without a set goal in place. You will be more productive and get more things done with daily goal setting as well. I number them in terms of priority, especially the ones that are money-making activities.

Now that you have set your goals, use the power of visualization daily for a few minutes. See what you want happening in your mind as if it has already happened, and visualize it happening perfectly the way you want it. Do this one to three times daily for a few minutes. You will reach a point where it's so ingrained in your mind's eye that there is no question in your mind that it will materialize.

When people who are now successful had nothing, they knew that they already had wealth and all of the things they desired before they even physically had them, and they had faith that whatever they set their minds to would work to make whatever it was they wanted to materialize come to them. In other words, they had already accomplished the end result in their minds with their goals before they had even attained it on the physical level. They had complete faith, and more importantly, the feeling of certainty that it would work out; this comes from seeing it perfectly working out in your mind through visualization. This process validated in their minds what they wanted, and it gave them the certainty, confidence, and excitement to follow through. Their subconscious minds were programmed to direct them toward their end goals, as opposed to subconsciously visualizing it not working out in their minds and leaving them uncertain and doubting. If you don't know whether or not something is going to work, or if you're doubtful, or if you keep visualizing it not working out, will you do it? Not very likely. This is the importance of complete faith and visualizing the perfect end result. Have faith that whatever you set your mind to, God, or the Universe, or whatever you want to call it, will create a way to bring it to you. Just stay focused on visualizing the perfect outcome as if it has already happened.

So, ultimately, why aren't you getting results? Because fear and doubt, resulting from wrong visualization and negative thought, close down the power of faith and activate darkness in your life! But the difference between people who get results and people who don't is that successful people are more connected to understanding the consequences of what life would be like if they don't follow through; by comparison, the other person is willing to settle for what he gets and be half in the game and half out and maybe take action on a goal that might help for the moment, but not follow through on it all the way because in the back of his mind, he is still doubtful.

The people in this latter category purchase any transformational products—for example, a gym membership—usually because of the feeling of moving toward their goals that they get with the purchase. They are progressing toward their goals by taking the first step. They will go to the gym, and they will feel better by doing so. All you have to do is simply take a little action or just make a little bit of progress to feel better and see that you are progressing. Unfortunately, these people will not take the middle or end step needed, which is to keep going. Instead, they quit the gym the third week, justifying it with excuses such as a lack of time. To succeed, they need to complete all of the steps necessary and make a permanent lifestyle out of the change they set out to do. Keep in mind that your authentic self always goes the extra mile over and beyond, and it refuses to be stopped by any obstacle. Your fake self always looks to cut corners, make excuses, and be stopped.

Enthusiastic overachievers usually have a psychology of associating a lot of pain and suffering with missing out on the abundance and opportunities that life has to offer. And this kind of programming typically happens because they usually hit rock bottom, where they are homeless, or in abusive situations for such a long time that they develop a hunger that keeps them going at their maximum! Not all, but many of the smarter ones also have the ability to create outrageous joy and love for their work and have tremendous enthusiasm and passion for what they do, which is the ultimate way to live and attract abundance because action then becomes easy.

Many people who don't get results aren't at the point where they are completely desperate, so they don't believe they absolutely have to take action to change their lives. These people are in comfortable situations; they do have greater ambitions and goals, but those factors aren't pushing them yet to the point where they will do what it takes to achieve whatever they want.

So how do you go from a situation where your desire is not strong enough to make you want to change your life, to one where you condition your mind to leave a situation that is average and pursue something greater that will expand you to deeper levels of yourself. In other words, how do you get all your desires fulfilled without manifesting severely negative situations such as extreme poverty or abuse that are so bad that you must change?

The answer is simpler than you may think. First off, you create your own reality; you can have a blast working day and night for hours, simply because you affirm it and visualize it. Loving your work is a choice and an affirmation within itself. Let it become your daily mantra. What can you love about it? How can you love it more? You are enjoying and loving your work because you say you are, because you affirm it daily. You have explosive energy because you say you do. You are enthusiastic because you say you are. You create the fun in whatever you want, including the things you procrastinate with. Use the power of visualization and affirmation for this magical creation. Try it now. Are you feeling sad? Affirm that you are joyful and notice what happens to your energy; do you feel better or worse? Affirming and visualizing starts to attract what you want almost immediately, and you can tell this by how you start to feel.

Secondly, take it one step at a time. Every day, adopt about ten to twenty minutes a day to say your affirmations and do your visualizations and look at your goals. Do these simple visualization and affirmation techniques every day to condition your mind to become enthusiastic, to take massive action, and to create the urge to do more within one day. Below are four affirmation tools I encourage you to use:

Create Emotion: You must get yourself into the emotional state where you will follow through. Emotion creates motion. So when doing affirmations or visualizations, make sure you are creating the feelings of passion, enthusiasm, urge, and inspiration. Play your favorite music while you do them if it helps you, or think of your positive future that you want to create. Dance. Do whatever works for you that will spark your emotion so you desire to follow through. Experiment until you find what works.

Use the Power of Why: Write down and post somewhere on your wall or vision board exactly why you must do whatever it is you desire, such as change your body or your finances. For example, in keeping with this book's purpose: Why is it that you want to reawaken yourself? The Power of Why is so important for making your affirmations and visualizations much more effective, as well as for taking action throughout the day. Again, as I mentioned earlier in this chapter— and it's worth mentioning again—the power of asking, "Why do I want something?" is absolutely necessary so you take action and complete your goals. To be clear, it's very important to wake up every morning pondering and asking this question. It really is the revolutionary foundation for anyone who takes action and succeeds. Personally, the more I do this, the more euphoria I experience, and the more I feel that it's absolutely crucial for me to follow through on my goals, especially when I focus on the strong enough "why" that moves me to action.

Follow Through: This tool might help you figure out your "why." You must follow through, take a lot of action, and go the extra mile: One of the reasons I followed through was because I sat down and visualized for myself what it would be like at the end of my life if I had not followed through. I saw myself as a sad old person, struggling to live. I took a good chunk of time so I could really see it in my mind's eye and really ingrain it in myself. It was so painful that I was grateful that I was still young, full of life, and energetic enough to make a difference in living a better life. For example, when people follow the regular junk diet that the masses follow, it makes them weak and disintegrates their bodies; simply picturing that gives me the desire to do whatever it takes to maintain my body in a youthful and healthy state for years to come. It is possible, as many youthful centenarians have proven! I do, however, realize that you don't have to put yourself through a painful visualization like I did, or make yourself feel bad. Maybe just thinking of the consequences might help you to avoid procrastination. Perhaps you can do the opposite—make yourself feel good by thinking of all the possibilities and the goodness in your future that you can create by deciding to take action. Do whatever works for you.

Find Others to Hold You Accountable: When I find a successful coach and am around people who are doing better than me, I feel like I want to do even better, follow through on my affirmations and visualization techniques even more, and accomplish more work in one day because I am being held accountable. If being held accountable means that you have to pay for high quality seminars to get around people who are doing better than you, or get a coach or friends to hold you accountable, then do it because it's worth the investment! You will become whomever you surround yourself with, so seek people who are doing better than you, and if you can make them your friends, take them out to dinner; their presence alone can change your life.

But again, take it one step at a time; achieve one small portion of your goal, and then master another part of your goal. You don't have to kill yourself by trying to achieve everything overnight if you don't have the urge to change things as soon as you can. After you have started doing the simple things, you might get more excited with your accomplishments. After you have proven to yourself that you can achieve things—that you are capable of materializing your goals—you may want to do more and immerse yourself even deeper in what you have to do on a daily basis. Collect the little pieces of success to reaffirm your belief that success is possible. I am going to say this one more time: once you break through to at least some level of success, even if it's just a small breakthrough, if you keep going to bigger and bigger goals and breakthroughs, you will condition your mind to activate the level of certainty, confidence, and habit of following through that you need to achieve your goals. Once you get momentum, nothing can stop you; it's just like the snowball effect—your success will grow bigger and bigger as it rolls down a mountain full of snow.

In essence, what you are really building is the emotion of confidence or faith within your being. When you believe or know in the entirety of your being that what you are doing is going to work, then you will do it, whereas when you think something is not going to work, you are never going to work at it to the fullest extent necessary.

To shift any reluctance or doubt you still have, you must start with visualizing and affirming it happening perfectly in your mind as if it has already happened, and if you want to make it happen faster, visualize and affirm it as if you are presently enjoying it. Visualize and affirm it daily, until it's so real in your mind that your body believes it has already happened; then you're taking enormous amounts of action and materializing it to become 100 percent reality. Just think about it; when you're unsure that it's going to work, what are you picturing? That it's not working. Because you're picturing it not working, that is what the Universe and your subconscious mind give you in return. This is worth repeating, so I suggest you read this paragraph again. I'm sorry if this section seems so repetitive. I just really want you to get this concept because it is such an important one for you to become successful.

This discussion reminds me of a time in my own life when I couldn't get much of my work for my new career done. I was so paralyzed with fear that I wouldn't be successful that I didn't even want to bother. But the moment I started visualizing myself as enjoying the work, enthusiastically getting it done, seeing the perfect outcome, and affirming my enthusiasm and joy for it, everything changed. I started to achieve what I thought was impossible, and I couldn't believe that I had been frozen about this situation for so long. I never achieved my goal until I made a shift in my mind about visualizing the outcome working out perfectly. I visualized it in my mind perfectly over and over again until my belief, faith, and confidence about doing it changed. This experience was a perfect example of how the subconscious responds to your beliefs about what you can and cannot do. Therefore, one of the most important tools to change your beliefs and level of certainty and faith that a goal can be achieved is to change your visualization process about it; begin to visualize it happening perfectly like you want it to happen.

It's important to state here as well that action without the perfect vision of what you want is not very effective. Even massive action with the belief that it is not going to work is not going to get you anywhere, at least not to a very high level of success. It's like a network marketer trying to sign you up as a distributor for her product, but she doesn't even believe herself that she can be successful at it. So please get visual results in your head and *feel* as if it what you want has already happened. Develop an obsession toward this to the point where it is inevitable and you're absolutely totally certain in your level of belief that it will happen. Then go through the day expecting to get what you set out to accomplish.

There is a story of a man who visualized his cancer cells disappearing and his immune system getting stronger. The doctors could not believe that his cancer went into remission just from him visualizing his cancer going away. That is the power of visualization—it is a real medicine, and it is real magic; visualizations are real things, just as thoughts are real things.

Also, keep your goals and dreams to yourself (other than the successful people you're asking to hold you accountable). Don't share them with people who will want to rain on your parade or cause you to create negative affirmations and visualizations that you will unintentionally implant into your subconscious. If you have negative friends or family members who aren't willing to do what it takes to change their lives, stay away from them. Whatever comes out of their mouths can work like a spell that keeps you from achieving your goals. Some of us are strong enough to overcome such attacks and move on with our goals, but why even put yourself in that position? If you are not strong enough to resist, their negativity will instill itself into your subconscious and affect your outcome.

Look carefully for friends who want to praise you and nourish you toward your goals, but even then, I wouldn't talk very much about a goal that is just in its baby stages of development. Develop sturdy, well-grounded roots first before you put the thought or idea into someone else's mind because everyone is very powerful and can affect what you are trying to create.

So let's use the example of perfect heath as a goal and see how using visualization and affirmation can lead us to getting radiant health so we can reawaken whom we truly are. Here is what you must understand to get the results you want. If you want to embody radiant health and be who you really are, then you must hold a perfect vision in your mind and daily practice seeing what you will look like over and over again. Let me repeat that because it's so important: you must visualize yourself as a fully reawakened, perfectly healthy being over and over again. You can visualize it in your head or you can have magazine cut-outs to look at that represent it. Notice that this is about focusing and giving energy to what you really want, as opposed to being in fear and visualizing what you don't want; it's important to be aware of the difference and catch yourself throughout the day if you are seeing in your mind's eye other than what you want. If you don't have a dream board of all the goals you want to accomplish with pictures that represent that, then get one, or at least hang up a picture of what you want; for example, if you want to lose weight and get into shape, find a photo of someone who has a similar body to the one you want to achieve. Maybe even chop the person's head off and put your head there instead. Or just visualize. You must picture yourself with vibrancy and full of energy if that is what you want for the rest of your life. This is the visual aspect of your mind.

You must also affirm, or declare daily, what you want as the end result. Here are some affirmations as examples:

- Nothing can stop me; everything I love is more than possible; it's inevitable and easy because I let it be.
- I am a fully awakened soul in this perfectly radiant and healthy body.
- My body is forever youthful; I get younger and healthier every day. I am full of massive amounts of energy. I am so healthy and full of energy that I can do the things I love for long hours.
- My immune system is strong and I never get sick.
- It is easy for me to change my diet to a better one.
- I am fully capable of doing juice fasts without any fear; I embrace their discomfort, for I know I will attract more joy into my life.
- I am fully nourished while I fast on water. God sustains me always.
- Eating a raw vegan diet is easy; it's healthy and it tastes amazing.
- Raw superfood greens like spirulina have plenty of protein. I am reminded that horses eat only grass.
- I know what to eat in this moment. My body guides me perfectly on what to eat.
- I am fully capable of eating 100 percent live organic foods. Where there is a will, there is a way!
- I have enough abundance provided always to eat healthily. I am creative enough to make it happen every day!

- I am fully present and aware of this moment, in this now. I enjoy this moment, and every step I have to take to achieve this moment.
- Avalanches of abundant health and wealth come to me quickly and easily by the grace of God for the greater good of all concerned.

These are just a few examples of the affirmations you could start saying to yourself daily. You don't have to say all of them, and you can follow your intuition and make your own. You need to listen in on what limiting beliefs you have, change them, and affirm different ones. And please don't fall into "This doesn't work." That within itself is another affirmation that will keep you from transforming your consciousness. Things take time to manifest and change, so please remember that the happier you are and the more love and joy you have, the faster you can manifest with visualization and affirmations, so take time to cultivate your love and joy.

Whenever you're blocked or having a problem, it is the perfect opportunity to make an affirmation to counteract it. Be certain that the affirmation will make a difference. Once you release that thought and embrace the power of how a thought can manifest and activate your subconscious, things will start shifting for you quite nicely. If you don't believe me, just look at some of the most successful people out there; all of them, whether or not they know it on a conscious level, have had thoughts that manifested into their outer realities.

Again, don't forget to add all the emotional intensity when you are saying your affirmations. Make sure you are in a place of peace and forgiveness. A sad and upset emotional body will block a lot of the affirmative power. Say it with true meaning within your heart and all of the emotional intensity you have. That doesn't mean you have to yell, but feel it; don't just say it mechanically from your head. Say it while you run or walk, or when you dance, or whenever you feel most intuitively guided to do so. As an option, move your body in a way that engages your affirmation to come out with emotion; for example, put your hands up with the emotion of victory, or punch a punching bag, run, jump on a trampoline, or even dance. Experiment to see which of these examples you resonate with the most.

I also suggest you record your affirmations and play them in the car on your CD player, or on your computer; listen to them while you are washing your dishes, organizing your house, or driving to the gym. You can also simply sit in meditation while you listen to your recorded voice; this tool is very powerful because it will sink the affirmations into your subconscious.

Probably the most powerful tool I have ever used is Mind Movies 2.0 (the current version as I write this). It's a software that allows you easily to plug in your affirmations, all of your compelling visual images to complement the affirmations, and your favorite music to give them that emotional kick while you're watching this movie vision board. The person who invented this program did so because when he was looking at his vision board, he understood the power of visualization, but he wasn't really motivated or emotionally moved (which is crucial to changing your vibration so you can attract what you want in your life), so he didn't really use it. Then he came up with the idea of making an affirmation/visualization movie with all of the pictures from his vision board and all of the affirmations to go with it. Within three months of watching his movie twice a day, all of his goals were achieved. That resonated with me because I already had an awesome vision board with affirmations and visual images, but I also liked that I could also focus with Mind Movies. Once I got my Mind Movies software, I made my first visualization and affirmation movie, and it was amazing. When I began to watch it more than twice daily, I noticed a dramatic difference in the way I performed to achieve my goals; trust me, it is truly a Divine Diet for your mind! You can find more information on Mind Movies at www.mindmovies.com.

PRAYER

Although affirmations and visualization are a form of asking for what you want, prayer, in the traditional sense, holds the same intention of manifestation, so if it's a tool that is available, why not practice it? It's a free and very powerful tool that must be exploited to its fullest extent like visualization and affirmation for the good of your life and all of humanity!

While using the tools to transform yourself in this book, you might go through some serious healing situations that might be very uncomfortable for you; in these hard times, you're going to need everything you've got. God cannot help you unless you pray so S/He has permission to give it to you. In the Bible, we are told, "Ye have not, because ye ask not" (James 4:2). Those seven words contain the answer for why so many people are struggling today. Another statement, "You cannot cast out your sins without fasting and prayer" is a paraphrase of a passage from *The Essene Gospel of Peace*. Prayer is so powerful, and God responds to it at every moment.

Yes, there is such a thing as unanswered prayers, but that's because there are some prayers that to answer might not be in your best interests. So when you pray, always ask at the end of your prayer, "Please give me this or something better." Pray with faith and with the belief and expectation that you will succeed and that the Universe has heard and is answering your prayers, even if they don't materialize exactly how you asked for them; just remember there is something divinely better awaiting you than what you requested. The bigger your faith, the more boldness your prayers will have, and the bigger your prayer requests will be. God wants you to pray with faith—to have boldness in your prayers because that indicates the level of faith you have in your prayers manifesting. Faith is power; it is the currency of God, so make sure you intertwine the power of faith and prayer to magnify and activate their greater power.

Remember that faith activates God's power, but fear that it might not work also activates the powers of destruction, so choose wisely when you pray. Pray often and pray big bold prayers instead of small ones. It's not about being greedy; it's about claiming every piece of abundance that belongs to you. You want to make sure that everything that belongs to you is yours because you asked for it. How do you know you are denying yourself a better future? Because you didn't ask for it. So I suggest you ask every day.

Here is what I do: The moment I get up, or I'm driving, or I'm in the grocery line, whenever I have time for prayer throughout the day, I say:

God, please protect me; please heal my body of any diseases; please restore my health; please bring massive prosperity now, the sooner the better; please protect my family, my friends, my team at work; please speak to me loudly and clearly about what you want me to do, say, and how to act; please guide my thoughts and my steps; please surround me only with positive people who will catapult my life to greatness;

please repel negative people; please have archangel Michael protect me for the rest of my life; please give me everything I need that is in my best interest that I have not asked for; please give me this or something better!"

You can adopt something similar to this. It's very powerful and it's free! Ask your creator for support always. The Universe want to help you, and it lovingly supports you, so why not ask?

Here are other forms of prayers that are really great to adopt as well. You can photocopy them and hang them on your walls or frame them, and you can read them daily if you are inspired to do so. These are popular prayers and suggestions for personal prayer requests that you might be inspired to say daily. This first one, by Saint Francis of Assisi, is one of my favorites. Please read it carefully to appreciate the profundity of it. I say it daily to set the tone for my day. And, as I've said before, if you're not religious or fond of the word "God," you can substitute it with "Universe," "Creator," or whatever term or belief suits you best:

Prayer of Saint Francis of Assisi
Lord, make me an instrument of your peace
Where there is hatred, let me sow love;
Where there is injury, pardon;
Where there is doubt, faith;
Where there is despair, hope;
Where there is darkness, light;
And where there is sadness, joy.

Oh, Divine Master, grant that I may not so much seek
To be consoled as to console;
To be understood as to understand;

To be loved as to love.
For it is in giving that we receive;
It is in pardoning that we are pardoned;
And it is in dying that we are born to eternal life. Amen.

I love this prayer so much because it's such a breath of fresh air. It's a mantra for living life that I think everyone can benefit from adopting. It's the reminder to be the beacon of love when there is hate—and there is so much hate within us and outside us—but we are blessed with the opportunity to choose the light and to grow into a better being. The second paragraph asks for us to be the leader, the giver. That's so important because we live in a society where selfishness is rampant. This is the secret of life; we ourselves need to stand up and give because abundance is created when we console, understand, love, give, pardon, and are willing to die to be reborn to eternal life.

The next prayer, the prayer to archangel Michael, is a prayer of protection. Whenever you feel you need it, especially in this world full of people who are looking to prey on your life, it's crucial that you pray this prayer, and I recommend you pray it even when you feel safe. I have seen clairvoyantly an angel who took away a dark being sending me negativity on the spiritual plane. Not sure if it was archangel Michael, but I did ask for his protection during that time.

Prayer for Protection to Archangel Michael
Saint Michael the Archangel, defend us in battle, be our protection against the wickedness and snares of the devil; may God rebuke him, we humbly pray, and do thou, O Prince of the heavenly host, by the power of God, thrust into hell Satan and all evil spirits who wander through the world for the ruin of souls. Amen.

Four Rosary Prayers: Our Father, Hail Mary, Key of Harmony, and Hail, Holy Queen

The four prayers below, you can pray as part of the rosary. Although Key of Harmony is not a traditional rosary prayer, there is no harm in creating it as part of your rosary prayer. I pray the rosary whenever I feel intuitively guided to. It's incredibly powerful, centering, and peaceful. I won't go over how to pray the rosary here since I just wanted to give examples of affirmative prayer, but you can ask a friend how to pray it, Google it, or find it at YouTube if you're interested in taking your prayers further.

Our Father
Our Father who art in Heaven
Hallowed be Thy Name
Let us go unto Thy Kingdom
Thy will be done
On earth as it is in heaven
Give us this day our daily bread, Lord
Forgive us our debts as we forgive our debtors
Let us not fall, Lord, into temptation
But deliver me and defend me, Lord, from all evil.
Amen.

Hail Mary
Hail Mary, full of grace.
The Lord is with Thee.
Blessed art Thou amongst women!
Blessed is the fruit of Thy womb, Jesus.
Holy Mary, Mother of God, pray to God for
Us sinners, now and at the hour of our death.
Amen.

Key of Harmony

I wish Harmony, Love, Truth, and Justice to
All my brothers and sisters. With the united
Forces of the silent vibrations of our thoughts
We are strong, healthy, and happy thus forming a
Link of universal fraternity.
I am happy and at peace with the whole Universe and
I wish that all beings achieve their most intimate aspirations.
I give thanks to the invisible Father for having established
Harmony, Love, Truth, and Justice among all His children.
So be it. Amen.

Hail, Holy Queen

Hail, Holy Queen, Mother of Mercy,
Our life, our sweetness, and our hope, hail!
To Thee, do we cry, poor banished children of Eve;
To thee do we send up our sighs, mourning and weeping
In this valley of tears. Turn then, our advocate, thine eyes
Of mercy towards us, and after this exile, show unto us Jesus.
Blessed is the fruit of thy womb, oh clement, oh merciful, oh
Sweet ever virgin Mary!
Pray to God for us, Most Holy Mother of God, that we may be
Made worthy of attaining the promises of our Lord Jesus
Christ,
Our Lord.
Amen.

Personal Prayer Requests

The following prayer requests are those I often ask for during
the day. You can borrow them or be inspired by them to make
up your own to ask for during the day:

- I pray for protection around my body. I pray for a
  golden bubble of protection around me so that all

positive energies can come into my body and all negative energies bounce off of it, including my own energy.

- I pray that God brings me everything I need today or something better.
- I pray for inspiration today.
- I pray to be shown new levels of enthusiasm today.
- I pray for God to show me how to have nonstop massive levels of euphoric energy even when I have been working long hours.
- I pray for the perfect ideas to come my way to cure my diseases.
- I pray for any diseases in my body to heal themselves.
- I pray for the health and wellbeing of humanity.
- I pray that God surround me only with people who will bring me up and not bring me down.
- I pray for good situations to happen to me today.
- I pray that my food be blessed today before I eat it.
- I pray that my body be filled full of light and nourishment when I am fasting.
- I pray for a deeper level of enlightenment today.
- I pray that all my worries go away.
- I pray that my life plays out perfectly, and that my purpose on this planet plays out perfectly.

You get the idea here for the personal prayer requests, please feel inspired to make up your own personal prayer requests according to your needs.

ASSOCIATING WITH POSITIVE MINDS

The number one reason why I have succeeded quickly is because of whom I associate with on a regular basis. I can trace back my failures to associating with negative people, and my fast successes to joining communities that catapulted me there because they all strived for excellence and lovingly supported me.

In this section, I want to leave you with something worth applying that is a very powerful part of creating a Divine Mental Diet. As you continue on your journey of feeding your mind, it is important to understand that you will have challenges with people whose minds are filled with negative thoughts. Not only will you have negative thoughts within yourself that "taint" your diet, but you will encounter people with negative thoughts who might want to bring you down as well. They can be friends, family members, acquaintances, or people in the media, movies, gossip magazines, etc. You must be very careful not to leave your mind wide open to being affected on subtle or not so subtle levels. Mediocrity is the norm, so don't let yourself get sucked into it by marinating around in it on a regular basis.

In his book *The Four Agreements*, Don Miguel Ruiz talks about thoughts as being very powerful spells that can either make or break you. It's a great little book I suggest you read. There are people who are stopped dead in their dreams because their family members tell them they aren't good enough, or they can't do something—for whatever reason. Once you have set your positive affirmations and visualization, I want you to guard yourself from people who contradict them. Don't talk about your most precious dreams or what you want unless you feel you have formed a solid habit and have total confidence that nobody can break your positive thoughts or vision. You might even want to visualize around yourself a bubble of protection against any negative thoughts within you or without you. Creating a bubble of protection is one of the most important things you can ever do because thoughts literally either make you or break you. It will make all the difference for you because once it's in your awareness, then as soon as someone says something and your spirit is down, you know why it's a happening and you can immediately change it through positive affirmations.

I might suggest here to surround yourself with successful people who are vibrant and encouraging and/or read their books and products if they have any. I can assure you that you will become like them because you'll think like them as a result of all the thoughts and ideas they shared with you. Again, as I mentioned earlier, if you can afford it, get a good coach either through my academy or through a referral from someone you respect and trust. Get a good success coach if you can; he or she will feed you with so much great information and inspiration that will guide you in your life like you wouldn't believe. Remember that who you become is the sum of your five closest friends. You don't have to know them personally; you can add famous and successful people if you like; read their books constantly or go to their seminars or workshops if they have them. Remember the power of association and the power of letting go of people who do not serve you.

The reason I created Reawaken Your Authentic Self Academy and its yearly membership programs was because I wanted to create a community of like-minded individuals who wanted to better their lives, love each other, and support each other for the purposes of spiritual growth on all levels. If you don't resonate with my academy, find a community that you do resonate with; it's that important, period.

BE JOYOUSLY PRESENT

Another aspect of the consciousness of your authentic self and a great part of your mental diet is being present in the present. Wholeness exists by living in the present moment and creating joy in it. But don't just be present; find, create, and cultivate so much joy in what you are presently doing that you cannot help but be engaged in it. Lack of presence has a lot to do with lack of enjoying it. The joy, no doubt, is always there; you just have to cultivate it.

So many of us fall into the trap of thinking that the joy comes only when we achieve all our goals and we are perfect, but then it still eludes us once we achieve those goals. The key is to realize that joy is cultivated in the mind, so it can be experienced now with your thoughts and creative ideas. Looking to the future and being attached to the fruits of your actions will only cause suffering. The only way to be at peace is to realize that you already have what you are looking for now; this joy or feeling that you want from your goals can be created now. You already are the prize; what you are really looking for is not the external symbols of success, such as money, but the feelings you believe you will get from them. I can tell you that the more present you are, and the more you indulge in the now and create space to enjoy it, the more you can access the innate gifts and overwhelming joy of being. If you want help in creating more joy, please contact my academy for coaching guidance on how to create a deeper sense of joyful presence.

From this feeling of wholeness (instead of the ego state of feeling lack and believing you need to attain something in the future to feel whole), you will experience a sense of happily achieving, instead of achieving to attain happiness. This state of consciousness is crucial if you want to live a life free of suffering. So all you have to do is practice. Practice living in the moment and enjoying it with appreciation. And practice noticing the things that fill you up and make you even more present. One of those things for me is dancing to music. Music can be used to enhance and enjoy the present moment, and from that enjoyment, an opening of inner joy can be felt. That joy can pour out to your future during moments in the present when you might find it harder to be fully present, such as when working at a job you don't fully enjoy. Use things you already enjoy and are fully present with as a starting point for you to expand and experience this state of enjoyment consciousness that can open within yourself. Be like a child exploring this experience and see where it takes you.

It is important to realize what an utterly amazing and profoundly joyful being you are. If you have spent a lifetime depressed and unhappy, that might not be as easy to see, but the truth is that your natural state is as a being who is full of joy and excitement, along with all the possible positive emotions. Your soul loves and enjoys the challenge of life. You came here to love the joy of expansion. To think that you don't enjoy it is an illusion of your ego; a joyful being is inherently who you are. If you don't feel that, it's because you have created mountains of disconnection to this aspect of yourself. When you clear your mind from negative thoughts by practicing being whole in the present moment, and especially when you practice the techniques described in the last two chapters of this book, you start to get a glimpse of who you really are.

Once you start going, it will be like a snowball effect; your wholeness and authentic self will begin to take on great momentum. You will soon start being engaged in the present moment with tremendous joy and enthusiasm, working on whatever goals you have set for yourself, and yet, at the same time, you will not be attached to the outcome because you know deep inside that the true fulfillment is in the present moment.

It's like a singer with a beautiful voice trying to sell millions of records and worrying that she hasn't yet when she should realize that she already has prosperity because she has the precious enjoyable gift from God that is her singing voice. The lesson is to enjoy singing at whatever capacity the moment presents itself with. Go with what's intuitive; don't focus on the future and how many records sales you should get. That's not to say that material success is not important, for wealth is your birthright, but to be attached and preoccupied with the future outcome is not being here now; it is a form of suffering.

Being engaged, focused, and joyously present gives a chance for your authentic self to cultivate and be present. Your authentic self can only be in the joyful now; it's nowhere else. You can be present in this world, or with your thoughts or images; the key is to stay in awareness, no matter what you are doing. When you're idle, you're not focused; you're thinking about something else, and you're not 100 percent on the task or action at hand; you're really setting an invitation for dark energy to fill in that void. It's so important for you to be present at every moment to protect yourself from that dark energy. Trust me; you will save yourself a lot of suffering if you have not noticed that already. I know personally I was horrible at being present, and I'm still getting better at it. It's a work in progress.

PUTTING IT INTO PRACTICE

Here are some suggestions for how you can put into practice what you learned in this chapter:

- Meditate thirty minutes a day.
- Consider joining a ten-day vipassana retreat.

- Believe in yourself and have faith! Affirm and know that you can do whatever you need or want to do daily! Then go about setting big goals for the next year; read them twice daily, morning and night.
- Pray for goodness to come into your life, and say prayers such as the Prayer of Saint Francis of Assisi.
- Affirm daily what you want to draw into your life. Affirm joy in what you don't want to do; create the joy in it.
- Visualize the things you want already in your life, and act as if things are as you want them to be.
- Set your goals. Then ask yourself, "What do I need to affirm to achieve my goals?" Then visualize yourself doing what is necessary to achieve them.
- When you get the urge to judge others, bless them instead.
- Surround yourself with positive minds only, and avoid negative minds at all costs.
- Stay joyously present and focused in the moment; don't tune out; stay fully focused in your goals for that particular moment. Ask yourself, "How can I make this a joyous experience?"
- The primary purpose of your life is to be authentically you. Take a moment here to take out your journal. Then, before you write anything, spend five to ten minutes in silence; listen in on what's going on within yourself. Where do you feel the pain in your life? Are you happy? Are you sad or angry? Are you frustrated? On a scale of 1-10, how productive are you and are you giving it your all? Are you afraid to be really you when you walk down the street or when you are around people? Do you walk tall and proud and sit straight up? Are you wholeheartedly immersed in your mission in life? Are you confident, and do you have faith that you can achieve whatever it is you want? Write what comes to your mind and see where you're

at in terms of where you're holding back and where you're wanting to be.

- Get a life coach to guide you on changing your mindset, experiencing more joy, and holding you accountable for your goals and taking action.

Chapter Three
The Divine Diet for
The Emotional Body

"Evolved people experience life as a celebration
rather than a problem to be solved."
— Michael Bernard Beckwith

EMOTIONS ARE YOUR LIFE

Your emotional body is probably one of the most important bodies, if not the most important, that you possess. If the happiest people are truly the most successful people in this world, rather than the most financially well-off people, then I would say a healthy and happy emotional body is the most important body you can possess. The emotional body is the gauge, the indicator of whether or not you are in alignment with your authentic self. An emotional body that is constantly feeling positive emotions of joy, happiness, gratitude, appreciation, confidence, ecstasy, nirvana, bliss, enthusiasm, passion, euphoria, love, excitement, compassion, peace, serenity, certainty, and any other positive emotion is an emotional body in alignment with your authentic self. Ultimately, it is the emotional body that everybody is working hard to get. Think about it—why do people do what they do? Every movement they make, every goal they set is, consciously or unconsciously, a move to try to feel better or be happier in some way.

For example, why do some people want fancy cars? Ultimately, when you get down to the nitty-gritty of it, it's because of the feeling the fancy car will give its owner. The most popular feelings that will result are richness, worthiness, freedom, and power. Another example is searching for a partner. People seek a partner because, ultimately, they are looking for a feeling of connection, love, and intimacy.

Positive emotions, such as the ones mentioned above, are the emotions you will feed yourself as part of your Divine Diet for your emotional body. This Divine Emotional Diet is so crucial for your wellbeing and the awakening of your authentic self because who you really are on an emotional level is someone immensely overflowing with all positive emotion! You cannot, however, have an effective and healthy emotional body full of positive emotions without first integrating the information we explored in the previous chapter on the Mental Body. It is crucial to find and cultivate joyous positive emotions because it is primarily our thoughts that affect our emotions.

The truth is that you don't have to wait until your outer circumstances materialize to feel the emotions you want; you can feel them right now and start to experience the emotional life you are really meant to live. Even in the toughest circumstances, it is possible to experience joy because you can control your mind to think thoughts that make you feel good. Again, as I mentioned, this great myth that you have to achieve something to be a happy and successful person is nonsense; you're a happy and successful person because you are a creation of God. That thought alone gives you permission to allow yourself to feel joy and cultivate it now. That belief and knowledge alone should start to make you smile. Really, if you haven't realized that, go jump up and down and celebrate this permanent success because nobody can take it away from you. Please read on to experience a further reawakening of your emotional joy!

So how do we get there? How do we maximize or strengthen the vast array of positive emotions at our disposal? How do we use those emotions so that whenever we are challenged in our daily lives with something we don't like, we can bathe it with a joyous experience instead? This chapter will give you those answers. It's about unlocking all of the major concepts, ideas, and strategies to allow you to dine on the most amazing Divine Diet for the emotional body.

Before we continue this chapter, I would like you to take a quick look at the topics we will cover below so you can get a better understanding of how we will break down the process to get you the positive emotions you really want:

- Understanding Positive Emotion
- Make This Now Moment a Joyous Experience
- Set the Rules and Beliefs in Your Mind So You Can Be Happy
- Happiness Lies in Constant Personal Growth
- Adding Emotion to Your Daily Affirmations, Prayer, Spoken Words, and Daily Action
- Using Focused Visualization to Create Positive Emotions and the Powerful Emotion of Certainty
- The Power of Gratitude, Confidence, Enthusiasm, Love, Peace, and Passion
- Set Your Intention to Enjoy Every Day
- Using Food and Physical Movement to Create Positive Emotion

UNDERSTANDING POSITIVE EMOTION

The first step toward having a divine, happy emotional body full of positive emotions at all times is understanding that being happy is who you really are; it's the authentic you. Positive emotion has the ability to heighten your perception to channel your talents, actions, and abilities clearly to the highest level, as well as fuel you with an abundance of energy to follow through on your goals.

God created you to be fully abundant with joyful emotion. Perhaps you don't remember this natural state because you have lived in a world that has perhaps beaten you down, you have surrounded yourself with negative people, you have abused your body with junk food and drugs for decades, or you have unconsciously chosen to feel emotions that are not good for you because you have not consciously thought about deciding or being determined to have healthy, vibrant emotions on a continuous basis. But, as I said, your emotional authentic self is full of joy, confidence, gratitude, ecstasy, enthusiasm, excitement, love, euphoria, nirvana, bliss, happiness, passion, certainty, peace, and every other emotional positive feeling that you can imagine! You are these emotions because the authentic you only chooses thoughts that generate those kinds of emotions. Remember that what you think about, focus on, visualize, or believe affects your emotions. You can generate either positive or negative emotions with your mind, primarily through your thoughts. These are sacred emotions given to you to experience on a regular basis by your creator. They are inherently part of your makeup as a soul! And when you truly are consciously aware and understand that this is what you really are, nothing outside of yourself can affect you, or at least not as deeply, because you are now aware and choosing to embody and feel your true authentic self.

Being your authentic self of positive emotions is a powerful experience and spiritual practice. It's like holding a torch of light for a world that mistakenly believes that in order to be happy, everything must always be going our way. When you embody the massive wealth and abundance that you really are, especially during difficult times, you start to see that the inner world of happiness has no connection whatsoever to the problems of the outer world. You start to understand that anything outside of yourself is a challenge that is meant to be dealt with joyfully, with an attitude of playful gratitude, a punch of enthusiasm, and as something you get the privilege to do because you were born on this planet to have fun with the problems that have been gifted to you.

A person who is authentically him- or herself always sees problems as positive opportunities to grow and become even better than what he or she already is. Understanding and embracing that opportunity is what makes life fun! Can you imagine a life without problems? There is no opportunity to grow without problems, so take full advantage of them and enjoy the journey. When you choose to be the real you emotionally, you will begin to see problems as opportunities. I can guarantee that you didn't come here to dread problems, but to enjoy the challenge! Be patient with yourself through this process of learning to see your problems in new ways—it takes time to create this new habit.

Think of dogs and their incredible sense of joy, excitement, and fun. They are the perfect examples of beings that embody their authentic selves. Have you ever noticed how dogs are so full of excitement and joy and so full of wanting to give love? And no matter what happens— they could lose a leg or get spanked by their owner—they will almost immediately whip back to an emotional state of excitement and joy. I want you really to think about dogs because these beautiful teachers can remind you that when you are not blocked in your mind with negative thoughts, you start to choose joy in the moment, no matter what the outer world demonstrates. Easier said than done, especially in the harder times of your life, but nonetheless, very possible; it just takes practice.

Positive emotions are always a choice, so decide to have them now. It's as simple as stepping into them—talk enthusiastically about them and you will create more of them; feel love for someone and you will feel even more of it. You can either be the authentic you, emotionally, or not the authentic you. All I can tell you is that you can't afford not to choose to be the emotional authentic you because choosing to be afraid, angry, sad, bitter, vengeful, doubtful, or depressed because your outer circumstances aren't going your way or just out of habit of feeling these things isn't helping you at all; it's robbing you of attracting better outer circumstances through clarity in how to take the best action; it's robbing you of the energy you need to take action toward your goals, and it's robbing you of all the creativity and insight that comes from within and can be accessed and activated when you're in a state of positive emotion. The Divine Diet for the emotional body is bliss, so simply decide to experience that bliss; it's not hard at all to move your facial muscles and crack a smile, even if you feel horrible right now. Just do it; enjoy it, and you will eventually have so much habitual momentum you can't help but cultivate even more positive emotion!

MAKE THIS NOW MOMENT A JOYOUS EXPERIENCE

All of us have things in our lives that we do not fully enjoy doing, so when we do them, we tune out a bit because we have not found the joy in them. The truth is that you really can create a joyous experience for every segment of your life. Whenever you find something that you are not fully enjoying in the moment, and you are tuning out because you don't find the joy in it, ask yourself, "How can I find the joy in this now moment with the task at hand?"

I realized that declaring something as simple as "I love my job. I enjoy it so much I can't stand it when I am away from it" could change how I felt. Making a statement about a moment or a task at hand, and stating what I want it to feel like, even though it does not feel like it for me, allows me to create greater access to those feelings I do want to have for a particular task at hand. It really is like a mind spell that allows you a different experience. The same thing happens when you say, "My life sucks. I hate my life." Haven't you noticed that that is what you are experiencing when you state those negative emotions in your head? Why not state ones that you really do want to experience over and over until they become your reality?

I want to give you an example from my own personal life. As I mentioned earlier, I do hot yoga six times a week. It's probably one of the most intense yoga workouts there is—probably one of the most intense workouts, period. But in the beginning, it was something I wasn't enjoying very much, so I found myself tuning out and not being fully present with it. I realized that my lack of presence during the sessions was partially because I wasn't enjoying it fully, so I asked myself, "How can I fully enjoy this workout more?" I started writing down all sorts of things that I could think about. I started to smile and invited my inner playful child to come out to play throughout the workout, which made it more enjoyable. I started to think of God loving me and nourishing me with every posture. I also started to think of the sensuality of it and started to feel how orgasmic the pain was. Then I started to laugh and humor myself by thinking of the discomfort as something sensual. I started to generate emotions of gratitude for what hot yoga did for my body and for how lucky I was actually to have a studio next to where I lived with beautiful and nice instructors. I created a reality in my mind for how I wanted to feel as I did it, and it worked! The discomfort and challenge may never go away, but that's just my ego that wants it to go away. My authentic self is always appreciative and always excited to go to the next class; it finds joy in the challenge of it as I get out of bed every morning to face it, and I experience every posture as a playful experiment to be rediscovered over and over by my inner child. Now it's what I live for! I now apply this joyful sense of appreciation to every single aspect of my life!

What are the thoughts or ideas that can make things exciting and joyous in your life? Can you tune in to your playful inner child? Can you adopt a sense of humor and laugh at your problems? Can you smile through it? Can you be appreciative of it? Can you lovingly do it? Can you think about all of the people or your family members whom you will help because you do this thing? Can you play music and dance as you do it? Now is the time to create a joyous now. The more joy in the moment, the more authentic you become, the more present you will be while you take action, and the faster you will accomplish your goals. Remember that life is supposed to be fun now, not later. You were born to play! Enjoy every drop of it!

SET THE RULES AND BELIEFS IN YOUR MIND SO YOU CAN BE HAPPY

Everybody has rules and beliefs, whether they are conscious or unconscious. Usually, they are set and programmed by society, friends, family, parents, peers, and teachers. In this section, we are going to explore and weed out all the rules and beliefs you have in your mind that do not serve you. It is important to understand that these rules and beliefs are controlling a good chunk of the emotions you are feeling.

Let me give you a popular example. Let's say that a woman would like to lose weight. She is overweight, and when she looks in the mirror, she feels awful because she is not thin, and she is not healthy. She is not letting herself feel happy because in her mind she thinks that being thin is when she can be happy. But say she does lose the weight and chooses to feel happy because of it; wasn't it her choice to feel the feelings of being happy? It's very subtle, but she made the decision to feel happy.

Although emotions can also be messengers when they speak of sadness, depression, or any other uncomfortable feeling, you can see them as indicators that your psychology of thought or beliefs needs to change so you can move to a more positive emotional state of being.

What I am trying to say here is that the rules you have that are keeping you from being happy usually are linked to outer circumstances if you are operating on a subconscious level. In the example above, this woman's rule was that in order to be happy, she had to be a certain weight. And, of course, there is a certain level of fulfillment to losing weight and moving toward a goal, but if she would have changed her rule to something like "I am happy because I am a divine creation of God, and happiness is what I truly am," then she could enjoy having a fuller life while she happily achieves her weight loss goals instead of dreading every moment of her life and feeling like less because she is not thin. The truth is that when someone happily achieves and is full of enjoying the journey, chances are her goals will be met a lot faster. I can tell you that if you need to lose weight and you dislike your current weight, you will most likely eat more to numb the pain, which is probably why most people are overweight in the first place!

Another example is if someone believes that most people are corrupt and out to get them. I had this belief for a long time. It made me feel constricted, agitated, and always on guard when people approached me. It might still be true that some people are corrupt, but I instead choose to believe that people are inherently good, and when they make mistakes, they are just doing the best they can and have forgotten their goodness. I also changed my rule that I didn't have to wait for people to be good in order to be happy; instead, I could be at peace now. Once I changed my belief, I was at piece within myself, and I was able to operate from a place of love and peace.

So, to make it clear, the rules usually go like this: "In order to feel happy, I must…." So ask yourself what must happen in order for you to feel happy or excited? And then if it's limiting your happiness to wait to feel it in the future, change your rules to easier ones in order for you to feel happy.

Another aspect of feeling happy has to do with your beliefs. What are your limiting beliefs that are causing you to feel sad? What are the empowering beliefs that are making you feel happy? Here are some common ones:

Disempowering Beliefs:
I have to wait to achieve my goals to be happy.
I am not worthy.
I am not good enough.
I will never figure it out.
I'm not smart enough.

Empowering Beliefs:
Every day I am alive is a great day to enjoy!
The Universe wants me to play at every moment.
I live in a loving and supportive Universe.
I have limitless energy.
Where there is a will, there is a way.
I am worthy.
I am capable of anything because I am a powerful creation of God.
I am the embodiment of happiness, love, joy, and ecstasy.
I am full of passionate joy.
Every moment is an opportunity to enjoy and be excited about life.
Every moment has joy in it!
Nothing outside myself can affect my euphoria!

These are but a few examples of empowering beliefs that you can adopt and limiting ones that you can let go. They certainly do affect your emotional life, so get out your journal and write down all of the limiting beliefs you have and replace them with empowering ones. Also write down all of the limiting rules you have and replace them with empowering rules that will set you up so you have energetic, positive emotions at your disposal now! Please do this exercise because it will make a difference if you actually write everything down as opposed to just doing it in your head. Writing allows you to focus and makes it more official, instilling the information into your subconscious.

HAPPINESS LIES IN CONSTANT PERSONAL GROWTH

In order to feed yourself a continuous divine banquet of emotional happiness, you must understand that when you're growing and working toward a desired goal, a level of joy and happiness is naturally being fed to your emotional body. That is because personal growth to become your authentic self is the reason you entered your body and chose to birth yourself in this planet. The Universe, in its infinite intelligence, knew that if it gave you an emotional dial to turn, you could use it so you could feel happy. That emotional dial is the range of high positive emotions and low negative emotions. By paying attention to your emotions and turning the dial up, you will eventually find your way back into your authentic self. Sure you might feel uncomfortable when you're growing and expanding, but that's just a sign that the aliveness of feeling more joy, happiness, and fulfillment is just around the corner. It is how we were all made! We were made to grow in joyous, positive discomfort and then be catapulted into a joyous fulfillment that comes after every wave of expansion that comes from hard work (or shall I say hard, joyous play)!

When you are not growing, and when you have decided not to push yourself or move forward toward your goals and become more authentically you, you will automatically feel depressed, sad, or another negative emotion. Your soul will always guide you with negative emotions, at least on a subtle level, if you're not moving in the right direction. The Creator has designed us in such a way that we are built to grow. It's why we came to earth! If you're not feeling good, it's an indicator that you have stopped growing and are not doing the things you were meant to do in order to grow and become a better, more authentic version of yourself!

So if personal growth is a major key in feeling happy, what are the things you must do to keep growing? First, it's important to have big goals that excite you. If you have too much time on your hands, are bored, or don't know what to do with your life, you probably don't have big enough goals to challenge or excite you. You must always and continuously have set goals and, more importantly, compelling and exciting goals. If you have done so already, it is essential that you write down your goals. Be clear about what you want, and make sure that when you think about your goals, it makes you want to get out of bed every morning and be excited about the journey toward them.

Remember, the key here is to harness positive emotion and cultivate happiness, so it is very important that you view every goal as having a high level of enjoyment. For example, if you want to lose weight, don't just write down that you want to lose weight because you might equate that with not eating your favorite foods, starvation, and long hours of torture at the gym. Perhaps your goal should be to have massive energy levels, to find the activities that will make you enjoy losing weight, and that you will achieve your weight loss in a healthy, enjoyable way. This goal, compared to the original one, is a lot more appealing and a lot more exciting. Think about your goals carefully and explore what you really want in them.

Once you have your goals written down, make sure you look at them daily so your subconscious mind can be programmed for where it's going and so your focus is in the right direction. And then, what's next? You take joyful action, of course. And lots of it, really focused, immersed, inspired joyful action. The best joyful action you can possibly muster type of joyful action! The kind of joyful action that wows people; that is the ultimate fulfilling emotion because you know you did your best and you took lots of joyful action every single day. The top successful people always over-deliver in their actions and take the time to enjoy them fully, so why not explosively enjoy going over and beyond what you think you're capable of in your daily action? You have the power to create it with your mind!

However, you may then start to feel the discomfort of what comes when you expand yourself beyond your comfort zone to attain your goals, and you could find yourself saying, "I thought this was supposed to bring me happiness, not pain." Here is the deal; I guarantee you that the pain that comes from not growing is far greater than the positive discomfort of growing and taking action. You might, at some level, feel comfortable where you are at, but a level of sadness is still eating at you, and sooner or later, the problem will become so big that it's just unbearable and you will wish that you took action a long time ago. Please note that the discomfort of expansion is your teacher; it's your "weights" to make you stronger and even more determined to stay in peace, love, and joy, despite any problems or discomfort. Discomfort when you're expanding is the birthing process of a new you, but it will soon pass.

I cannot tell you how unbelievably good it feels to me to accomplish something that took me out of my comfort zone. I remember when I went from a size 12 to a size 4 and I made the decision that I was going to exercise six times a week doing hot yoga. The discomfort for the first six months was unbearable at times. I had so much toxicity coming up, and my body was tired from all the energy I was putting into the exercising. It was not easy, but I chose to let go of resisting it and to have love, joy, and a sense of peace with whatever experience I had, so I stuck with it. I then felt the joy of being passionate about moving forward like a warrior, but also as a playful child. The pain of doing the things I had to do was there, but I was happy and proud of myself; that's a feeling of accomplishment I wouldn't trade for anything.

And then the times when I didn't do the things I should have done began eating at me, so I didn't have much of a choice and I just kept going. So every time you feel like quitting, fill yourself up and enjoy your warrior spirit; remember that when you grow into a more expanded person, the activities that you once thought were unconquerable are eventually going to become easier because you will have grown to be a stronger person.

And then, obviously, you move on to bigger and bigger goals that keep taking you out of your comfort zone. The expansion into the discomfort never ends; it's your magnificent state of being, so just get used to diving into positive discomfort and accepting that it isn't going away, but that doesn't mean you cannot enjoy yourself while it's present in your journey. Remember that everything you want comes after the joy of stepping outside your comfort zone!

ADDING EMOTIONS TO YOUR DAILY AFFIRMATIONS, PRAYERS, SPOKEN WORDS, AND DAILY ACTION

I have noticed that the majority of people, especially in English-speaking countries, are more focused on living in the mind and making it superior to any other part of the human body, especially the emotional body. Although I do see this situation changing as more spiritually-integrated teachers and students emerge, living in the mind and identifying with it still seems predominant. Some people only associate themselves with the mental body without really honoring the emotional body and its power to attract authentic abundance. But I can tell you that the link between the mental and emotional body is crucial to activate and awaken yourself as well as the manifestation of an abundant life.

One of the major areas where I see this importance is in affirmations. As we discussed in the last chapter, affirmations will be part of your daily routine on the Divine Diet, but affirmation without positive emotion has less power and effect in getting results. If you are monotonously just saying the words without high vibrational positive emotion, a level of disconnection is there. Affirmation, with boredom, disbelief, fear, and uncertainty about what you're saying, is really just affirming those emotions. Positive emotions are what truly activate the power of affirmation, visualization, goal-setting, and setting intentions. Mind and heart in spoken word is a divine activation of your true spirit just like fire and wood burning together. Don't forget that spoken word is more powerful than just thoughts.

If you're just going to be like a machine, bored out of your mind and just saying words over and over, your subconscious mind isn't going to believe or pick up what you're saying as something that you really mean or intend on doing. So be fully present with the expectation that you're going to get what you want, and with as much emotional intensity as you can, affirm this within yourself. Your whole body will respond very differently, and your subconscious will guide you to take action on levels you never imagined. So go somewhere alone, like an empty room or your car while you're driving somewhere, and say your affirmations with emotional intensity. Also, remember that you can always say things quietly with just as much emotional intensity if you have people around you and you do not want to disturb them. From now on, please play and have fun with these spiritual practices, and add to your daily affirmation practices an emotional intensity of love, faith, confidence, joy, passion, gratitude, excitement, enthusiasm, or whatever emotion is appropriate to match the affirmation you are affirming to yourself.

This process can also apply to daily prayer so you can make your prayer even more powerful, and it can apply to your daily spoken word or even singing, if you're a singer. I am reminded here of singer Christina Aguilera's quote, "It's always worked for me to sing from the heart." A person who embodies an intense emotional love for humanity and goes about his or her day talking to people and taking action to help people has a far more profound effect on others and him- or herself than when just going through the motions and getting things done without being connected to the emotional body. It's magnetic to see people connect their spoken word with deep emotion; it's apparent in preachers, teachers, singers, and speakers who are famous and draw large crowds; you can't help wanting to watch them because, whether you know it or not, their positive emotional energy is being sent out and is feeding everyone around it. Just notice how good you feel with someone you admire who is a positive speaker who engages his emotional bodies when he speaks or is just around you.

Also, it is important to remember not to do the opposite. How many times have we spoken negative words, swearing and arguing with all the negative emotional anger we can muster? That's a very destructive way to live, so I want to suggest that you be highly aware of how you're living. When you're in a negative emotional state, you can change it immediately by focusing on something you're grateful for and focusing on things that make you feel good and proud; it's that simple. It is easy to get back into your positive emotions because you have the power to choose the thoughts that make you feel better.

In general, your overall background emotion should be a deep peace and love for God, for yourself, for humanity, and for all of the other parts of creation on this planet. Then when you speak and take action through the day, these emotions can have a much more profound effect on your daily thoughts, spoken words, and prayers. Simply affirm this, visualize it, and create it within yourself.

USING FOCUSED VISUALIZATION TO CREATE POSITIVE EMOTIONS AND THE POWERFUL EMOTION OF CERTAINTY

In the last chapter, we touched on the power of visualization and adding it to your daily routine to visualize the perfect outcome and attract what you want into your life. In this chapter, we will touch on how this technique can and does create positive emotion.

Like affirmation, visualization without positive emotion has a less positive effect on the results you are trying to get. However, in my experience, it takes less effort to create positive emotion when it comes to visualizing positive things. Positive Visualization is so powerful that, for almost anyone, a strong positive emotion comes with it, but being aware of your emotions and how powerful the emotional body is, I can guarantee you that just by this awareness, you can intensify the emotion as much as you want during your visualizations.

Before I delve into visualization, I want to mention here the power of focus. You must constantly focus throughout the day and picture the things you want, especially the yearly goals you want to attain. When you are focused and picturing the things you don't want, especially the things you fear happening, you move toward those things, and that is not what you want to do, so whenever you catch yourself, change the vision into what you do want. A lot of us just go through the day thinking about dreadful things and thinking and visualizing things not working out because we are afraid they won't work out, but that's precisely why they don't and why what we fear ends up happening. It's important to understand and start being aware and present of the thoughts and visualizations that you have throughout the day. Sometimes, for no reason, we think about an old boyfriend or girlfriend who betrayed us or a job we lost, and then we start feeling negative emotion. So change your focus by thinking about and visualizing only the things that make you feel good and excited about moving on with your life.

When you picture and visualize things going perfectly, you eventually start to feel emotions of absolute knowing that things will work out—emotions of certainty that you can do it, and there's no question that it will come to fruition. Visualizing things as if they already happened makes your subconscious mind give you the feelings that come with already having attained a goal, and in return, you eventually do. But it is important to understand that that feeling of faith, that feeling of absolute certainty, is crucial to attaining your goals because it opens up the high vibrational frequency that is in harmony with attracting what you want.

Have you heard the saying, "If you believe it, you will see it"? That's what's happening here because the more you see it, the more your subconscious tends to believe it's on its way, and then when you focus on it enough, it will materialize in the outer world. In your head, see it perfectly happening over and over every day; make your emotional feeling so confident and certain that there isn't an ounce of fear within you that it's not going to work out. That's the way to all of your dreams and goals—at least the ones that are in alignment with your highest self; sometimes you don't get what you want, but then, in turn, you get directed to a higher purpose that is in alignment with your path.

Also remember that you can use the power of visualization to change any negative mood you have. Perhaps thinking of your family or having a picture of them next to you will help. Also picturing yourself in the Bahamas, experiencing a newborn puppy, a happy baby, your favorite date, or anything that you think will uplift you is always a powerful remedy to get your attention and focus away from any negative thoughts or visions that are causing you to experience negative emotion.

THE POWER OF GRATITUDE, CONFIDENCE, ENTHUSIASM, LOVE, PEACE, AND PASSION

The emotions of gratitude, confidence, enthusiasm, love, peace, and passion are the top emotions I believe everyone can gravitate toward daily to reap the rewards of true success. The foundation of your success always comes from how happy you are or how high your frequency of positive emotion is. Understanding the power of these emotions as described below will give you a deeper perspective on how to benefit more fully and enjoy these emotions even further to attract even more abundance in all areas of your life.

Gratitude is one of the most powerful emotions you could ever feel on a daily basis; it holds a vibration as high as love. Gratitude and appreciation must be a way of life for you and part of your overall attitude in how you look at your life because they have the power to attract even more good things into your life. When you feel gratitude and appreciation, you're basically saying, "Thank you, Universe, for all I have," and in saying that, you're allowing more abundance to be attracted to you. A joyous moment is always filled with gratitude and appreciation. It has the power to make you look at the glass as half-full instead of half-empty. It has the power to dissolve fear when you feel it, and the power to attract even more goodness and prosperity into your life because you feel appreciation for however little or much you may already have. When you're grateful, you see that you are truly abundant and that lack is only an illusion and an attitude. True abundance is not the money you have, but the ability to see that no matter how little you have materially, you always have blessings all around you, so take the time daily to notice them, appreciate them, and give thanks.

A great example of how gratitude works is partners in a loving relationship. Imagine a husband and wife saying, "Thank you" to each other and appreciating everything they each do for their marriage and family. Do you think the husband would then want to do more for his family? Their sense of appreciation and gratitude is bringing them even more abundance. What about the opposite? Do you think a husband who is being taken for granted will be motivated to do more for his wife, or less? I think you know the answer. Perhaps being thankful to the Universe works the same way; the Universe then wants to bring more abundance into your life because you are grateful and appreciative of everything it has given to you. Allow yourself to receive more goodness into your life by being grateful.

It is also always good to be reminded that someone always has it worse than you. You may not be in a wheelchair like many people who will sit in one for the rest of their lives, and you may have all your body parts as opposed to many who are missing their arms, legs, eyes, etc. Whatever you have, therefore, it is important to start being grateful for it. Other good examples are maybe you were not sent out to war, or you have a roof over your head. Think about all the lack that other people have in areas where you are rich. It's important to add feeling strong emotions of gratitude to your daily practice so they spill out throughout your day to make it even more enjoyable. This practice is just as important as visualization and affirmation. I highly recommend that you practice writing down or talking out loud about all of the things you are grateful for in a journal every day or say them out loud in front of your altar, if you have one, or in some other special place where you think it would be nice to honor what you are grateful for. Taking the time to do this will enrich your emotional life at a high level and make you feel like a million dollars; it's that important.

Confidence is such a crucial emotion to your success, especially when it comes to your talents and your life purpose. If you are monetizing what you are meant to do and making it your career, your ability to attract clients or prosperity will depend very much on your confidence level. Anyone who wants to work with you, whether she knows it or not, will want to work with someone with confidence who knows what he is doing. Confidence is very much related to faith and certainty. When you have faith that things are going to work out, you trust that the Universe or God has your back, and your confidence level increases.

Another way to increase confidence is to list all of the things you have accomplished in the past. By doing this, you have a reference point and you see how you have the power to achieve more. Also list all of the ways you have seen the Universe assist and help you in challenging situations. This will serve as a reminder to you that you are not alone, you are being lovingly supported, and the Universe is guiding your steps; knowing this alone can make a tremendous difference in your level of confidence. How can you not be confident when you know the Universe is at your side and at your disposal to make your life happen the way you want?

Enthusiasm is another great emotion to adopt. The word enthusiasm originated from the Greek words *Theus* (God) and *En* (In), which means "In God." That's a pretty amazing and magical definition! To have this emotion is to be inside or a part of God—that's a pretty sacred experience, so look forward to cultivating enthusiasm every day, no matter what problems you may have around you! Do you see and feel how much more powerfully your life can unfold and grow when you are in God?

I find that enthusiasm not only tickles you with blissful emotions as you enthusiastically go through the day, but it blasts you with massive amounts of energy to keep you going. You find yourself spending longer and longer periods of time doing the things you love because you are so enthusiastic about them. Enthusiasm has the ability to attract so many people to you; it is such a magnetic quality. Napoleon Hill talks about enthusiasm's power in his classic book *Think and Grow Rich*. A smart salesman or anyone with a product knows the power of enthusiasm; salesmen always add a strong element of enthusiasm to their sales speeches when talking to people about their products and or services. When you go about achieving your goals, set the intention of adding enthusiasm and you will not only feel good, but you will have so much more energy fueling your body to achieve your goals, and that energy will fuel your clients or friends as well. Start to expand this emotion by affirming enthusiasm in your daily work and activities.

How do you cultivate enthusiasm to such a high degree within your body that it becomes habitual and is easy to access the moment you get out of bed and every single moment until you go back to bed, despite any problems you might face throughout the day? One of the easiest ways is to move your body in a celebratory way, moving up and down, dancing to dance music, raising your hands, clapping your hands with excitement, smiling, breathing more fully, raising your eyebrows, speaking loudly, being childlike and silly, cracking up with a fake laugh until you're truly laughing, and rehearsing in your mind by pretending that whatever it is that you want to be enthusiastic about is actually exciting for you. Enthusiasm cannot exist for you without faith and seeing a bright future in your mind's eye. Start talking about whatever it is in an enthusiastic way. Keep acting enthusiastic and practicing it over and over until you start to see your body and mind believing it and feeling high levels of enthusiasm. I do it with dance music over and over two to five times a day for five or ten minutes until I experience a level of emotion that does feel exciting and I am passionately enthusiastic about my subject or activity.

I also write down all the ideas that come to me after I ask myself, "What about this topic, product, or service makes me enthusiastic?" After I write them down, I check my emotional gauge to see how I respond to them, and if I am not quite enthusiastic yet, I keep working at it. I keep moving; I keep asking until I find that level of enthusiasm.

Be aware of your focus. If you focus on your problems or negative doubtful visions, it will suck out all of your energy and enthusiasm. Focus on things working out; see your final outcome as if you already possess it; focus on the excitement of your life as something that must be celebrated because life is meant to be fun, and then stay at that level of focus. Remember that it's a choice to feel good, so decide to focus on it.

I cannot stress enough how important it is not only for your emotional wellbeing to experience and enjoy this fun emotion of enthusiasm, but that it can win you customers, clients, and new friends, and it can draw a new level of abundance into your life and the lives of those around you who have not even dreamed about it. Just take a look at the salesmen in commercials; the good commercials are the ones where the person is speaking with a high level of enthusiasm. Don't customers usually buy when a salesman speaks about a product with this level of positive emotion? Enthusiasm is so energetically nourishing that everybody wants it, so why not cultivate it within yourself and apply it to every single day of your life? Decide to be the torch of fire, not the blown out one. Hold your torch up high every day, and let it nourish you and everyone around you. Finally, it's great to have upbeat enthusiasm, but you can also have a more quiet enthusiasm when appropriate.

Love is such a popular emotion, but, unfortunately, it is too often taken for granted. Love is the mother of all positive emotions and the gateway to enlightenment. It's what holds this planet and the entire Universe together. It's the very essence of the Universe or God. Love has the power to open and activate so much within you if you consciously intend to expand this emotion. When you feel deep emotions of love, then without question, you are open to receiving from within yourself the right spiritual guidance and level of actions you need to take, and the thoughts and feelings you need so you can accomplish what you are meant to do. When you're in the opposite emotion of anger or fear, bitterness or resentment, you close your doors to heightened divine guidance, creativity, inspiration, and right action. Cultivate the feeling of love daily, even if it's just five minutes spent focusing on your heart and feeling love for your children, parents, brothers, sisters, family, friends, and the world. You might, for example, want to take the time to volunteer at a homeless shelter or nursing home and cultivate those feelings of love there. I find that hugging people helps a lot to activate a deep emotion of love. Doing my "Sunflower of Positive Emotions Meditation" or playing with children or pets, especially dogs and cats, are also very good ways to activate and cultivate love within your being.

Below is a paragraph I wrote years ago and recently rediscovered in my journal. I thought it was intriguing so I want to share and elaborate on it:

> I lost my will to live completely alive and passionate, failed many times, burned and backstabbed so many times, so many awful feelings of depression, resentment, and anger...yet here I wake up today with a miracle I prayed for, an overwhelming love for all of you, for me and God, and to serve humanity, a love so big it brings tears to my eyes. All of a sudden, I feel like nothing can stop me. I have a reason to live fully again.

I was surprised by the level of love I felt that night. It was like I never felt it before, as if God were hugging me from within. I simply asked for it, and there it was. The emotion of love can often be overwhelming; it's always there, no matter how deeply sad or depressed you are. I recommend you do your own personal love meditations, focusing your attention on your heart, thinking about the people you love, loving yourself, sending love to yourself, and recognizing how much you love yourself. Make a commitment to see beauty in this world and to love it so completely, no matter how many times you have been betrayed or hurt by others. When you make that commitment, you have great power to transform the world. I cannot tell you how enjoyable it is to have love in your heart and truly contribute to humanity.

I remember realizing that the more you want to contribute to humanity, the more insight and wisdom can be activated within yourself. Can you imagine that? When you make a conscious decision to expand your love within yourself and give your all as much as you can because of that love to serve, the Universe rewards you with a new level of insight you were not able to access before. And, of course, there is the Law of Reciprocity: What you give always comes back to you. Do not wait for someone to fill the void of love within you; go ahead and give it freely; then you will feel it, and you will get it in return.

Perhaps you can relate to what I wrote in my journal passage above; maybe you're going through a similar experience. I think every one of us at some point in our lives goes through tremendous struggle and heartache, and we can sometimes get lost and forget what truly is important in our lives. What is it that is going to guide us to our real desires, dreams, and goals? One of the pieces that really helps me is expanding my love in my heart for humanity. I often visualize myself giving this love to humanity through my performance art, through my clothing designs, through my seminars, books, and products. In the back of my head, I always have the desire to visualize my love expanding so much that it makes me unstoppable. It makes me want to keep going even when I am tired or scared to keep going. It's like a drug, only it has no side effects; it truly is amazing! It almost feels like making love to every aspect of God, loving God in everyone so much that you're just willing to give your all because of it. It's a natural high; it's like making love 24/7 through my talents and my life purpose! For me, visualization is the key to strengthening this love and performing at a higher level of service to humanity.

It's also key for me to remember how powerful it is to play music that activates love within myself. You know what your love songs are and which ones do it for you. I think that using music when you're not feeling so well is so key to accessing and enhancing this powerful aspect of yourself. I can remember very clearly when I visited Texas how all the country music on the radio was all about love, and I remember how good it made me feel. I wondered whether that country music had anything to do with everyone in traffic being kind and letting me cut in front of him! In Los Angeles or New York, you'll get the finger instead. I really believe that people in Texas, just as one example, are so much more relaxed and in tune with their emotional bodies of love because of the country music they play. Music's vibration is so helpful to access the loving part of ourselves, and it doesn't have to be country music, or any music—again, I am just giving you ideas here to get in tune with this powerful emotion of love because love is the ideal foundation of all your emotions. It is beneficial for love to be your foundation, and then you can add different colors of emotion to it.

This paragraph may be the most important one I'll write about the powerful emotion of love. I am going to tell you a story about something that completely changed my perspective on love and the importance of having conscious loving people in one's inner circle. I have a wise teacher and friend who transformed me. After attending her second event, I realized the power of giving and receiving love authentically and strongly to people. There is such a thing as giving love like you have never given it before to people. Many of us have a dimmer light and perspective on the fire of love, while others have practiced it so much that their fire for feeling and expressing it has become vast in their lives. My teacher has this type of love. She can reach down and love you like you have never felt loved before. I was loved before, but the way she expressed it even triggered a love in me that I had never felt for people and humanity. I broke down crying for a week on and off, and I realized that my love had layers to be built. You think you know love? You know nothing of it. Love along with any other emotion might surprise you with a different energetic frequency you have never felt as it grows inside of you. Years might go by before a massive breakthrough on an emotion happens for you like it happened for me when I came to understand love more deeply. Surround yourself with people who love like there is no tomorrow; these are the people who are going to change your life and set the example for you to love more. My career as a public speaker, life coach, and author changed completely after that experience. I was fulfilling my life purpose, but that fire of love I felt for her ignited a different kind of love and delivery of my services to my students and clients. I felt a new level of fulfillment for what I was meant to do on the planet that I had never felt before. A new life was being rebuilt within me. My intention is now to love to the best of my capacity so you may be transformed to a higher level of consciousness like I experienced with my teacher. I can promise you this: the deeper and closer you step toward me, the deeper my love and commitment will be to you and to awakening your life purpose and prosperity.

Peace, to me, is the king of all emotions, it comes before love because it feeds the foundation and very essence of who we are. It comes from a place of stillness and nothingness. It's an element that accompanies meditation very easily. The essence of the Universe is quiet stillness and peaceful nothingness—that is a very profound energy that feeds and creates everything else. Without peace in your heart, no matter what is going on in your life, the very essence of you cannot build in a healthy way. Without peace in your heart, all other positive emotions, including love, cannot come in a profound and rich way.

To obtain peace, the most important thing to do is never to panic or resist, no matter what the circumstance, because panic or resistance always makes the situation worse. Breathe peace and calmness into your heart and it will always make everything easier. If you can't find joy in the moment, or if you are suffering, you can always cultivate peace to bring you through any situation, just by accepting what is and not resisting it. Peace is the foundation of your emotions that makes love blossom more effectively. Remember to breathe peace into your meditations and daily challenges; it will certainly ease your experiences and ability to follow through.

Passion, like enthusiasm, has the ability to activate great energy within your being. Passion is my favorite emotion to tune into, especially when I am tired and not willing to keep going because of the hard obstacles and challenges ahead of me, or when I want to channel anger into a positive emotion. Passion will keep you going even when you are tired. Passion is the emotion of a warrior who will not be stopped! The best way I have been able to cultivate passion is to say, with all the emotional passionate intensity I can, "I will not be stopped. I will take massive action." When I say it over and over for about five minutes, it builds such intense energy in me that it fuels me to get through everything I need to get through. It fuels me to be the best I can be in every area of my life. To have a passion is to have an obsession for a righteous life.

If love is wood, then passion is the fire that makes it burn. I don't know too much about astrology, but I have been told that my sign carries a lot of fire. I have channeled that fire into anger and used it very destructively many times (and boy, did I cause problems and negative pain). If you have fiery emotion like me, learn to transmute it into passion. I have learned to transmute that fire more effectively into passion to get things done. I think for most of us, we have so little passion within ourselves that we don't even know how to start to activate it within ourselves. I can tell you that it is very simple. Movement follows emotion. If you clap your hands very quickly, it will activate a certain intensity of energy within yourself. If you punch a bag and think of certain things that have hurt you in the past as you punch it, I guarantee it will activate a certain level of passion within you. You don't have to destroy anything; it can be as safe as dancing to upbeat music, running, fencing, or doing what you love. You can call in help from God or the Universe to help you activate what movements and thoughts you need to activate within yourself. I remember channeling my highest self once when I started punching an imaginary bag; it was teaching me how to move fiercely, telling me it was my "power move," and explaining how the punching activates a certain level of passionate power. Another good example is visualizing yourself holding a sword up high and speaking loudly with passion, or repeating emotional affirmations, such as "I am full of personal power and passion. Nothing can or will stop me now" or "My passion now guides me to the most productive day possible." Please say it with emotional intensity, and monitor your body and the way you say it. Make sure you're completely feeling what you say or it won't work. When you feel this powerful emotion of passion, you will automatically be inspired to follow it with a greater level of effective action toward your goals.

This emotion of passion is so important because every day when you wake up, your body is sort of in a "dead" state. If you don't move your body with exercise and activate your passion 100 percent, then you're just going to go through your day with a less effective way to get things done.

I recommend you figure out your passion formula—what makes you passionate. Because everyone is different, I can't really tell you what will and won't work for you, so experiment until you get it right, and do it daily. My passion formula is singing and dancing in a vigorous way and using punching movements; this movement activates and fuels me to keep going throughout the day, and it deviates me from destructive emotions like anger.

SET YOUR INTENTION TO ENJOY EVERY DAY

Setting your intention to enjoy every day is one of the most important lessons to understand because when you feel enjoyment and enjoy every moment of your life, it is a magnet for wealth and abundance of good on all levels. Setting the intention and determination to enjoy every single moment and then doing just that is true wealth; it's the number one true success secret. Your level of success equals the level of enjoyment and happiness you have in your heart for this moment, not the amount of money you have in your bank account. When you have joy, you are strong and powerful, so ego and dark forces have less power over you! You are putting up a shield of light around yourself to protect you against the dark forces within yourself and on this planet so you cannot be weakened. Plus, the joy and power you feel will attract even more goodness into your life because like attracts like.

Some people don't allow themselves to feel joy because they believe they don't deserve it or it just feels too foreign to them. They think they need to be on drugs to be happy. Don't let the darkness fool you; you are meant to have ecstatic joy even in the discomfort of growth; it's your natural state! The Creator wants you to feel deep oceans of joy. Allow yourself to feel joy because it is what the Universe wants for you and it is rightfully yours! Pray to God to fill you. Visualize yourself swelling up with joy or simply dance with music to start cultivating it within you. Let God make love to your emotional body with joy, a sense of humor, laughter, and fun!

Enjoying your life despite what is going on or no matter how hard it gets is true success! You can have peace even though you have the toughest struggle of your life. You have to build the habit daily so you can be a strong, giant, joyful oak tree that no wind can knock down. When you're not enjoying things and not positive, you're flowing against the stream of life. God, the universal flow, is always positive and full of joy. In order to enjoy life, start by changing your thoughts, your focus, and be grateful for every moment. If you see yourself as rich, then you are more able to enjoy your life. You might have lost your leg, but at least you have your other body parts! You might have learned your most profound lesson because of it! Don't make any excuses not to feel joy or enjoy your day. Don't let the outside world rob you of this most important emotion; your future abundance, prosperity, and joy depend on it; your health and abundance depend on it.

Also, get rid of the idea that in the future you will decide to enjoy yourself when you have everything perfect because that will never happen. Your end goal is really ecstatic joy for this moment—not the future. This is your moment; there is nothing else, so decide every day when you wake up to enjoy your day! Put a smile on your face and enjoy the heaven out it!

Adopt the idea that everything is exciting, full of fun and joy; you just have to unlock the door to see it that way. Your chores are full of joy; your job is full of joy. The Universe wants you to experience joy in your daily activities; just find the right thoughts; the Universe is whispering to you so you can tune into the fun of it! Get quiet and listen; it is there for you! And then once you have tuned into it, don't let it go; grab on to it enthusiastically and juice up the joy!

And one more thing: Think of joy and enjoyment not only as your shield of protection that you put on every morning, but as a way to unblock any disconnections you might have with the inner wisdom you already possess. God feeds you daily with thoughts and actions; His purpose is to work through you to radiate positive energy and to heal humanity through your gifts and talents. When you are full of enjoyment, you are better guided on how to increase your finances, upgrade to better friends, and move to an even deeper level of happiness in all areas of your life. So no matter how hard your situation is, meet it with a smile because that's what's going to get you out of it as smoothly as possible.

Also, remember that your Creator is waiting to turn your life around when you choose to enjoy and have happiness now. Most think it's the opposite—that happiness is something to be attained when you achieve your goal. But instead, why not happily achieve? Why not enjoy this moment because I can guarantee you that just that one happy moment after you achieve success is not fulfilling enough because your emotions are ongoing. You consciously need to decide to train yourself every day to have enjoyment, happiness, and euphoria as your state of being. Stop depending on the idea of an outside situation of success for your inner condition of happiness. Decide now to condition yourself habitually to enjoy every moment in a celebratory, funny, enthusiastic, exciting, and loving way.

Here are some affirmations you might want to add to your daily routine: (Please remember to say them with all the excitement and emotional enthusiasm you can muster.)

- I am excited about this day; I am surrounded by a massive permanent shield of joy, happiness, ecstasy, and sense of humor that is unshakable despite my outer circumstances.
- I have an unshakable massive permanent shield of ecstatic enthusiastic exciting joy that attracts all the overflowing abundance of God.
- This is a great day; I am joyfully enthusiastic to serve the children of God through my beautiful talents and services.

Please remember to make these affirmations your own; adjust them as needed or make up your own personal affirmations that best suit you. These are just examples of possibilities that might serve you. Most importantly, don't forget to say them with joy.

I also want to mention the power of having a sense of humor and laughing often as part of your daily enjoyment process. When you set the intention of seeing things with a sense of humor and laughing about them, it creates feelings of goodness that overflow into the rest of your day and make it even more enjoyable. When you laugh and smile, it sends a signal into your brain to release pleasure hormones into your bloodstream, which elevates your mood. So make jokes often, be silly, see the humor in everything, cultivate a good sense of humor, and crack up laughing even without a reason! Yes, you can also laugh for no reason! Try it! It's unbelievably euphoric! Why not? Your inner child will love it! You may also join laughter yoga meet-ups in your local area. Google to find them and practice laughing in groups!

USING FOOD AND PHYSICAL MOVEMENT
TO CREATE POSITIVE EMOTION

Although diet and body movement will be addressed in detail in the next chapter, "The Divine Diet for the Physical Body," I wanted to mention them briefly in this chapter because they have a huge effect on the emotional body. Obviously, all mental, emotional, physical, and spiritual bodies are interlinked so they affect each other. Therefore, here I will give some of the core elements and understandings of diet, exercise, and body movements that will affect your emotions drastically. This will be a perfect way to transition into the next chapter.

Let's start with movement. Movement, as I mentioned earlier, does affect emotion. Even the word emotion has the word motion in it. Facial movement, especially smiling, is so important to feel good. So smile more, even when you don't feel like it. Smiling helps your brain produce endorphins to make you feel good. Jump up and down in joy with your hands raised up and smiling or dance to create more excitement and joy. Throughout the day, choose the movements that help you feel emotionally uplifted, and keep practicing them until they become daily habits.

In terms of exercise, I recommend you do it daily, but then take off one day a week to recover. A body without daily exercise is a tired, stagnant, unhappy body that is less able to be emotionally charged with positive emotion. A body that has the lymphatic system stimulated and oxygen levels and muscles worked on a daily basis will automatically help you feel more energized, alive, and happier. I personally do hot yoga six times a week, and I feel more emotionally stable and in a happier mood because of it. You can choose whatever it is that appeals to you; however, I will highly recommend you do hot yoga as it was recommend to me by my highest self in a clairvoyant communication. If you already have an exercise program, add an extra thirty minutes after the daily practice for joyful movement after your hot yoga practice. Make sure you move your body daily with some form of exercise if you can't find yourself in a hot yoga studio. Studies have shown that those who exercise on a regular basis are much happier and are less likely to be in a bad mood or in some form of depression; exercise is that important. Hot yoga makes the body healthier, energetically charges your body, and extends lifespan.

Food has a more subtle effect on the body; however, it does affect your emotional wellbeing for the long term. The number one thing I see that affects overall mood is how alkaline the body is. An acid body is not a happy body and can catch colds and disease easier. I believe that a diet with an emphasis on alkaline foods is like a natural high. That's why people smoke—it's alkalizing to take deep breaths, and it alleviates the body of acidity. Introducing at least 16 ounces of freshly juiced alkaline vegetable juice from dark green, leafy vegetables will slowly but surely transform and balance out the body's acid alkaline balance and give you so much more energy. Drinking this juice daily will eventually give you a natural high.

Eating dead foods—basically all cooked foods—has an effect on the body as well. Although they may taste good for the most part, they gradually numb the nervous system of feelings and emotions without us noticing it because it's such a slow process. Eventually, we start feeling so much less, and we wonder why we are not happy. It's like a frog being slowly cooked in water in a pot; it will eventually die because it was slowly warmed until boiling so it doesn't realize it needs to jump out, whereas a frog that is thrown into boiling water will immediately jump out. This is a great metaphor for people who prematurely take years off their lives and numb their feelings by eating cooked foods. A raw diet full of living foods can correct this problem and intensify and amplify the level of emotional intensity, feelings, and aliveness that you can feel. For recipes on how to live a raw diet lifestyle to influence your happier mood, check out my books available on Kindle at Amazon.com: *Divina's Hearty Raw Foods* and *Divina's Living Caribbean Cuisine*.

So remember to smile, dance, move your body, exercise, and eat and drink as many living foods as you can daily. And if there is one thing you change about your diet to change your mood, let it be to drink 16 ounces of freshly juiced, cold, pressed, dark green, leafy vegetables every day. This section is just the beginning to the importance of how diet and exercise have an effect on the emotional body, so let's explore now in the next chapter how to take care of the physical body to activate a deeper wealth of positive emotion.

PUTTING IT INTO PRACTICE

Here are some suggestions to put into practice what you learned in this chapter:

- Set aside ten to twenty minutes a day to feel grateful, peaceful, enthusiastic, passionate, and loving whenever you are feeling negative emotion.

- Affirm daily what you want to draw into your life with all the emotional intensity you can activate.

- Visualize the things you want as if they are already in your life and as if things are as you want them to be. Be present and add as much feeling as you can to your visualization. Focus only on the positive visions in your mind's eye. When you catch yourself focusing on the negative, switch it back to the vision of the end goal you are wanting to accomplish. Remember that you always move toward what you focus on.

- Use the power of physical body movement to feel good. Move your body daily, smile often, laugh, exercise, and dance to feel good.

- Set your intention to enjoy every day. Be silly, have a sense of humor, and laugh!

- Set the rules and beliefs in your mind so you can be happy. Write down the ones that are not working, and then write down ones to replace them with that will work. Revisit your rules and beliefs for at least twenty-one days to reprogram your subconscious into your new routine.

- Make sure you have your goals written down and you look at them daily so you have something to look forward to working toward. Happiness is in personal growth; you can't grow to your maximum without set goals.

- Enjoy raw living foods and juice—at least 16 ounces of cold, pressed, dark, green vegetable juice every day. An alkaline body is a happy body! It's a natural high.

Chapter Four
The Divine Diet for the Physical Body

"For if you eat living food, the same will *quicken* you, but
if you kill your food, the dead food will kill you also."
— Jesus Christ, *The Essene Gospel of Peace*

THE FOUNDATION OF UNDERSTANDING

This chapter is about giving you the most explosive, massively energetic, and vibrant physical body you will ever have for the rest of your life! That statement makes me laugh a bit because it's quite a big promise, but I am confident that I have channeled great information from my highest self that will help you get just that! It's about giving you the energy to fuel you even more than you have imagined to keep you going with stamina in your career and personal life and to clear dark energy so you may channel your life purpose more easily from the divine! It's about building a virtually ageless body for the rest of your life; it's about building a body that is authentically reflecting who you are; it's no longer about leaving the body because it's full of diseases and sick and disabled in your mature years; it's about having the freedom of leaving because your soul chose to. But, ultimately, it's about reconnecting back to who you are by building a body that attracts the real you into it in a much more expansive manner. My dream for humanity is to have nursing homes be extinct and to have people strong enough and vibrant enough in their last stages of life literally to be able to dig their own graves if they want to.

If you have always wanted high levels of sustained energy throughout the day to get all of the things you want done, then read on! I'm excited to share with you the top amazing techniques to achieve extreme health, a long-lasting, ageless body, and massive energy! You will finally experience who you really are—a massively energetic, extremely healthy, continuously youthful being even well into your last years of living. Your body will be so clean that your soul can seat itself properly and finally channel your life purpose more clearly. The most important part of this chapter is what it teaches about the massive energy you can get, as well as the massive amounts of soul energy you can activate within your body, so buckle up because your productivity levels in getting the things you want done are about to take a 360-degree turn in the right direction, and you are about to discover who you are on a physical level!

In today's world, the physical body is probably the most neglected and polluted of all four bodies. Physical health, for the most part, is not honored at a high level. It could be, but it's not because most people don't recognize they are living in a sacred temple for the soul so it must be treated with utmost respect. People must have the same reverence and respect they feel when they enter a church or a temple when they wake up and enter their sacred body temples after sleep. The House of the Lord, whether it's a church or temple, is always clean, holy water is present, complete peace and stillness reign, and there is a sense of respectful holiness. Now is your opportunity to use that same energy to have your sacred body temple always clean, bathed with clean water, nourished with only natural food to maintain its peace and stillness, and respected as part of the holiness of creation that was given to you.

What I call "healthy" is, for most people, too extreme in their minds, but it's actually closer to the way we were designed to live. We live in a society where mediocrity is the norm; pizza parlors, fried foods, dead foods, and junk foods are rampant, so we subconsciously think it's okay to eat such food, although it's really out of alignment with our authentic sacred body temples and the vibrancy they are meant to reflect. It is absolutely essential that if you're going to change your health, you do it at a high level of "extreme health." It's really not extreme. Believe me, it is the norm in the sacred kingdom of heaven to worship the sacred body temple in such a holy way through practicing the Divine Diet of the physical body.

"Extreme health" is normal health. Do you really think enlightened beings and archangels and angels in their normal authentic state would choose a mediocre diet? Why should you? If you're not willing to be what you most likely see as extreme, then you don't really understand how valuable your body really is; it's your only connection to this planet. You can't just grow another body when your current one gets old and then slip into the new one. You wouldn't give away an arm of yours even for a million dollars, so why ruin your body with junk food and incorrect forms of food consumption? Is peer pressure, fear of looking different or being ridiculed or laughed at from the masses going to stop you from honoring yourself and God in this way? If people understood the magnitude of souls waiting to get their own bodies, and how a body provides the opportunity to advance faster spiritually by following this diet, people wouldn't take their bodies for granted or eat any junk food that takes life away from them. The longer lifespan you have, if you know the right spiritual practices, the more you can use that time to advance and grow spiritually before you leave your body and go back to the spiritual world.

It baffles me when I see expensive cars roll in to the drive-thru window at McDonald's, Kentucky Fried Chicken, Burger King, In-N-Out Burger, Domino's Pizza, or even parked at junk food restaurants or grocery stores. People then go home with the worst foods for their bodies to consume. They get the best and latest model cars, yet they have no sense of what the real value is for their bodies, so they trash them with junk food. If people treated their bodies the way they treat their expensive, high class cars, then they would start to get somewhere. Think of a race horse, a champion, top of the line breed. If you owned one, would you feed it junk food? No, because you want that horse to perform at its highest level, yet we trash the sacred temple of our soul with just about anything because it tastes good. It really is prostituting your body that opens the doors to dark energy and or entities in your body when you choose to eat something that tastes good just for the taste; junk food really is empty food that disconnects you from your light source. The truth is that healthy food doesn't need to be tasteless food. The ways and tastes of God in terms of health are a little simpler, which wisely teaches and enhances our sense of peace with what is, yet the feeling of wellness is undeniably more appealing than how junk food numbs your body and robs you of good feelings in the long term.

And then, so much has been written in thousands of books and so much of it creates confusion about diets and misunderstandings about what real nutrition and health are. So many diets are out there that it's hard to choose or know which one really is the healthiest and most well-grounded for our bodies. Furthermore, since the majority of people are not placing high priority on their physical health, they are ignorant of good health and pretty much take the degeneration of the body for granted like it's something normal that we inevitably experience. A body that is decomposing due to aging is usually out of alignment with source and is lacking correct information on how to take care of the body. I can tell you that we don't have to become less vibrant or have decomposed bodies as we age—at least very little decomposed compared to how most people do today. A vibrant body is achievable, and it is definitely something that can be attained by following what I will talk about in this chapter. You are about to experience huge levels of energy you never experienced before, a complete sense of wellbeing, and a body to make you proud that's vibrant and full of radiance.

But before you take action to change your health, first you must understand that your psychology about health is more important than the diet changes because it will make you take action long-term to prevent disease in your body. The one thing you need to change in terms of that psychology is deciding how important it is for you to have extreme health. Because if it's that important to you, you will find a way; if it's not, you will just find an excuse. Make it an extreme priority. One way I have made it a high priority is to understand that my body is a sacred temple. Your primary place of worship is not the church or any sacred temple where people choose to gather spiritually. Your number one sacred temple of worship is your body. You can best worship God by caring for and using the body He gave you. You do that by keeping it clean from any junk food, pornographic sexual behavior, nourishing it with sacred natural food that Mother Earth has provided for you, and through sacred spiritual practices like hot yoga. Cleanliness is next to godliness; may I say, "Amen" to this truthful statement. Your godliness, your highest self, is waiting for you constantly to reach new levels of internal cleanliness so you can make space for it to inhabit your body. The less clean you are internally, the less your highest self can activate and take its seat within your sacred body temple.

Below is the list of topics for the Divine Diet for your body that we will discuss in this chapter. A better understanding of each topic will transform you and bring you a step closer to your authentic self. However, please note that this chapter only covers the very foundation of what you need to get started. I am just scratching the surface here. I have created a two-year program that also includes two three-day events that not only cover the advanced level of the Divine Diet that I have channeled from Spirit, but that also coach you through two years of advancing spiritually in this Divine Diet with the support of other members, as well as myself, from the academy so you can resurrect your authentic body. I really am excited to share with you this two-year program to resurrect and magnetize not only your sacred body temple but more of your authentic highest self into your sacred body temple, which is your ultimate life purpose. I also plan soon to have an advanced program for this Divine Diet for people who have already completed the two-year program.

So here is what we will cover in this chapter:

The Mind-Body Connection
- The Psychology Behind a Healthy Body
- Using Affirmation/Visualization to Create Massive Energy, Health, and Wellbeing

The Body Movement
- Hot Yoga
- Rebounding
- Dancing
- Deep Breathing
- Smiling

The Food Principles
- Do Not Cook, Freeze, or Rot Your Food
- Vegetarian/Vegan: Honey, Milk, Grains, Vegetables, Fruit
- Combine No More Than Three Kinds of Food in a Meal and Do Not Eat to Fullness
- Eat Once or Twice A Day—No More
- Do Several Colon Cleanses
- Practice Increasing Your Food Intuition
- Fast Once a Week
- Do Colonics
- Vegetables: The Importance of Alkalinity, Vegetable Protein/Minerals, and Chlorophyll

- The Power of Juicing and Liquids
- Adding Superfoods to Your Lifestyle
- Probiotics
- Green Superfood Formulas/Supplements
- Eating Locally-Grown Food
- Nourishing Your Outer Body

THE MIND-BODY CONNECTION

THE PSYCHOLOGY BEHIND A HEALTHY BODY

Understanding your mind-body connection is essential for you to have a healthy body. All the tools discussed below will not do you any good without a solid mental psychology that will make you take joyful and plentiful action toward your goals.

You must start in your mind first and make it a priority to change any thoughts holding you back. If you do not believe extreme health is of extreme importance, you must shift your mental attitude regarding health. If you don't have the health you want, then taking care of your body is not important enough to you, so you must ask yourself why it is not important enough? Is suffering from ill health and old age in your future something you have not considered? Is visualizing yourself forty years in the future as an ill person with no energy a big enough motivator for you to change? Is thinking about having massive energy and perfect health enough of a motivator for you to change your attitude? Take out your journal and write down all of the limiting beliefs you have about health. Then write down all of the things that will motivate you to make changing your health an extreme priority and an absolute must.

Personally, I cannot fathom seeing myself in the future with a disease-filled body that is not vibrant and alive or that does not allow me to move freely and openly. I don't sit well with the idea of not being able to dance and perform in my body because I want to dance for the rest of my life as a profession. I know how amazing it feels to have a body that feels so vibrant and alive and is so full of energy. I know having that vibrant body is worth all the effort I put into it because this body is all I have and is the gateway to reconnecting with God and enlightenment; it is worth more than millions of dollars or anything else that I could ever own. Therefore, getting to the bottom of your limiting beliefs so you can change them is the most important objective of this entire chapter. Get your mental psychology right first, and then everything else I'll cover in this chapter will be so easy. It's true that achieving great health is 90 percent psychology and 10 percent using tools to take action. You can't get results without a correct attitude and the right thoughts. So find a way to create fun as you develop the right mindset to achieve your now expanding physical health!

USING AFFIRMATION/VISUALIZATION TO CREATE MASSIVE ENERGY, HEALTH, AND WELLBEING

Now that you understand the psychology about your health that you must have, it is time to write down what you think are the most empowering affirmations for you personally and the perfect visualization for the outcome you desire for your body, as if you already have that healthy body. I have already talked about the power of visualization and affirmation as a daily practice in Chapter Two so please refresh your memory by rereading that section if you're not entirely familiar with the concept.

Below are some examples of health affirmations you can say to yourself daily and couple with your own creative visualization:

- I am perfect health. The longer I live, the healthier I get.
- I am overflowing with massive and abundant amounts of energy.
- I only crave healthy food.
- I have high standards with my health.
- I exercise every day, and I eat extremely well every day.
- I have so much energy and enthusiasm that I can produce for long hours.
- Transitioning to the Divine Diet for my body is easier than not changing, and it's fun!
- It's easy to exercise six times a week, and I enjoy it.
- I get massive euphoric enjoyment out of extreme health.
- I am permanently and perfectly ageless and radiant!
- I am permanently overflowing with massive energy.
- My body is always guiding me. I always know what it needs to eat and move.
- I now accept the full truth of perfect health, and I completely surrender to practicing it every day.
- My body gets younger and stronger every day.

Remember that if you want to make your affirmations more effective, you should visualize your goal as you say them. If you can't visualize and affirm at the same time, it's okay; you can do them separately. I also recommend you say your affirmations and do your visualizations whenever you're sitting in traffic, driving or standing in a grocery line, or waiting at the doctor's office. You can affirm with all the passion in your mind and visualize quietly. You can add this process to a daily affirmation and visualization morning routine you already might have. This process is beneficial because it prevents your mind from thinking disempowering thoughts, so you can achieve your goals in a more productive and efficient way.

THE BODY MOVEMENT

Movement is so powerful. The right physical moves can unlock massive levels of energy within you, make your muscles toned, and help your cardiovascular system to nourish your body with fresh, energizing oxygen so you have sustained energy throughout the day. Movement can create the right levels of endorphins, moods, and emotions to get you fired up for your day. The exercise routines I will be recommending and discussing here are primarily focused on sustaining a body on a long-term basis so your body actually improves and increases its sustained energy. Although the routines will tone muscles and make your overall body much more slender, the focus here is not to give you chiseled abs and massive biceps. I want to maximize your time so you get what you really need, which is massive energy, a body built for sustained longevity, and a healthy clean body that elevates positive emotion. If you have the time to do 500 sit-ups because you want washboard abs, go right ahead, but the focus in this chapter is on energy and how to maintain a fit, well-nourished, and healthy, internally clean, toxin-free body.

I have learned to adopt a daily lifestyle of body movement where I get into my body and ground myself in it. I have learned to move in ways that channel my authentic self to a deeper level. When you take a break from your mind and daily drop down into your body to move it, it engages your physiology and takes you away from the danger of losing yourself completely in the unreality of your mind chatter. Even more importantly, it tunes you into the wisdom of yourself; your physical body has so much intelligence within itself, so it will help you embody the power of your true authentic self.

Many beautiful exercise programs are out there. I generally recommend yoga because it is really a moving meditation that encourages being present. It activates being in the moment and being aware of your body as you receive instructions for your postures. I know a lot of us are looking for physical strength, toning, and shaping the body, and yoga can definitely address this, but the ultimate purpose of yoga is linking the outer movement with the inner journey to awaken your authentic self. Yoga is so amazing because of its ability to wring out toxins from the body so you can live longer.

BIKRAM YOGA

A few years ago, I had a clairvoyant experience where I was divinely guided by my highest self to do Bikram yoga also known as hot yoga. I highly recommend it to everyone, and it's especially great for dancers. I will be as bold as to state that not many, as of yet, touches the profundity of this practice. Bikram yoga is different from other yoga techniques because the studios where the postures take place and are practiced are heated to well over 100 degrees Fahrenheit with about 70 percent humidity depending on the studio. The heat's purpose is to loosen and stretch the muscles so they can enhance the postures, but it helps the body sweat and detox as well. What is impressive to me is that this practice has twenty-six postures that allow the movement of more oxygenated blood to each fiber and organ of your body so it can restore all systems to a natural and healthy state.

I believe Bikram yoga is one of the best, if not the best, form of yoga out there. Many people superficially only focus on building muscle, with no real focus in restoring overall authentic heath into the body. The Bikram yoga sequence addresses every system of the body including internal organs and glands.I highly recommend this program because even though you might feel tired like I did for the first six months of practice, it's so hardcore that it awakens energy in you that you never felt before. It's a complete workout; it's aerobic, it tones all of your muscles, it works on every area of your body, and the magical stretching somehow activates so much energy and unblocks your body channels so that energy can flow through you more freely.

Bikram yoga makes my body feel stabilized, centered, and grounded, which I absolutely love; I don't feel that way after weight training or aerobics exercise alone. It feels as if practicing Bikram yoga long-term will make me stronger than anything else I have practiced as an exercise program. Bikram yoga has also strengthened my positive emotions in a sense that every time I walk in for a session, no matter how hard it is, I have made the choice to strengthen my peace, love, and joy in the practice despite the discomfort. When you can be at peace in Bikram yoga's hot muscle burning workout, you can be at peace with almost anything.

I have dabbled with other exercises such as popular aerobics and weight routines, and they're great fun, but I don't consider them as strong foundations for my intention to sustain my body long-term; they are more like a dance warm-up that I might do for fun after my yoga practice. But I consistently practice the original hot yoga six times a week. I also find that doing other programs with hot yoga can be a little too much, so I have primarily stuck with the original hot yoga.

Please listen to your heart to determine whether this practice is for you; however, If you want my opinion, I will say that I am incredibly convinced it is. I just hope you don't waste your valuable time with other workouts that don't work. If you like strength training, for example, do this yoga first, then do an extra few minutes with weights. This recommendation on Bikram yoga came to me in a communication with my highest self during an entheogenic journey (more on entheogens in the last chapter). I know if my spiritual guides speaks so highly about it, there is no question in my mind that it will be of tremendous benefit to you. Also, while some teachers recommend changing your routine, I believe sticking to just one practice every single day can be very powerful; it allows you to laser beam your focus to activate the same areas every day. With Bikram yoga, you build that area to be stronger as opposed to spreading your energy all over the place and not working on those areas over and over. If it is your choice to do yoga, please pay attention to that focus as you move along.

I also want to mention that in my opinion, taking classes is better than practicing at home. You then gain momentum from being with the other students and a teacher, which is more motivating; plus, the teacher can correct you, and you can gain overall inspiration from group practice.

Personally, I have done many other yoga practices and loved them. In the beginning of my venture to find a workout, I loved getting myself out there and exploring new things; however, you need to get honed in on the routine you are going to practice if you want to be effective with your time. I have currently been only devoted to Bikram yoga six times a week, and then if I wanted, I would add on an extra thirty minutes of anything else I wanted to explore on top of that like dance, other yoga, pilates, aerobic, and/or weights to tone up extra muscle.

REBOUNDING

Rebounding is a great exercise for moving your lymphatic system, which is really good for you. After one to four hours of working on the computer, I turn on my dance music and jump, punch, and jab with my arms and smile and be silly with all the enthusiasm, energy, and excitement I can muster. I do it as much or as little as one to five times a day for about five to ten minutes per session, and I recommend it for you as well.

The great thing about rebounding is, first off, it doesn't hurt your knees like running. It's so much fun to be bouncing up and down, and you're giving your lymphatic system a cleaning because you're being aerobic, which cleanses toxins from your body by increasing your oxygen intake and waking up your body after several hours of inactivity. Your energy levels are then more sustained throughout the day.

The human body needs to move because the lymphatic system stimulates every cell, carrying nutrients to the cell and taking waste products away. The lymphatic system is fully dependent on physical exercise for it to circulate effectively. Without proper movement, the cells are left stewing in their own waste products and malnourished with no nutrients, a situation that contributes to arthritis, cancer, and other degenerative diseases, as well as aging. Proper effective exercise such as rebounding is reported to multiply lymph flow by up to thirty times. The more your lymphatic system is stimulated with exercise, the greater your energy levels will become.

DANCING

Dancing is the body's expression of celebrating life; it awakens those feel good positive emotions that guide you to channel your daily activities in a much better way! If you're not a dancer, that's okay. You don't have to be, and you don't need to worry about how bad your dancing is; this discussion is about bringing your inner child out to have fun through movement. Like rebounding, dancing is another option for you to reawaken your body after one to four hours of long work and being sedentary at your desk throughout the day. Even if you have to dance to your iPod in the bathroom for five minutes after you've finished some work in your cubicle at the office or whatever your work situation may be, dancing can give you tremendous benefits. It feeds your body with an exhilarating level of new energy to sustain you throughout the day. Have fun doing it, and notice how much more refreshed you feel and how much more you accomplish when you go back to work! Another suggestion with dancing would be to take up some dance classes, or some aerobic dance classes to have fun and open up the feeling good energy in your body. Enjoy!

DEEP BREATHING

Deep breathing and breathing techniques are an ideal daily practice toward reconnecting yourself with your authentic self. The authentic you can translate better in a calm, relaxed state, so what deep breathing does is stimulate a still, centered, and relaxed state in your body. When you are in this state, you are more present and less likely to be thrown out of balance as you go through your day.

Many Eastern cultures have long recognized the importance of breathing to cultivate a positive relationship between the body and the mind—a relationship that results in a more tranquil state of being and a more resilient physiology. Kriya yoga, yoga, Kundalini yoga, qigong, and tai chi are such healthy practices in large part because they combine deep breathing and movement to support a steady central nervous response. The hot yoga's first practice is breathing similar to kriya yoga that helps bring in more prana or energy to the body.

Studies have shown that yogic deep-breathing techniques are extremely effective in handling depression, anxiety, and stress-related disorders. These techniques can serve as an excellent substitute to taking drugs to calm ourselves down, or in some cases, as a great substitute in treating myriad psychological disorders, as well as eating disorders and obesity. A lot of people might be taking drugs, overeating, or harming their bodies to relax when all they need is to take five minutes of their time to take long, deep, slow breaths.

Shallow breathing (or chest breathing) causes a constriction of the chest and lung tissue over time, decreasing oxygen flow and delivery to your tissues. Deep, rhythmic breathing, by comparison, expands the diaphragm muscle, the cone-shaped muscle under your lungs, which expands the lungs' air pockets, invoking the relaxation response, and massaging the lymphatic system.

When someone is frightened or stressed, he tends to hold his breath or take rapid, shallow breaths. The heart pounds and muscles clench as the adrenaline kicks in. When the stressor is resolved, the person lets out a deep breath, signaling the brain that everything is okay again. If deep breathing continues, the heart rate decreases, the lungs expand, and the muscles relax. Equilibrium is restored.

One thing I like about hot yoga is that you get your deep breathing for the day at the beginning of the exercises before the postures. This breathing relaxes, centers, and infuses your body with energy from the oxygen to nourish your body, and it has the power to transform your consciousness.

This technique is very empowering, and I am fascinated by its transformative abilities. I am also very fascinated and intrigued by Kriya yoga breathing. It is very similar to hot yoga's first breathing technique as taught in class. Kriya yoga's breathing technique is taught by the famous Yogananda's Self-Realization Fellowship. Unfortunately, it takes one to two years to get initiated into breathing with Self-Realization Fellowship; however, you can get initiated to an almost identical practice through one of the teachers of Yogiraj at HamsaYoga.org if you feel so guided. I cannot teach the technique here because I do not have qualifications.

Yogiraj does teach the deep and profound teachings of the Indian enlightened being named Babaji, including his Kriya yoga breathing technique. I currently practice this technique, which is seventy-two breaths of deep breathing every day. Some people practice the complete 144 breaths of Kriya yoga, but for now, seventy-two fits my schedule. HamsaYoga will initiate you into four other techniques along with the breathing, but I personally just practice the first two techniques. Visit www.HamsaYoga.org or google your local Kriya yoga teacher for more information if you would like to explore this type of breathing. You don't necessarily have to attend a Yogiraj retreat to learn the techniques; you can also set up a private class with one of their teachers for a in your local area.

Also, it's very important for you to understand that you don't have to get initiated in this form of breathing to practice and get the benefits of deep breathing. Kriya yoga is just an added bonus I wanted to mention. You can practice hot yoga's deep breathing technique alone if you decide you want to do it. And you can also watch your breath and breathe deeply for about five to ten minutes a day by being present with your breath, filling your lungs slowly and completely, and breathing out all of the air slowly and completely. I do this technique throughout the day whenever I feel the need to oxygenate and relax my body and feel more centered. You can research other techniques as well; the only reason I recommend Kriya yoga is because it allows the body to absorb pranic energy in your body, and it awakens your consciousness at a deeper level.

As I mentioned earlier, I highly recommend deep breathing because it allows the body to center itself and calm itself down. Deep breathing is highly energizing to the body, and it allows it to nourish the body cells with oxygen. Oxygen is the number one nutrient we need to survive. It makes us more alert, present, and better able to function. If you do not have oxygen in your body, you will die within fourteen to thirty minutes. Oxygen is that important of a nutrient for the body. Most of us are not breathing deeply enough; we are breathing shallowly, and yet we wonder why we feel anxious or disconnected. Most of us just take shallow breaths and are not breathing from our belly but from our chest instead. It's important to be conscious and aware throughout the day how we are doing in regards to our breathing and to make sure we take short breaks to take deep, full, slow breaths because breathing is a foundation of our essential being. Breath has a very strong connection to your being, to who you really are, and to your creator. When you take a full breath, you are more present in being within your body opposed to when you are practicing shallow breathing. I recommend practicing deep breathing to focus and center yourself at least once a day.

SMILING

Have you ever noticed how when you're smiling, you feel really good? Try cracking a smile right now and see how it feels. Does it make you feel better? Almost always, no matter how bad you feel, a slight smile or a big smile sends a signal to your brain that all is well! Smiling makes life a lot easier! Smile during intense workouts, long hours at work, or whenever you don't feel so good. Moving your body in certain ways has a similar effect; for example, sitting up straight instead of slouching might help correct depression or a slightly down mood. Even when you don't feel like smiling, smile with faith and allow yourself to melt into feeling better. Make it a spiritual practice to smile; it always elevates your vibration and alleviates any negative mood.

I would often see clairvoyant visions of my highest self smiling all the time even in the most depressing dark times of my life. I would see this big encouraging smile in my inner eye assuring me everything is all right and every moment is a joyful play. I always wondered why I looked so happy in those visions and was smiling a lot. Then a revelation came to me. I smiled a lot because I knew it was my sword against negative thoughts, negative dramatic people or circumstances; smiling is the light that made it all disappear. Every time I wake up in the morning with negative thoughts telling me not to go to the yoga studio for another intense workout, I just smile. I smile when things don't go my way, and I smile for no reason at all;

it is the medicine to bring me more joy in my heart, and the more joy I have, the more I abundance I attract.

THE FOOD PRINCIPLES

Before I give you any information in this section, I want to say that this chapter would not be possible if it weren't for the scriptures that Jesus Christ left behind in what is now called *The Essene Gospel of Peace*. I highly recommend that you read this book; it's a short read and you can purchase it online for only a dollar or two. It is so inexpensive because its translator wanted the information to be readily available to everyone on this planet—rich or poor. Don't be fooled by its price; it's worth more than its weight in gold. In this section, I will address the importance of the laws written in this sacred book while sharing my personal experiences of how to apply them to living in this modern world.

Every time I hold the book and read it, I sense how its vibration holds tremendous power; it's a book that will make unclean toxicity and disease in your body disappear. Be aware as you read this information of how you feel; watch your thoughts and see whether you feel any resistance as you read this section. Sit still whenever you feel a discomfort rise up as you read. Then write down in your journal what you're feeling to clarify your process.

I know it might be hard to fathom that Jesus Christ actually wrote this scripture. I still have trouble believing it myself. Perhaps He didn't, but I do know, without a shadow of a doubt, that it contains real spiritual practices for taking care of and nourishing your body so you can resurrect your authentic self to its full potential. After a decade of following *The Essene Gospel of Peace*'s basic practices, I intuitively knew I was raising my vibration and alignment to my authentic self because my highest self communicated to me that I was to advance to a higher level of this practice consistent with modern times. For that reason, I have created the advanced versions now taught in my one-year and two-year programs. The more I practice this Divine Diet, the more I see how karmically I suffer if I get out of alignment with just one of the principles that I will teach you in this book. The communication I channeled was that there were no juicing or blending strategies or modern colon-cleansing machines when *The Essene Gospel of Peace* was written, so I needed to teach new levels of the Divine Diet so the sacred body temple could reach its optimum vibrant state and substantially stabilize its decomposing and ill health. Once I received the new teachings, I knew and understood the sacredness in *The Essene Gospel of Peace*, despite my disbelief about who wrote it.

I want to start with the foundational teachings that *The Essene Gospel of Peace* talks about. In the last twenty years or so, I have seen many books written on raw vegan food that were primarily branching off these teachings, but they do not really align to this book's overall teaching. So many raw plant-based diet books out there give a lot of great information on raw food, but I wanted to write a book that aligns closely to the teachings of what's written in *The Essene Gospel of Peace*. Although I do enjoy being a raw foodist and the vegan/vegetarian lifestyle, and it's a great way to get started to better health, I would rather call myself an Essene practitioner because I understand the value of and honor every single word in this book. I have since created my own name for the advanced diet that I follow—The Divine Diet.

So, basically, this section will go beyond the raw vegan lifestyle that has become popular in the mainstream media;

the Divine Diet is about looking at food as a spiritual practice with more specific principles to reawaken your consciousness and authentic self. It's about the spiritual laws of how to eat your food, when, and what is the deep divine understanding of this Divine Diet. It asks: What does it really mean to be in harmony with how the Universe, the sun, and Mother Nature want to nourish your body. I want to clarify and really give you the truth of the matter. I see so much confusion, so many people giving certain advice, even raw foodists, and that's great—I don't want to "bash" any of it because, for most people, the raw food or raw restaurants' meals really are transitional, easy, and delicious ways to move out of the junk food diet. I even lived the raw foodist lifestyle myself for a few years and wrote recipe books supporting the raw vegan lifestyle, but then I was asked to teach from my highest self and to stay true to what it truly is to be extremely healthy and raise your level of spiritual practice through nourishing the body into alignment with your authentic being.

If you want the best rewards that the Universe has to offer, you have to raise the bar from mediocrity to excellence. The universal energy abundantly rewards outstanding behavior, not the average mediocre performance. If you really want to experience a deep communion with your creator, then setting your standards high is the way to go. It may take you several years—it took me a decade—but I want to fine tune your next step after you decide that you want to go all the way because every single thing, no matter how small, that you do with your diet affects you; it affects your consciousness, so I wanted to address every "i" that needs to be dotted and every "t" that needs to be crossed because this book is about aligning yourself with who you really are, not about taste satisfaction from a delicious, creative raw food vegan cuisine because that only offers temporary satisfaction. I want to give a taste of longer-term satisfaction with tools to help align you with your deeper level, which is what you really are looking for anyway, or at least, what your highest self wants for you.

One other note: I will not be covering the history of *The Essene Gospel of Peace*, although it's important to know a little about its history. I'm going to stick to writing more about transforming you, the core of the teachings, my experience with them, and the messages I believe it is really important to pay attention to and apply to the modern world. If you want to read more about *The Essene Gospel of Peace*, I encourage to purchase a copy and read it many times.

Here are its foundational principles:

DO NOT COOK, FREEZE, OR ROT YOUR FOOD

The following is an important scripture quote from *The Essene Gospel of Peace*: "But I do say to you: Kill neither men, nor beasts, nor yet the food which goes into your mouth. For if you eat living food, the same will quicken you, but if you kill your food, the dead food will kill you also." The passage continues on to say that rotten food will rot your body, cooked food will cook your body, and frozen food will freeze your body.

This teaching is so important to understand, and it is probably the practice from this scripture that has been most popularized in the raw food movement's recommendation not to heat food over 115 degrees Fahrenheit so you keep living nutrients intact. The raw food lifestyle is very popular now, so it's too bad that people don't really talk about the scripture that started it all. If the raw food lifestyle is foreign to you, then go to the nearest raw food restaurant and familiarize yourself with it. I can tell you that it means far more than just eating cold salads—some very delicious meals are available, but I won't get into them here. I'll simply state that the lifestyle's rule about heating your food comes from this scripture. Dehydrating food has also taken the place of cooking food in the raw food lifestyle.

It is also important to understand that freezing food kills it so that should be excluded as well. Stay away from foods that are cooked, frozen, or rotted (fermented foods such as kombucha, wine, those blue moldy cheeses, or cheeses with worms in them that they call a delicacy!).

Raw food is truthfully defined as food that has not been heated over 115 degrees, not been chilled to be frozen, and not been rotted. Your food needs to be fresh and not altered in its composition at a cellular level at the very least. Food that is as close to its freshest state as nature delivered it is the healthiest and will make your body the most vibrant. Food that has not been cooked, frozen, or rotted has a complete vibrant light aura that can be seen through Kirlian photography. By comparison, the light aura of cooked, frozen, or rotted food is considerably less with holes in it. Think about it: you're a being who is alive and has your own aura, so you don't want to feed yourself food that has less of an auric field to restore and rebuild your cells because that only weakens you and makes you less vibrant and alive.

As described in *The Essene Gospel of Peace*, cooked food cooks your body, frozen food freezes your body, and rotted food rots your body. Think about all the people who eat cooked food—do they look vibrant in their sixties, seventies, or eighties? They have conditions like dry skin, loss of hair and hair color, and they are tired because of all the enzyme depletion the body experiences from the absence of enzymes in the food they eat (because those enzymes were killed by heat). Even starting as early as age thirty, people start to show signs of aging and having a low-energy body because they are expending so much energy, especially from eating cooked food.

And what about alcohol and wine (rotten grapes). Not only does alcohol impair you when you're driving, but it eats out your liver, kills brain cells, and weakens the body. Nor are foods that have been sitting in the fridge for too long and have a bit of a smell ideal to eat. Always buy raw foods, especially produce from farmer's markets because they are usually freshly and more recently picked, so they will contain more nutrients. Keep your fermented foods like wine and kombucha to a minimum, and preferably, don't consume any at all since they are really rotted food that impairs and weakens the body.

Although I wouldn't consider freezing your food to be as bad as cooking it, frozen foods are dead foods as well. I do see many raw foodists freeze their fruit to make ice cream with it, and there are a few raw ice cream places with frozen ice cream. Those are definitely a better alternative than regular ice cream, but they are still frozen. The choice is yours. If you're an ice cream junkie and absolutely cannot live without ice cream, then definitely go for the "raw" ice cream and then upgrade to opt out in the future. But, in general, it is important to preserve food at cool temperatures in the fridge and not freeze it so it doesn't lose its life force and become dead food.

VEGETARIAN/VEGAN: HONEY, MILK, GRAINS, VEGETABLES, FRUIT

No meat or eggs. In *The Essene Gospel of Peace*, the foundation for a correct diet is laid. The first thing mentioned is the importance on not eating meat. Basically, it says eating meat causes an abomination to your body and gives dark forces more power over it. Although not eating meat fits my lifestyle and I resonate with not eating it in general, I have had circumstances where I was shown that meat was not good for me because it attracts dark energies around me. In a dream, I received a message from some changelings that some people do need meat and it was recommended only to eat fish. In the dream, I was catching salmon from a waterfall; the salmon were jumping up the waterfall, and I was like a bear, catching them. I gave the fish to a woman to consume, and while I knew the fish wasn't necessary for me, I realized some people do need to be pescetarian. Since then, I have seen several of my friends being guided back to meat from a vegan diet and become healthier. One of them was vegetarian and was guided to eat fish during an entheogenic journey, although she did go back to being vegetarian.

If your intuition is telling you that you need meat, I would recommend raw fish like ceviche, sushi, or sashimi since its alive and unheated meat. Heating meat heats the oils in it, which causes free radical damage in your system and ages the body. Leave the eggs and the other meats for your dogs; you don't need to be eating all of that; it's not very appealing eating it uncooked, and raw fish is a lot easier to digest; plus, everyone always talks about how red meat is not good for you.

Although *The Essene Gospel of Peace* does say not to eat the meat of beasts, my interpretation of this statement is to avoid meat from more sentient beings. Although fish is flesh, it does tend to have a less sentient feel to it, and many people who consider themselves vegetarians even eat fish, perhaps because it has a different energetic frequency than eating meat from four-legged or two-legged land animals.

Fish lovers, please know that you cannot get your omega-3 fatty acids with cooked salmon because the cooking oil causes free radical damage; you're better off eating it raw and preparing it as ceviche or buying cold pressed flax oil, hemp oil, or any omega-3 oil that has not been cooked. One last note on fish and mercury toxicity: please research and eat the ones with lower mercury in them or the ones that are mercury free. They are worth eating, despite the mercury, more than your land friends that come with their karmic toxicity. If you are consuming greens juices and super foods and following the Divine Diet, that will clean out any fish toxicity.

The Essene Gospel of Peace goes on to say that every fruit here on earth and every herb shall be substitutes for your meat. "Herb" here doesn't just mean herbs like rosemary, basil, and oregano but all the vegetables, such as kale, lettuce, collard greens, spinach, cauliflower, cabbage, parsley, broccoli, celery, bok choy, and all the others available for human consumption. Personally, my vegan meat is mostly spirulina; I recommend three to ten tablespoons of it per day to thicken any soup or smoothie. This vegetarian meat is not only a complete protein, but it has so many minerals, such as calcium and trace minerals. It's the number one appetite suppressant for me, and it helps me not to crave much food because of its nutrient-dense content. Of course, I know some people need more protein than others; I have a low metabolism so I can live off of very little protein compared to other people. I probably consume 100 grams a week, but for my body, it's more than plenty. I have no hair loss, skin or nail or muscle problems, and have normal monthly heavy periods.

According to the scripture, an ideal diet is the vegetarian diet. Raw honey (royal jelly and bee pollen included), milk, grains (rice, seeds, legumes, nuts), vegetables (leafy greens, roots, herbs), and fruit are all listed in *The Essene Gospel of Peace* as acceptable foods. A growing number of vegans don't consume raw milk/cheese (but do consume bee products, while more extreme vegans don't consume bee products at all) because of all the hormones and toxins that animals accumulate today due to unhealthy animal farming. It's a good idea to stay away from raw milk/cheese products from cows raised on farms without organic standards. If you are going to consume dairy products, I recommend you do so minimally and on an irregular basis and make sure they come from grass-fed goats and cows, as is typical with Amish or Third World farming where animals are not bred en masse or given hormones to produce milk that is then unhealthy. Raw milk is a lot different from pasteurized milk, and it is more beneficial, but it's hard to get it in high quality or quantity, so check your sources before you consume it.

Personally, I am not opposed to the consumption of raw organic milk, and I received a couple of clairvoyant messages regarding milk and cheese that told me they were fine to consume, yet I still live close to a vegan lifestyle. I do, however, consume royal jelly and bee pollen on a regular basis for their amazing superfood qualities. I don't consume milk because I don't require much food since my highest self has instructed me to live on no more than one meal a day, and I know that milk/cheese tends to block entheogen healing work in the body, which is a big part of my life for expanding my consciousness. (More on entheogens in Chapter Five.) I do consume raw milk, but no more than once a year and from the Amish community where animals roam freely, unlike at standard milk farms. Raw milk and cheese is a great substitute for the pasteurized versions. If you're a big dairy lover, these raw products don't cause dark cavities because the sugar in the milk has not been cooked and lactose-intolerant people can actually drink it because the milk still has its enzymes intact. I'm going to be bold and say here that milk does not cause cancer despite what the book *The China Study* suggests; in that study, pasteurized milk was tested. Raw milk, however, that comes from a grass-fed, organically grown animal, can be very beneficial. My only suggestion is not to go crazy on dairy and limit it, especially if you decide to use entheogens to expand your spiritual body as will be discussed in Chapter Five. You might want to abstain a few days before trying this kind of healing work.

Some vegans do not consume bee products because they think it is cruel to consume animal products. That's your decision, but I believe bees were put on this planet in the service of other beings so we could consume their beautiful food.

Then there are leafy greens, roots, herbs, and grains, including rice, legumes, nuts, and seeds. Be sure to check out my raw food recipe books *Divina's Hearty Raw Foods* and *Divina's Living Caribbean Cuisine* to demystify the raw food lifestyle and learn how to prepare all your raw meals so they are even more delicious than cooked food and ten times more nutritious!

What about salt? Salt is not mentioned in the Essene diet. However, some raw foodists swear by it and recommend sea salt, such as Celtic or Himalayan. It's not really necessary to have salt in your diet, so I would replace salt with dulse, which is a salty sea food already. Many dark green vegetables also already have sodium in them. If you can't live without salt, I recommend Himalayan or Celtic sea salt instead of regular table salt, which is really not good for you. I once experimented with a not-so-smart cleanse involving massive amounts of salt; I lost bone and a tooth of mine chipped. Salt seems to leach calcium out of the body in large quantities. Of course, small amounts of salt are not noticeable, so avoid it; consume only sea salt moderately, or stick to foods with salt naturally in them.

My rule of thumb is to avoid table salt entirely, avoid too much sea salt, or replace it with dulse or other salty seaweeds in your meals if you are craving it. I also recommend juicing celery and dark green veggies since they have a lot of sodium in them. A lot of the raw food meals prepared still use a lot of sea salt; I would rather they replace it with dulse because the salt in dulse, in my opinion, is activated and more readily usable. I often think eating salt is similar to eating dirt for its minerals rather than eating the minerals when they're passed into a plant. You would never do that, and the comparison may seem extreme, but you get my point, I'm sure.

So, in summary, in the diet law of the Essenes, you are allowed to eat fruits, grains, and grasses/herbs/veggies, the milk of beasts, and the honey of bees without it being cooked. Everything else can cause problems because they contain energy that is not in harmony with God and can, therefore, work like an enemy against your body.

COMBINE NO MORE THAN THREE KINDS OF FOOD IN A MEAL AND DO NOT EAT TO FULLNESS

It is important to be conscious of food combinations. In general, mixing too many foods confuses your body. If you choose to eat meat, eat it with vegetables, not fruit. A meal should consist of fruits, vegetables, and grains. Ideally, I would combine the vegetables and grains, and in another meal, combine the vegetables and fruits. I have found that fruits, vegetables, and grains/legumes/nuts go well together;

however, I wouldn't go further than that. Perhaps leave your bee products and milk for another meal or a fruit smoothie.

Make sure you eat slowly to digest your food thoroughly, and let your stomach give you the signal for when it's full—it takes about fifteen minutes for it to tell. Also, don't overdo the eating. Your stomach should feel comfortable, not exploding with food. When Thanksgiving and Christmas come, avoid overeating until you are in a coma! That is so bad for you, and you must not be bloated. *The Essene Gospel of Peace* tells us that combining too much food together and overeating in a meal "Casts out the angel helpers and causes an abomination in your system."

In terms of not eating to fullness, *The Essene Gospel of Peace* also states that your food intake shouldn't exceed two pounds a day or be less than a pound. Two pounds is not a lot, so I would fill that weight with superfoods like spiraling, wheatgrass, juiced vegetables, and all of the essentials first to get your nutritional value out of your daily two pounds of food.

On a personal note, when I started juicing vegetables and fruit to make my vegetable soup meal, I was guided in a clairvoyant vision to juice only a cup. Until then, I was doing twice that amount, but when I cut back, I had a lot more energy. My stomach had a lot more space, and I felt a sense of liberation from the energy drain of just too much juice. I didn't realize you can overdo juiced veggies in one meal, but they are so powerful that they can overwhelm the body, depending on the person; experiment to find your balance.

EAT ONCE OR TWICE A DAY—NO MORE

This rule is one of the most important aspects of the Essene diet lifestyle that I have adopted. Just eating once or twice a day is such a subtle technique, but the resulting level of mental clarity and amount of energy I receive throughout the day is immense. You will feel the same after practicing it daily for about two months. The power you will harness from this practice will increase as you go along.

I'll admit I don't understand the full science behind eating when the sun is at its highest and eating once more after the sun sets, but I can tell you, from my experience of just eating at these two times and leaving my stomach empty at others, that it is unbelievable. I'm not bombarding my stomach then with so much food, and I'm letting it digest lunch and dinner, as well as giving it space between meals to use even more energy for body regeneration. It's like dialing a code to be in alignment with how the earth orbits around the sun to nourish yourself properly. When I changed to eating solely at these times, I was able to think better, my mind was clear, and I was better able to sense what I really needed to do each day to better my life. All that from eating once or twice a day? Yes! Try it for yourself and see how your consciousness changes. It is amazing and much smarter than eating six small meals a day, which dilutes your digestive juices and doesn't allow your digestive tract to rest and regenerate. If you want to keep your blood sugar up through the day as you change to eating just once or twice a day, I would drink lots of coconut water or juice to sustain yourself until you get use to it. Coconut water digests extremely fast and quickly hydrates so it's a better replacement than a snack since we are mostly water anyway, so the more water we consume, the better.

If you are in the habit of eating all day, switch to eating twice a day and keep it that way for a few years, or at least one year before you consider eating once a day. For me, eating nutrient-packed superfoods once a day has been the most energy-boosting technique I have ever done. Once my body adjusted, I couldn't believe how light and fast I could think and move. My body no longer felt sluggish from all the food I was eating. I now just feed myself the most important nutrients: 70 percent greens (50 percent of it from superfoods like wheatgrass, seaweed, spirulina, and green powders), 20 percent fruit, and 10 percent fats, grains, legumes, seeds, royal jelly, bee pollen, etc. This ratio keeps me full and nourished. I'm not saying this is the ratio for you because some people need more calories since they burn a lot. So adjust accordingly! My point is that when people feed their bodies superfoods and foods at the estimated percentages above, the body doesn't need to eat so much because it feels satisfied. But it all starts with twice a day first because if you came from a typical cooked diet, you're most likely very malnourished, so you need to build up the body again with larger amounts of good raw food.

What about breakfast? Isn't that the most important meal of the day? And what about snacks—are they allowed? I know many well-respected people in the nutrition field who advise eating breakfast, but from my experience, the concept that you need breakfast to be healthy is a myth. When you lighten the load on the body with less frequent but highly nutrient-dense meals (unlike the three meals a day with no nutrition that most people eat), the body fasts and gets rid of toxins at a higher rate, and you are able to use that digestive energy for your day at work or at home to get things done, as well as extend your lifespan! When you stop breaking your fast at breakfast, extend it to a longer time period, and have two to three liters of water instead, then imagine the extra time you will accumulate! First off, your authentic self can better infuse itself into your physical body, so you will be vibrating at a closer energetic match to your highest self, meaning you can channel more of you and access greater levels of you on this planet!

Lightening your load of food over a lifetime and eating more concentrated superfood powders can make you live a lot longer, and if you are eating superfoods like spirulina and wheatgrass in high quantities, your need for more than two meals a day will subside. Personally, when I moved to two meals a day, I started with having brunch and moved it along to lunch just to get used to the new lifestyle; sometimes, my schedule didn't permit me to eat lunch, but I was still eating twice a day until I eventually cut down to just once a day.

Remember my story in the introduction where I had the miraculous experience of my highest self screaming, "I'm here! I'm here! I'm in my body!" during a healing ceremony? The primary reason that happened was because I listened to my inner guidance that I was designed to eat no more than once a day. There is something very profound about this spiritual dietary practice that calls in your highest self at higher levels, so I want to inspire people to take it more seriously if they want to get ahead in their lives.

DO SEVERAL COLON CLEANSES

If you have been eating processed dead foods all your life, you probably have a colon that has been clogged up through the years. If you're going to start cleaning your body, the first step is to change your diet by introducing massive amounts of produce. Choose the ones you like the best and start looking at raw recipes for how to make juices, soups, smoothies, salads, and other meals with them.

After a month or two, the second step is to start a colon cleanse. When I took this step, I rid myself of several feet of mucoid plaque (black rubbery junk material!) attached to my colon and I erased my body's memories and desire to eat cooked and processed foods. I couldn't believe that after a year, every time I got off a colon cleanse, my desire to eat unhealthy foods diminished. When I was on the cleanse, the herbs I took had a magical way of making the desire for food, especially bad food, go away. You're supposed to be nourishing yourself with raw fruits, vegetable juice, and meals during the cleanse. It was a tremendously helpful tool to transition from eating a diet of meat and lifeless cooked and fried foods. I was eating 100 percent raw food within one year. I had a tremendous desire to be healthy, to avoid a troubled, diseased, and decaying body when I was older, and to get away from being sick, tired, and full of acne. You must condition yourself toward an extremely healthy lifestyle to achieve these results, so please read Chapter Two again to learn how to program your mind this way.

If you are coming from a standard cooked and meat diet, you will have to do colon cleanses if you want to be healthy because that type of diet builds what is called mucoid plaque in your colon. It's basically old food and mucus built-up to protect the body from all the junk you feed it. When you clean out your colon, this plaque detaches itself from the colon and comes out rubbery, black, and rope like during your bowel movements. I recommend that you immediately apply the principles discussed above and then purchase a colon cleansing kit to clean out your colon as soon as possible.

Personally, I did a thirty-day colon cleanse every other month for a year, and at the end of the year, I was eating only raw foods. The reason I did so many cleanses was because when I was on the colon cleanse, the herbs were so powerful that all I wanted to eat was raw food. I didn't crave any cooked food. It was only when I was off of the cleanses that I became a witch and ate all of the bad cooked food my tongue could get ahold of. The cleansing kit I purchased seemed to have a cleansing effect on the memories I had of eating cooked food. Every time I completed a cleanse, I craved cooked food a lot less.

Let me add that once you have cleaned out your colon, it will be very hard for you to go back to eating cooked food, especially cooked fats, sugars, and refined grains. When you remove that protective layer in your colon, and then you eat fried foods, you are doing a lot of harm to yourself. What I recommend is that if you then have a temptation to eat cooked food, make it healthy cooked food, like steamed vegetables, boiled sprouted quinoa, or sprouted grains. Also, keep your fats and oils raw (cooked fats create a lot of free radicals) on top of your cooked meals.

I only recommend one colon cleanse out there. I tell you I have never seen anything like it. No other colon cleanse compares to how powerful this one is. I have no affiliation with this product or its company and I don't make any money by endorsing it; I am just simply recommending it because it has literally and profoundly changed my internal life!

Here is the company I recommend: Arise and Shine. I have never seen anything more powerful than Arise and Shine products. To me, it is the number one colon-cleansing company in the world. You can find out more about it at www. AriseandShine.com.

PRACTICE INCREASING YOUR FOOD INTUITION

As you move along with your diet, make sure you pay attention to what your body is telling you. When you shop for produce, try running your hands along foods and see how your body responds. How does your body feel? Is your heart or stomach telling you something? Are you clairvoyant? Do you get pictures of the foods you need? For example, I'm very intuitive, so when I run my hands over vegetables, usually my heart tingles when I touch the ones my body wants and needs.

This is not a, "I'm craving junk food right now, so I must go eat it" craving; it's deeper than that. Make sure you feel intuitively with your gut or heart. You might be doing this technique already without even knowing it. But being more consciously aware will save you energy in terms of what to eat so you can fill the "spot" more immediately.

My intuition tells me that people need diets high in dark green vegetables because the basis of a body, besides water, is muscle, blood, and bone, and these vegetables feed all three. Aquatic water vegetables are the best, such as kelp, arame, dulse, sea lettuce, wakame, and spirulina (a lake vegetable); they are the kings of complete protein (60 percent more protein than meat!), and they are not only protein-rich, which is great for muscles, but mineral-rich. The primary cause of overeating is your body looking for minerals.

Land and sea vegetables are rich in calcium, contrary to popular belief, and they feed the blood because chlorophyll is a blood builder and feeder. If you are eating meat for protein, I recommend ceviche or raw sashimi since the raw version doesn't cause as many free radicals as the cooked. I would also supplement with plant protein such as spirulina anyway because too much animal protein is acidic and can lower your pH levels too much. Vegetable-based protein from greens alkalizes and helps reduce dangerous acidic levels in the body so if you're not eating/drinking vegetables, you're not feeding your blood with the chlorophyll and alkalinity it needs, which is just as important, if not more important, than protein. It is hard for the body to get any diseases on an alkaline pH level. I want you to pay attention to your intuition here with green vegetables first since this is the diet's foundation, and to me, it's the ultimate hunger killer. Most people don't know it, but they are hungry even when they have a full stomach, such as one filled with pasta, for example, because they are not feeding themselves primarily with green superfoods.

FAST ONCE A WEEK

I recommend fasting once a week for everyone on this planet. It is also recommended in *The Essene Gospel of Peace*. According to the Bible, God rested on the seventh day of the Creation, so we should let our digestive tracts rest on the seventh day also; they deserve a vacation. I generally recommend the weekend since most of us are off work then. Sunday would be ideal. I dedicate that day to regeneration, rejuvenation, and to God, honoring my body by giving it a rest. Although this book's final chapter will cover fasting more extensively for longer period fasts, here let me just say that fasting once a week is easy to do, and I recommend you do it with coconut water. Water fasts, in my opinion, are too rigorous and less hydrating and effective than fasting with coconut water. Coconut water seems to get rid of toxins a lot faster because it has the ability to penetrate your cells deeper than just spring water. It will keep your blood sugar up, and you will be able to concentrate better on whatever you want to do. I only recommend this weekly water fast after you have been doing two meals a day for at least six months because you will already be detoxifying if you're doing only two meals a day after years of eating more, and probably unhealthy, food. You might want to start also with fruit and vegetable juice for your fasting day, and then work your way to just coconut water and then just plain water.

Fasting once a week allows your body to recover, detoxify, and rejuvenate from the week-long digestive process it goes through. The absence of food is just as important as the presence of live raw superfoods in the diet. The key here is to do it in the right balance. Fasting will allow your body to be even more energized when you start your coming week, and it is also activating a higher vibration for the body that will be a closer match to your authentic self or soul. Food gives off the densest vibration you can put into your body, and it can disconnect you far from your high vibrational authentic self very easily if you overeat. Fasting is yet another powerful tool for harnessing large amounts of energy. When you never give your body a break, the body starts to break down so its ability to regenerate is diminished. When the body takes a one-day break every week, over the long-term, you are giving your body an accumulation of consistent rebuilding that will build energy resources instead of deplete them.

Another benefit from fasting is that it will give you the strength and willpower to overcome your eating habits. As *The Essene Gospel of Peace* states, "Live by the spirit, and resist the desires of the body." You need to remember this advice every single day for the rest of your life because you're going to be tempted; be consciously aware of the temptation and let it subside, especially during your fasts. I promise that after you drink tons of water and go to bed, you will feel better in the morning.

When you realize you can go one day without eating, every week for the rest of your life, you will ask yourself, "What else can I do that I thought I couldn't?" Your weekly fasting day really is a sacred day where you let your body nourish you with cleansing and a sacred spiritual practice to honor the body temple you reside in. When you're ready, start applying this Essene lifestyle.

I want to mention one last thought here along the lines of fasting. You have probably heard of Nobel Prize winning Dr. Carell and how he proved the cells are immortal. They simply need to be fed the right nutrients and be cleaned out of their wastes. What stood out for me about his test that proved cells are immortal was that the chicken cells he had in his laboratory lived several years until they died because someone forgot to clean out the waste in them.

What do cells have to do with not eating? When you allow the body a more ample time to rest from digestion, the energy works to eliminate toxins and waste from the body. We live in a society where the norm is to eat three meals a day and snack in between. When we socialize, eating is usually part of the activity; we order dessert, we overeat at Thanksgiving and Christmas, and so on. Even many raw foodists eat in larger quantities than what the body needs in a given day. But I really want to stress here how important it is to go without food to the highest level your body can sustain without compromising your nutrition.

You might say here, "How am I supposed to get everything I need if I'm not eating through the day?" The answer is concentrated nutrition in the form of superfoods, juicing vegetables and fruit, and blending superfood supplementations into juices to make soups and smoothies. You can also add superfoods such as spirulina and wheatgrass powder to your raw cakes, purees, salad dressings, dips, dehydrated crackers, etc.

The powerful nutrient-packed and nutrient-dense superfoods I will mention in the paragraphs to come will help every cell of your body to be happily nourished with everything it needs, so much so that you reduce your eating uptake to once or twice a day.

Your diet for optimal health could consist of an estimated 60 to 80 percent or more of water-rich fruits and vegetables. Unfortunately, eating them with their fibers doesn't necessarily guarantee 100 percent of their nutrition will be absorbed into your body, and eating too much fiber doesn't allow larger doses of the food to be consumed in any given meal, which is why I recommend juicing. Most of us do not chew fifty times or more till the food is liquid in our mouths. Juicing these amazing nutrient-packed foods allows us to receive 100 percent of their nutrition and, most importantly, maximize the amount of energy the body uses to eliminate wastes because less breaking down of the food occurs since no fiber is involved. If you want fiber in your diet, I would concentrate on the fruits and veggies that are hard to juice such as mango, blueberries, avocado, papaya, mushroom, eggplant, and olives as well as superfoods such as spirulina and wheatgrass powders. Juicing is such a ingenious way to save your body some extra energy—energy that it can instead use to accelerate detoxification, while at the same time, you're getting probably as much as 40 percent more nutrition. Is it becoming easier now to picture eating less and increasing your nutritional consumption more?

Next, we have the blending of foods into smoothies and soups. I recommend that you mix your juices with the superfoods, such as spirulina, into delicious smoothies and soups. (I'll discuss how in more detail as you read along.) This way you can make a super-nutrient rich meal that conserves so much energy, which can go toward precious detoxification of the body and fat flushing and will make your fasting easier to deal with. Please also check out my recipe book *Divina's Hearty Raw Foods* for ideas for soups and smoothies.

DO COLONICS

I already talked about colon cleansing by taking a formula, but colonics is a procedure to cleanse your colon. It is specifically talked about in *The Essene Gospel of Peace* as something that should be done during fasts. Although in ancient times, gourds were used, today we can visit colon hydrotherapy clinics. Colonics basically means filling up your colon with a machine that has a tube; the tube is inserted into your rectum and cleaned out several times and filled up with water several times. The process takes about one hour, and you will lay down on a special bed during it.

When fasting, I recommend doing a colon cleanse at least one to four times, depending on the length of your juice or water fast. If it's thirty days for example, I would fast at least once or twice a week.

If you become fanatic about colonics and can afford it, a colonic once a month would be beneficial. In general, I would stabilize yourself to doing at least four colonics a year with the change of seasons. They not only clean out your colon of old material, but they make your bowel movements function better and more efficiently.

VEGETABLES: THE IMPORTANCE OF ALKALINITY, VEGETABLE PROTEIN/MINERALS, AND CHLOROPHYLL

Green for Life

An important habit you can start today is to set a goal to make 60 to 70 percent of your diet be green leafy vegetables with a strong emphasis on superfood vegetables, such as sea and lake vegetables like spirulina, chlorella, E3Live, and wheatgrass. The rest of your diet should be about 20 percent fruit and 10 percent essential fatty acids, nuts, seeds, and grains; however, for those with a higher metabolism, a higher content on the nuts, seeds, and grains is appropriate. I can tell you that when I started eating the raw vegan way ten years ago, this was not the case for me; my diet was 70 percent nuts, seeds, grains, and fats, but at least I was eating raw, not cooked, gluten-rich breads and pasta. My body was so toxic and I was so used to eating heavily cooked carbs that the easiest way to transition was to start off with heavy acidic raw foods first (nuts, seeds, grains), neutral second (fruits), and alkaline last (the green leafy veggies). As you progress, you will see your body change its frequency, and as you introduce at least one salad and one vegetable juice a day, your body will start craving these foods and you will recognize how good they make you feel. It is literally a high to have a high alkaline diet. Just as the body can learn to crave junk food, the human body can learn to crave green leafy vegetables! I can tell you that it has been such a lifesaver for me to eat mostly produce, especially high in alkaline vegetables. I have massive amounts of energy, and I have lost about twenty-five pounds as of today. I am still losing since my lifestyle is now a liquid diet. You can eat and make delicious meals and still lose weight when you make this switch.

The reason it's so important to eat 70 percent raw green leafy vegetables is because they are so alkaline and protein rich. (Yes, I said protein rich—spirulina, in particular, for those of you who believe that meat is the only high protein source!) They are also chlorophyll rich. (This is so important because chlorophyll mimics the blood and is one of the primary sources to feed your blood properly.) Finally, raw, green, leafy vegetables are so dense with minerals, in particular, sea vegetables and lake vegetables like chlorella, E3Live, dulse, kelp, wakame, and spirulina, just to name a few. You're mostly made up of water, including your blood, so don't just drink massive amounts of water, but nourish yourself primarily with water-rich foods, in particular juiced vegetables.

Another big, super-alkaline source is green superfoods like raw wheatgrass powders and superfood green powder mixtures that have a vast array of vitamins and minerals. Please purchase these powders raw and mix them with your juices daily. I cannot repeat enough the importance of this. I remember checking my alkalinity level after consuming raw wheatgrass powder, and it spiked up so high so quickly I was shocked! As a society, we focus so much on acid level foods it's insane! We can overeat grains, meat, roots like potatoes, and too many nuts, especially those of us with low metabolism. Your body then has to hold on to more fat to protect itself because the body is so acidic. The body will not lose weight naturally until the body is fed massive amounts of alkaline foods, and if you have any form of disease, including cancer, it cannot survive on a highly alkaline diet. An alkaline body is a healthy body.

What Is Alkalinity?

Our blood is slightly alkaline, with a normal pH level of between 7.35 and 7.45. The benefit behind the alkaline diet is that our diet should reflect this pH level (as it did in the past before our modern-day diet). Alkaline diet concepts believe that a diet high in acid-producing foods disrupts this balance and promotes the loss of essential minerals such as potassium, magnesium, calcium, and sodium, as the body tries to restore equilibrium. This lack of balance makes people more open to illness.

In the year of 1931, Otto Warburg discovered that cancer is caused by weakened cell respiration, which is caused by fermentation that causes an acidic pH level in the human body. This acid condition destroys the cell's ability to control cell division which unfortunately then cause cancer cells begin to multiply. The main cause for cancer as tested is acidity in the human body.

Most doctors never address the pH levels in the body and instead focus more on getting blood pressure. The truth is that high blood pressure and fever, do not cause cancer—although they can cause other health issues—but definitely an acidic condition in the body does. Mr. Warburg has stated what's the cause of cancer, yet it is not given very much importance in most doctor's offices or hospitals. The body's pH level is most likely the most important aspect of human health, so it should be focused on with a highly alkaline diet, especially of juiced dark green vegetables.

It is very important for you to cherish this information and incorporate it into your lifestyle; alkaline foods should be introduced as a habit that is so ingrained in your system that it becomes second nature to you, like brushing your teeth every day. They say an apple a day keeps the doctor away. I say, a glass of juiced kale, spinach, broccoli, collard greens, parsley, and cilantro keeps the doctor away!

Food is not the only factor to affect our pH balance; any form of stress, acid water or argument, anger, or negative emotions created by the ego can leave an acidic residue in the bloodstream. On the other hand, any activity that is calming, relaxing, joyful, passionate, or positive can make your body more alkaline. Some situations that can make our pH more acidic are arguing with a partner, not being willing to forgive ourselves or others, holding a grudge or being resentful, being unable to surrender to what is happening in a particular moment, feeling jealous, wanting revenge, overworking, over-exercising, stress from the job, feeling depressed, anxious, or angry, watching scary or stressful movies, watching TV for a long time, or having your cell phone close to your ear for too long.

Some examples of good things that can make your body alkaline besides food is giving to charity with love, smiling, laughing, enjoying a favorite hobby, spending time with a romantic partner, watching a funny movie, spending time in nature, relaxing, deep meditation, deep breathing, dancing to your favorite tunes, receiving a soft massage, enthusiasm, excitement, and enjoying a healthy tasting alkaline meal with green leafy vegetables!

Having an at least 70 percent alkaline diet is probably more important than just being a raw foodist. Being a raw foodist is great, but without this 70/20/10 ratio, or close to it, depending on your metabolism, you cannot really reach optimal health. That's how important pH is in your life. And also after more than a decade on the raw food diet, it's impossible to have an alkaline diet without high levels of green leafy vegetables, and since 70 percent is a lot, I highly recommend that you juice daily your deep leafy greens and you fill up at least 70 percent of your glass with it; then mix in fruit or make a soup of green leafy veggie juice with tomato juiced with it and season to taste. This mixture will shoot your alkalinity levels to where you want them. I also recommend you do alkaline superfood powders like wheatgrass or spirulina and mix them with your drink. This mix is so alkaline it is unbelievable; I would not go a day without at least two tablespoons of it, and you can take up to six tablespoons daily. It will transform your life.

So out of all the choices you have in eating, if you were to eat just one thing a day, it would be your alkaline smoothie or juice drink, with 70 percent green leafy juice. This is the foundation of your daily nutrition. Your body can absorb it so quickly, there is no energy depletion from breaking down so much fiber, and you don't have to spend all day masticating large amounts of greens; instead, you can drink them in just a few minutes. It's fresh, and it is a perfect meal in a glass. Plus, the green powders contain beneficial fibers from the wheatgrass and other ingredients that are so nutritional and full of trace minerals that they are equivalent to pounds of produce.

Here are just a few examples of acid neutral and alkaline foods:

- **Most Alkaline:** raw milk, kale, collard greens, parsley, baby broccoli, broccoli, arugula, spinach, dandelion greens, and all dark green veggies
- **Alkaline:** cabbage, bok choy, baby bok choy, lettuce, celery, cilantro, green onion, and all lighter green veggies

- **Neutral:** apples, pears, oranges, berries, all other fruits, durian, coconut water, plant fats like olive oil, avocado oil, grape seed oil, and flax oil
- **Slightly Acidic (close to neutral):** avocados, strawberries, bananas
- **Acidic:** meats, nuts, grains, and seeds. Some nuts like almonds are considered alkaline, but they are only slightly-above-acidic scale, so they do not really have the potential to transform your pH balance to alkaline on a deep level.

An alkaline diet is the only way to healthy and permanent weight loss. So what happens when we go on a juice fast or water fast? After building your alkaline reserves and continuing to supplement on alkaline superfoods such as raw wheatgrass powder, you end up discovering how easy it is for your body to lose weight. Your body doesn't really let go of fat during exercise; your body lets go of it when your body is alkaline enough to buffer the toxic acidic fat deposit out of your system. This is the only reason why people struggle to lose weight, and I have permanently kept weight off by juice-fasting on alkaline juices and building my alkaline reserves, even when I decided I would eat solid foods such as with salads. If I would overeat, for example, it would be a hearty wholesome veggie green meal with tasty dressing and full of sea veggies as well. When your body has built up its alkalinity levels, it's efficiently getting rid of actual fat in your body so much faster than if you were to fast with just an acid condition alone. The traditional American diet, as well as traditional diets from other cultures, such as a Mexican, Chinese, Indian, or Italian diets, are all very acidic in general. It's important to go back and establish a high alkaline diet!

Where do you get your chlorophyll?

Another reason why an estimated 70 percent or so of your diet needs to be vegetables is because of the high chlorophyll content in them. A lot of meat eaters ask me, "Where do you get your protein?" I reply, "Spirulina, kelp, dulse, arame, sea lettuce, E3Live, nori, kale, spinach, non-GMO soy beans, nuts, seeds, grains, bee pollen, goji berries, royal jelly, and broccoli." Then I ask, "Where do you get your chlorophyll?" Is it all coming from that one lettuce leaf on a meat burger? And we wonder why America is so fat! I bet most people are not getting enough chlorophyll and don't realize vegetables need to be a portion of their protein source—not just meat!

If you want more energy, consume chlorophyll-rich foods; the deeper green color the leaves, the richer the content. As I always say: What works in nature, surely works in man. Some of the strongest animals in nature are full of energy and vitality, and they live only on green vegetation, which is full of chlorophyll. These animals include horses, pandas, gorillas (mostly greens), zebras, and deer, just to name a few. Wild horses have so much more strength and power than humans, yet all they eat is grass. Would you ask a horse, "Where do you get your protein?" If you look at it that way, wouldn't it seem a little ridiculous? Grass, like wheatgrass, is one of the richest sources of nutrition on the planet. That's why I recommend the consumption of raw wheatgrass powders.

Chlorophyll is the molecule that absorbs sunlight and uses its energy to synthesize carbohydrates from carbon dioxide and water. This process is known as photosynthesis, and it is the basis for sustaining the life processes of all plants. Since animals and humans obtain their food supplies by eating plants, photosynthesis can be said to be the source of our lives also.

When I look at the sun, I think of what an amazing gigantic star it is. It truly sustains life on this planet, and without it, none of us could exist. That is pretty profound. All life existence here on the planet is dependent on the sun. The sun is the source of all nutrition; it feeds us all. It really is love incarnated on the outer level through light. That said, wouldn't you think that the foods that directly absorb its awesome power would probably be the strongest foods to consume? Of course, so ask yourself: Where does sunlight get trapped first? It's not in fruit; it's not in animal meat; it's not in nuts, seeds, or grains. It's in green vegetation. Yes, that's right: green leaves, both land and aquatic, are the first places that sunlight gets trapped. That is what chlorophyll does; it traps the love and light nourishment of this magnificent star. That is a very powerful thing to understand. Are you starting to understand how powerful a piece of kale or spirulina is? Eating green vegetables is as close as your body can come to nourishing itself through the most powerful life-giving force for our planet. Do you understand now why 70 percent of green vegetation can be so powerful? If you juice your greens, you can absorb even more, and how much more powerful will that be? I mean, when I switched, and after I detoxified my body (which initially made me tired), I started feeling the high you get from consuming high doses of juiced deep greens. It really is a high! No amount of grains or nuts can give you that; sure they can fill your belly, but the reality is, they make you lose so much energy due to digestion, and then if you keep eating high quantities of these foods, before you know it, you're walking half-asleep, not really as alert and attentive as you could be. That is because these foods are secondary to the nourishment of the sun; they are denser forms of nutrition. These plants' leaves transfer the sun's energy into them, so they are secondary, not primary, sources of the life force. Once you realize the power of green vegetation and you see how a tall glass of green veggie juice a day makes you feel, you won't go back to such heavy food. Chlorophyll is truly sunlight's liquefied form. Just visualize, as you drink deep green juice, that you're bathing every single cell of your body in the most powerful loving force of the solar system. Doesn't that just give you goose bumps? No life is possible without sunshine, and no life is possible without chlorophyll.

Plants' lives depend on the loving, vibrant, energizing light of the sun, and we depend on plants to live. Even when people eat meat, they are eating the animal that ate the nutrients that came from the plants that directly absorbed the closest thing you can get to the sun's nutrients. This is most likely why humans eat vegetarian animals. Some ancient cultures, such as Islamic and Jewish ones, prohibited consumption of carnivorous animals. I remember reading a story of some people who got very sick from eating carnivorous animals. But even carnivorous creatures such as dogs and cats enjoy nibbling on green grasses now and then.

The chlorophyll molecule is very similar to the molecule of hemoglobin or human blood, and it really is the foundation for building a healthy bloodstream. If you think about it, 70 percent of our bodies are water-based, and most of that is blood; therefore, it's a good idea to consume water-rich foods such as green juices to feed the blood. Chlorophyll nurtures us like a mother; it takes care of our organs and blood by cleansing them; it even destroys many of our internal enemies like bacteria, fungus, and cancer cells.

Another great thing is that chlorophyll enhances the wellbeing of good bacteria in the intestines. To have optimal health, we need to have about 80 percent good bacteria in our intestinal tract. These good bacteria manufacture essential nutrients for us, including B vitamins, vitamin K, and helpful enzymes to assist in breaking down our foods, among other things. These good bacteria require the presence of oxygen, so if we don't have enough oxygen in our bodies, bad bacteria takes over and starts to destroy the body with infections and disease. Chlorophyll really is a profound powerful healer because it serves to keep good bacteria flourishing since it carries a significant amount of oxygen within it. The more chlorophyll we consume, via green juiced drinks or salads, green wraps, soups, etc., the better our intestinal flora and overall health will be. As I mentioned earlier, green juices are probably the easiest way to get this needed nutrition readily and easily in abundance. Although chewing is fun, and a salad a day would be fun, tasty, and joyfully crunchy, I highly doubt you'd want to eat ten salads a day when you can just juice the nutrient and have it all packed in one or two glasses. Remember, you can always mix it with fruit to make a tasty drink or a delicious soup! Consume chlorophyll at least six days a week with 12 ounces of liquid chlorophyll daily. (You can reach this quota by juicing and supplementing with superfood green powders such as raw spirulina or wheatgrass.)

Chlorophyll has been proven helpful in preventing and healing many forms of cancer and arteriosclerosis. Research shows that chlorophyll can help cure and prevent almost any illness. Chlorophyll has so many healing properties, but I'll just name a few below:

- Enhances energy
- Detoxifies the liver
- Eliminates body odor and bad breath
- Cleans the digestive tract

- Aids in the prevention of liver cancer
- Is beneficial in all cancer therapy
- Helps with anemia
- Aids in the elimination of mold from the body
- Builds a healthy high blood count
- Helps cure and prevent cancer
- Provides iron to organs
- Alkalizes the body
- Helps the body remove toxins
- Cleanses the bowels
- Improves hepatitis
- Balances menstrual cycles
- Improves milk production for breastfeeding mothers
- Helps heal cuts or sores more quickly and also prevents them
- Helps clean teeth and gums
- Heals ulcer tissue
- Helps catarrhal discharges
- Improves inflammation
- Improves eyesight

Without chlorophyll, also known as the "green blood" of plants, life as we know it could not exist. Chlorophyll is the natural plant pigment that lends its color to grass, leaves, and many of the vegetables we eat. Chlorophyll may indeed play an important role in prevention of certain cancers. Researchers in the early 1980s discovered that chlorophylls and related chemicals could inhibit the ability of certain DNA-damaging chemicals to cause mutations in bacteria.

Supplementation benefits with chlorophyll-rich chlorella was shown to reduce high blood pressure, lower LDL ("bad" cholesterol), accelerate wound healing, and improve immune function in colitis and fibromyalgia. In a 2000 study by Marchant, supplemental chlorella was given to a few dozen fibromyalgia patients. The results demonstrated a 22 percent decrease in pain intensity in patients with moderately severe fibromyalgia after sixty days of daily chlorella supplementation. Another study by Brazilian researcher M.S. Miranda showed that spirulina, rich in chlorophyll, phenolic acids, alpha-carotene, and beta-carotene, showed powerful free-radical antioxidant protection.

So, no more excuses for not getting your greens! You can introduce high levels of chlorophyll from chlorella, blue-green algae, spirulina, kelp, nori, arame, green barley, wheatgrass, fresh juiced green vegetables, and alfalfa.

With the high levels of oxygen in chlorophyll and high mineral content in greens plants and their extremely alkalizing properties, greens are the most important foundational nutrition for our bodies on this planet. Just by including one green juice smoothie packed with green superfoods such as wheatgrass powders or spirulina or a combination of superfood green powders, and any fruit to your liking, you can transform your amazing God-given body temple and truly have an aliveness in your existence that you never thought possible.

Why Are Minerals from Vegetables so Important?

Often when we are hungry and eat something, we can't figure out why it isn't "hitting the spot" to satisfy our hunger or taste buds. Why is it that you have to consume so much? The most likely reason is that your body is mineral-deficient and looking for minerals so that's probably why you keep eating. But you're probably just eating the wrong foods, like donuts, cooked gluten-rich unsprouted grains, breads, pasta, potatoes, and cooked meats; you're going for the heavy acid stuff, so your stomach feels full, but you aren't feeding the real hunger in your blood cells and at a cellular level for mineral rich foods.

Some of the best mineral rich vegetables, besides land vegetables, are sea vegetables, and I highly recommend you eat them regularly. I would recommend making a sea vegetable salad several times a week; it's so filling it's unbelievable; it will cut back on your eating so much. Some sea vegetables are spirulina (actually a freshwater vegetable, but nonetheless, super mineral dense) dulse, wakame, seaweed, sea lettuce, and nori. Make sure the labels say they are raw because often they have been roasted. For land vegetables, the deeper the green, the generally higher in minerals. Some land vegetables are arugula, spinach, kale, collard greens, broccoli, baby broccoli, dinosaur kale, parsley, cilantro, mustard greens, radish leaves, turnip leaves, and beet leaves. Radish leaves are high in silicone, which is good for bone-building, but broccoli and all of the above are really good bone-builders. Kiss your osteoporosis goodbye!

An Abundance of Protein in Greens

Before I discuss getting protein from greens, I want to say that some people, like myself, do poorly on animal protein. I actually have received clairvoyant messages that animal proteins attract dark spirits to me and darken my consciousness. *The Essene Gospel of Peace* says:

"For I tell you truly, he who kills, kills himself, and whoso *eats* the flesh of slain beasts, *eats* of the body of *death*."

This quote feels like it was written for me and many others who were destined to be vegetarians. For a while, I believed everyone should follow this rule and be vegetarian, but then I saw a couple of people who tried but could not sustain being vegetarians due to health issues. Who knows? Maybe they didn't try high enough levels of raw spirulina-rich protein daily, but everyone is a little different. For me, it's suicide to eat meat; clairvoyantly in my inner eye, I have been shown internal problems I will have from eating or even smelling it, and I know I'm not alone.

This is the case for many, whether or not they know it. If you don't know whether you're meant to be vegetarian, try it first and see how it goes. If you're concerned about protein, get a large portion of your complete protein from spirulina or combine your sprouted grains, nuts, and seeds for extra protein; then add secondary sources like vegetables, grains, nuts, and seeds. If, however, going without meat is not the way for you, don't do anything to harm yourself. Many of my friends have gone vegetarian, only to have had problems. The Dalai Lama, himself, was a vegetarian, but when he became sick, he regained his health by eating meat. One problem I see with eating cooked meat is that it ages and weakens the body. But who wants to eat raw cow meat? If you want to follow the raw diet and eat meat, then try ceviche, sushi, or sashimi. Raw fish is a lot more palatable and healthy, and our culture already embraces eating raw fish. My recommendation is that if you're going to eat meat, eat raw fish only and avoid all eggs and other meat; you don't really need it to get your protein. Also, those of you cooking your fish, like omega-3 rich salmon, who think you're getting omega-3 fatty acids, think again because your cooking oils make the omega-3 fatty acids rancid and not raw anymore so they are causing free radicals in your body and aging you faster. If you want omega-3s, try buying the vegetarian version cold pressed in bottled form. If you plan to eat cooked fish or meat anyway, drink two to six capsules of enzymes for better digestion and so you don't have to drain your own natural supply in your body. Cooked and raw meat does require a lot more enzymes than vegetables and fruit.

Can you get enough protein from vegetables? Most people seem to think that protein is the most important component in a person's diet. I wish people would ask, "Where are you getting your light? Where are you getting your enzymes? Where are you getting your chlorophyll?" The reality is if you're eating mostly green veggies, in particular the ones considered superfoods, such as spirulina, wheatgrass, and all seaweeds, you're getting an abundance of protein, and even more completely than you would from meats, plus it's an even cleaner protein source if its organic. Spirulina alone has 60 percent more protein than meat, and it's a complete protein.

I think what most people are afraid of when they get off a meat diet is facing the body's detoxification symptoms. The reality is that we aren't meant to be eating super-heavy foods all the time. The body needs good nutrition, but it's not meant to be overloaded and stuffed with these supersized meals offered by fast-food and other restaurants. When you feel weak and a lack of energy, you can often blame it on the diet, but the reality is the body now has more energy to get rid of toxins, which makes the body appear to be losing energy.

The following pages contain charts where I supply a list of high-protein vegetables. Please familiarize yourself with them to get an idea of how much protein is in different vegetables. The important thing to keep in mind is that you can get your protein from vegetables (among other plant-based foods), and they are a superior protein source to meat, which is high in cholesterol and the number one reason for the number one killer in America: heart attacks!

Vegetables/Quantity (grams)/Protein Content (grams)

Asparagus/100/3
Aubergine/100/1
Beetroot/100/2
Broccoli/100/3
Brussels sprouts/100/3
Cabbage/100/1
Carrot/100/0.5
Cauliflower/100/3
Celery/100/0.5
Chicory/100/ 0.6
Courgette/100/2
Cucumber/100/ 0.5
Dandelion greens/100/2
Endive/100/1
Garlic/100/6
Lentils/100/9
Lettuce/100/1
Mushrooms/100/2
Marrow/100/0.5
Okra/100/2.43
Onion/100/0.7
Onion Spring/100/2
Pumpkin/100/1
Parsnip/100/1.5
Potato/100/2
Radish/100/0.7
Spinach/100/2
Swede/100/0.5
Sweet corn/100/2.5
Squash/100/1.64
Sweet potato/100/1
Tomato/100/2
Turnip/100/0.8

Watercress/100/3
Yam/100/2

Beans/Quantity (grams)/Protein Content (grams)

Asparagus/100/2
Baked beans/100/5
Black beans/100/9
Chickpeas/100/15
Kidney beans/100/9
Lima beans/100/7
Mung beans/100/7
Navy beans/100/8
Pinto beans/100/9
Refried beans/100/5
Soybeans/100/12
White beans/100/9

Apart from vegetables and various kinds of beans, here are some more items on the protein rich foods list:

Almonds/100/21
Buckwheat/100/3
Cashews/100/15
Cornmeal/100/8
Kamut/100/10
Oats/100/3
Peanuts/100/24
Pecans/100/9
Pumpkin seeds/100/38
Quinoa/100/14
Sunflower seeds/100/19
Wild rice/100/3

Osteoporosis and building the strongest bones

Osteoporosis usually results from a lack of alkalinity in the body. Most of American society lives off foods that are so acidic that over time the body has to use its own bones to alkalize the body in order for the body to survive. A body that's too acidic can cause death if the body does not have enough alkalinity, so to compensate, the body draws it from the calcium in the bones. Acid foods like cooked sugar leach calcium from the bones; that's why alkaline foods such as green juices, vegetables, and, in particular, wheatgrass powders are so alkaline and buffer the acidity in the body; that is why it's so important to do alkaline juice fasts to flush out the acidity and nurture and restore the bones in the body to prevent osteoporosis. Taking calcium alone from prescription is not going to do it; neither is drinking pasteurized milk. Perhaps raw milk, but most milk these days is not so good in value; most animals are shot with hormones and locked in cages, so who knows what the quality of raw milk is. If you're drinking raw milk or eating cheese, buy organic and make sure the animals were free-range and grass-fed. I have occasionally consumed raw milk from the Amish community, which has really great milk because its animals are treated humanely; however, Amish raw milk is so rare to come by that I would recommend sticking to a vegan diet for the most part and focusing on the alkaline foods. Remember, an alkaline body cannot get sick.

Also, worth mentioning again, is that some books, including *The China Study*, state that milk causes cancer. The studies this statement is based on were performed with cooked milk, not organic raw milk. Raw milk has a different effect on the body and does not cause cancer. Also, the myth that cholesterol is bad for the body is not true. If it were true, then why do babies whose human mothers feed them with their cholesterol-rich breast milk not get cancer? Cholesterol is cholesterol; it's more cooking the milk than the raw milk that causes problems. Lactose intolerance can be corrected by drinking raw milk because its enzymes were not killed by cooking it.

THE POWER OF JUICING AND LIQUIDS

Juicing is the best, most important, and probably most delicious habit you can start today. Get a Juicer. The latest and most advanced juicers are the cold pressed juicers. They are the best because they create less oxidation while you juice your produce, and the juice lasts longer and retains more nutrients than regular juicers. One of the best is the Breville Juicer brand, and it does carry a cold pressed juicer. It is by far the best and the most reasonably priced for the average person. You will get the best amount of juice extracted at a reasonably easy pace while you juice.

Juice every single day. For starters, juice two 12-16 ounces of fresh fruits and vegetables. One for lunch/brunch and one for dinner. If you really want to be healthy, juicing is probably the most important thing you can do. And in particular, juice the green leafy vegetables because of their alkalinity. I know many of you do not like your broccoli or dark bitter greens like collards, especially raw; I only wish the general world diet would have more dark nutritious greens in it rather than just a lettuce leaf in a burger, or a Caesar salad, which is only lettuce, croutons, and cheese. But when you are conditioned to eat really soft-cooked foods, it's not appealing for the body to eat these raw, dark green strong foods. You can juice kale, spinach, or broccoli along with an apple to hide the taste of the vegetables you don't like, but at the same time, you're getting all of the nutritional benefits that come along with them. You can also make a delicious green soup with the green-juiced base and blend it with sprouted peas, chickpeas, nuts, avocado, tomato, sea salt, spices, or oil to your taste.

Juicing is so beneficial because, first off, it unlocks all the fruits and vegetables' nutrients. If you eat the fruit and vegetables, you're most likely not going to chew everything thoroughly and unlock almost all of the nutrients for your body to nourish itself. Secondly, you can get your serving requirements of daily fruits and vegetables so much faster; you can get so many more nutrients than just by sitting there and eating pounds of veggies to get the same requirements. Also, your body can absorb the nutrients in less than twenty minutes because the extraction of the nutrients has already been done for you! This is amazing stuff!

If you don't see the power of juicing from just reading these paragraphs, I don't know what to tell you! There is so much aliveness in raw juices, and there are so many delicious recipes! The amount of light and aliveness in a juice can energize you so much for your work throughout the day! Think of it as like having a blood transfusion. How many of us are doing daily blood transfusions? Your blood is the most important aspect to feed! More so than what heavy foods like nuts, seeds, and grains could ever do. Let's become vegetarian vampires, preying on the life force of green blood in plants by juicing! Drink your greens, and forget about coffee, if you want to be energized! In the long-term, as your body gets use to this lifestyle, and as you cut back more and more on dead cooked foods, you will notice a tremendous difference. Please be patient with your body; juice daily, build momentum, and you will see results!

Also, I want you to mix your juices with superfood greens among other superfoods. But if you're on a budget, there is one superfood in particular that I recommend among all others. Please get yourself Superfood Raw Green Powders that contain things like wheatgrass, dried green vegetables, and spirulina. I swear by it, and it is the most comprehensive product in terms of giving you all the vitamins and minerals as a supplement; it is better than any vitamin or mineral tablet I have ever taken. It literally detoxifies the body and gets rid of fats in your body when you're juice fasting because it's so alkaline. I was amazed when I did a juice fast with superfood green powders mixed in my juices because what came out smelled like old stored fats. No amount of exercise, no matter how strenuous, ever did that, and I would always gain the weight back. It was like a miracle the first time I saw that happen. Other great superfood products are also online; just google them.

If you go to a health food store, ask an employee to show you what is available. Remember, however, that not all superfood products are created equal and not all companies make the best; some of them are filled with filler and fibers to dilute the product's potency and save money; some companies also process the product. Be sure that it is dried at low temperatures so the nutrient content and enzymes are still intact. But if you want a safe bet, go with a raw green superfood powder, or just buy spirulina or wheatgrass powder alone. Several great superfood companies are listed on the index pages of my recipe books *Divina's Hearty Raw Foods* and *Divina's Living Caribbean Cuisine*. If you want to rotate and try out different superfood green powders, I suggest you go to raw food restaurants and ask the owner about them or look at what they are selling on their shelves; you're guaranteed 100 percent to have a quality product in your hands when you visit a raw vegan restaurant. These people know what they are offering you, and it is most certainly offered with love. So many raw vegan restaurants now exist that you're bound to bump into a great one in your area. Just search for them with Google or on YouTube.

ADDING SUPERFOODS TO YOUR LIFESTYLE

Superfoods are the most important nutrients you could ever consume. Superfoods need to be the foundation of your diet because they are so nutrient-packed that they literally kill cellular starvation and hunger. By using them, you will be so nutrient-dense that any fast you do will be as easy as it can get for you, and you'll get away with one or two meals a day without feeling fatigued or hungry because you are so well-nourished.

A superfood is a food that is considered to have more nutrients compared to other foods, is essential for human sustainability, is high in antioxidants, and is a food that makes you live a lot longer and healthier.

Here is a detailed list of the essential superfoods and their benefits that you should consider adding to your lifestyle:

Wheatgrass (Powder)

Generally, I recommend the raw powder version of wheatgrass instead of the juiced version because I personally had it freshly juiced and it's too nauseating for my taste. I believe you can get so much more out of the dried powder version because it tastes neutral so it's easier to consume. That said, wheatgrass is probably the most powerful land vegetable there is.

One shot of freshly juiced wheatgrass equals one kilogram of vegetables. Wheatgrass increases red blood cell count and lowers blood pressure. It cleanses the blood, organs, and gastrointestinal tract of debris. It also stimulates metabolism and the body's enzyme systems by enriching the blood. It aids in reducing blood pressure by dilating the blood pathways throughout the body. It stimulates the thyroid gland, correcting obesity, indigestion, and a host of other complaints. Finally, it restores alkalinity to the blood. The juice's abundance of alkaline minerals helps reduce over-acidity in the blood. It can be used to relieve many internal pains, and it has been used successfully to treat peptic ulcers, ulcerative colitis, constipation, diarrhea, and other complaints of the gastrointestinal tract.

Wheatgrass is a powerful detoxifier and liver and blood protector. The enzymes and amino acids found in it can protect us from carcinogens like no other food or medicine. It strengthens our cells, detoxifies the liver and bloodstream, and chemically neutralizes environmental pollutants.

Wheatgrass also fights tumors and neutralizes toxins. Recent studies show that wheatgrass juice has a powerful ability to fight tumors without the usual toxicity of drugs that also inhibit cell-destroying agents. The many active compounds found in wheatgrass juice cleanse the blood and neutralize and digest toxins in our cells.

Wheatgrass contains beneficial enzymes. Whether you have a cut finger you want to heal or you desire to lose five pounds...enzymes must do the actual work. The life and abilities of the enzymes found naturally in our bodies can be extended if we help them from the outside by adding exogenous enzymes, like the ones found in wheatgrass juice. Don't cook wheatgrass. We can only get the benefits of the many enzymes found in it by eating it uncooked. Cooking destroys 100 percent of the enzymes in food.

Chlorophyll's second important nutritional aspect is its remarkable similarity to hemoglobin, the compound that carries oxygen in the blood. Dr. Yoshihide Hagiwara, president of the Hagiwara Institute of Health in Japan, is a leading advocate for the use of wheatgrass as food and medicine. He reasons that since chlorophyll is soluble in fat particles, and fat particles are absorbed directly into the blood via the lymphatic system, chlorophyll can also be absorbed in this way. In other words, when the "blood" of plants is absorbed in humans, it transforms into human blood, which transports nutrients to every cell of the body.

When used as a rectal implant, wheatgrass reverses damage from inside the lower bowel. An implant is a small amount of juice held in the lower bowel for about twenty minutes. In the case of illness, wheatgrass implants stimulate a rapid cleansing of the lower bowel and draw out accumulations of debris.

Externally applied to the skin, wheatgrass can help eliminate itching almost immediately. It will soothe sunburned skin and act as a disinfectant. Rubbed into the scalp before a shampoo, it will help mend damaged hair and alleviate itchy, scaly, scalp conditions.

Wheatgrass is also soothing and healing for cuts, burns, scrapes, rashes, poison ivy, athlete's foot, insect bites, boils, sores, open ulcers, tumors, and so on. Use it as a poultice, and replace it every two to four hours. It also works as a sleep aid; merely place a tray of living wheatgrass near the head of your bed to enhance the oxygen in the air and generate healthy negative ions to help you sleep more soundly. You can enhance your bath by adding some wheatgrass to your bath water and settling in it for a nice, long soak.

Dental hygiene benefits also can be derived from wheatgrass. It sweetens the breath and firms up and tightens the gums. Just gargle it in some juice.

Toxicity is reduced with wheatgrass. It neutralizes toxic substances like cadmium, nicotine, strontium, mercury, and polyvinyl chloride.

Wheatgrass offers the benefits of a liquid oxygen transfusion since the juice contains liquid oxygen. Oxygen is vital to many body processes: it stimulates digestion (the oxidation of food), promotes clearer thinking (the brain utilizes 25 percent of the body's oxygen supply), and protects the blood against anaerobic bacteria. Cancer cells cannot exist in oxygen's presence.

The aging process can be slowed down or reversed by using wheatgrass. It returns gray hair to its natural color. It greatly increases energy levels when consumed daily. It is a beauty treatment that slows down the aging process and helps to tighten loose and sagging skin. Wheatgrass will cleanse your blood and help rejuvenate aging cells, making you feel more alive right away.

Wheatgrass also lessens the effects of radiation. One enzyme found in wheatgrass, SOD, lessens the effects of radiation and acts as an anti-inflammatory compound that may prevent cellular damage following heart attacks or exposure to irritants.

Finally, wheatgrass restores fertility and promotes youthfulness. It can double your red blood cell count just by soaking in it. Renowned nutritionist Dr. Bernard Jensen found that no other blood builders are superior to green juices and wheatgrass. In his book *Health Magic Through Chlorophyll from Living Plant Life*, he mentions several cases where he was able to double the red blood cell count in a matter of days merely by having patients soak in a chlorophyll-water bath. Blood-building results occur even more rapidly when patients drink green juices and wheatgrass regularly.

Spirulina

Spirulina is my favorite superfood because it is protein, mineral, and nutrient rich all at the same time, and it has tons of chlorophyll. It got rid of my adult acne after I had tried for years, and it reduced my voracious appetite when I began to take just 4-6 daily tablespoons of it. My hair, skin, and nails are more vibrant and thicker and healthier now because of my religious, continuous use of it. Spirulina is one of a family of nutritional algae, along with chlorella. They are usually found in warm and alkaline waters all over the world, predominantly in South America, Africa, and Mexico. The name "spirulina" is derived from the Latin word for "helix" or "spiral." Its name reflects the physical configuration of the organism as it forms in swirling, microscopic strands.

Spirulina is a water-grown, 100 percent vegetable plankton. It is a blue-green algae that grows or is grown in fresh water. Spirulina has been used by humans for thousands of years. It was very popular with the ancient Aztecs, who thrived on the spirulina that grew in Lake Texcoco in Mexico. For the people who live around Lake Chad in Africa, spirulina has been a mainstay in their diet for thousands of years.

For me, spirulina is the number one hunger killer of all foods. It's so nutrient dense that it's dark green, almost black, in color. It contains a vast array of vitamins and minerals, has concentrated non-toxic absorbable nutrients, and is the elite food of choice to substitute all your protein powders. The protein in spirulina contains all eight essential amino acids, making it a complete protein. Spirulina also contains vitamins A, B-1, B-2, B-6, B-12, E, and K. As if that were not enough, spirulina provides minerals, trace minerals, cell salts, phytonutrients and enzymes, and an abundance of chlorophyll and other beneficial pigments. Raw meat is 27 percent protein, and even soybeans are 34 percent protein. Spirulina is 65 percent complete protein, making it the world's highest known source! Make sure to get spirulina that is dried at low temperatures because the enzymes are so important for its digestion and its protein utilization is maximized compared to cooked protein. If you go the vegetarian route and somebody who eats meat asks you, "Where do you get your protein?", this is it.

Spirulina is widely used as an ingredient in most green superfood powders, and it is beneficial as an aid in weight-loss programs. Spirulina has surprisingly been found to have significant positive effects on people suffering from type-2 diabetes. Studies show that spirulina has the ability to reduce fasting blood sugar levels in the body after six to eight weeks of intake.

Spirulina contains the essential fatty acid gamma-linoleic, which can help prevent conditions such as heart disease, arthritis, diabetes, and even cancer. Spirulina helps support a healthy pH balance in your body. A diet heavy in acidic foods such as animal proteins and grains can be effectively balanced by the alkaline properties of spirulina.

Among spirulina's many other benefits are the following:

- Inhibits the power of many viruses—including HIV, flu, mumps, measles, and herpes
- Helps diminish allergies such as hay fever

- Helps protect the liver from toxins
- Helps reduce blood pressure and cholesterol
- Helps control symptoms of ulcerative colitis
- Exerts strong antioxidant and anti-inflammatory effects
- Helps boost the immune system
- Creates stronger nails and hair

Finally, Spirulina has cleansing and detoxification benefits that remove dangerous toxins from the body. When you put your body under extreme stress, such as intense physical training, toxins and free radicals are released from your tissues. The chlorophyll in spirulina helps eliminate these waste products, and it cleanses your liver, kidneys, and blood. When the liver and kidneys are working more smoothly, everything else in the body works better, too and acne problems tend to disappear. Other benefits of spirulina include protection against environmental toxins, air and water pollution, and other contaminants you're exposed to every day.

Seaweeds

Sea vegetables, such as wakame, hijiki, mozuku, aonori, ogonori, nori, kombu, arame, kelp, sea lettuce, and dulse are some of the most nutrient-dense, protein-rich vegetables on this planet. And when compared with plants that grow on land, seaweed or sea vegetables are roughly twenty times more nutrient-dense. Sea vegetables have a high protein (30-50 percent) content and offer the broadest range of minerals of any food; they are an excellent source of the B-vitamin folate, potassium, sodium, copper, zinc, and magnesium, as well as a great source of iron, calcium, and the B-vitamins riboflavin and pantothenic acid. In addition, seaweed contains significant amounts of lignans, which are plant compounds with cancer-protective properties.

For centuries, the Japanese and Koreans have been known for the powerful health benefits they derive from seaweeds. Cultures that traditionally eat seaweed diets have been proven to suffer less from obesity, diabetes, Alzheimer's, and other diseases.

Another interesting study shows that women who consume seaweed on a regular basis tend to have less breast cancer than those who eat more meat. The female population in Japan, for example, has a lower risk of breast cancer than women in countries with high meat diets.

The lignans present in seaweeds also have been shown to block blood cell growth, which is the process through which fast-growing tumors not only gain extra nourishment, but send cancer cells out in the bloodstream to establish secondary tumors or metastases in other areas of the body. Lignans are also known to prevent colon cancer due to their high levels of vitamin B content and folic acid.

Healthy thyroid function is another very popular benefit of eating seaweed. Seaweed is probably one of the richest sources of iodine, a nutrient associated with the thyroid hormones thyroxin and triiodothyronine, both of which are essential for human life. Without enough iodine, your body cannot make enough hormones. Thyroid deficiency causes obesity and an enlarged thyroid gland called goiter.

Folic acid, which is highly present in sea vegetables, plays a very important role in protecting the body. Studies have shown that adequate levels of folic acid in the diet are very essential in the prevention of birth defects.

Sea vegetables also are a great weapon against heart disease, and they decrease the risk of heart attack. They are a potent source of magnesium, which is well-known for reducing high blood pressure and preventing heart attack.

Another interesting benefit of seaweed is its ability to give support through any stress by providing magnesium and the B vitamins pantothenic acid and riboflavin, which are necessary for energy production. Pantothenic acid is essential for the adrenal glands' health. Adrenal glands control a number of the body's functions and are very important for stress resistance. When these nutrients are not present, stress can more easily damage the adrenal glands, which would reduce the body's resistance to infection.

E3Live

E3Live is an edible, wild-harvested aqua botanical superfood and vegetable. It has sixty-four easily absorbable vitamins, minerals, and enzymes, and it also provides antioxidants and protein. It's a great trace mineral food to satisfy hunger for those hard-to-find minerals the body wants and craves.

In its raw organic state, E3Live is easily digested and full of antioxidants. It is extremely rich in minerals and has a higher concentration of beta-carotene than broccoli.

This blue-green algae also contains 60 to 70 percent vegetable protein, and it provides all the essential amino acids. All these benefits can be achieved without the risk of consuming meat, which is high in cholesterol and difficult to digest.

A rich source of calcium, iron, vitamin B12, enzymes, and antioxidants makes blue-green algae an ideal food for both adults and children and offers numerous benefits to our wellbeing, including:

- **Anti-aging properties:** E3Live is packed with a lot more essential nutrients and iron than most foods we consume. Its high concentration of antioxidants means our bodies can combat more free radicals and toxic waste, which reduces aging.
- **Relief from headaches and other aches and pains:** Our immune systems are strengthened because of its alkaline properties, along with its other qualities.
- **Energy boosting:** It works on the adrenal glands, providing rejuvenating effects.
- **Better digestion:** It coats the stomach lining and is packed with enzymes that help to improve digestion.
- **Better sleep:** It is detoxifying, resulting in better rest.
- **Weight loss:** Its high mineral content results in less food cravings and a more balanced appetite.
- **Greater concentration and focus:** Increases energy and clarity of mind; it's a great brain food.
- **Strengthens hair, skin, and nails:** It's high in protein, which is the main building block for healthy hair, skin, and nails.
- **Less anxiety and stress:** It has beneficial effects on our brain development and can help us cope better with stress.
- **Improves memory:** Because it has effects on our brain development, regular consumption of blue-green algae has also been shown to have an impact on our memory.

PROBIOTICS

Although probiotics is not technically a food, I wanted to mention it here for its amazing benefits in the digestion of food and assimilating not only your regular foods, but your superfoods. Probiotics (from "pro" and "biota," meaning "for life") are beneficial microorganisms that assist in the digestion process. They can help aid in irritable bowel syndrome. Many people are deficient in probiotics due to their diets' high-cooked content.

These good bacteria should be present in the billions in the intestinal tract because they are responsible for keeping the digestive system working properly. They help break down food and other substances, making digested nutrients more available for absorption. In an unhealthy digestive system or one compromised by medications, specific health problems, or even travel or stress, many of these beneficial intestinal bacteria have been destroyed. This situation can result in the proliferation of "bad bacteria." Such an imbalance can cause decreased absorption of food and nutrients, the growth of potentially toxic, harmful bacteria, sluggishness, and other digestive problems.

Healthy colonies of intestinal flora contribute to overall good health and wellbeing. When a healthy balance of intestinal bacteria is present, digestive challenges can lessen, so the growth of harmful, toxic bacteria is hindered. The right bacteria in the right amounts is essential for: a strong immune system; the assimilation of vitamins, proteins, fats, and carbohydrates; and the manufacture of B vitamins (including B-12), vitamin K, and various amino acids. Probiotic supplements, in conjunction with a balanced diet, can reduce and may even eliminate or avoid some of the most common discomforts associated with an out-of-balance intestinal system such as diarrhea or constipation; it may also give support in times of stress, poor diet, and use of antibiotics/prescription medicines and antacids. Replacing beneficial bacteria through supplementation, especially after antibiotic use, can re-establish the good bacteria and help boost the immune system.

GREEN SUPERFOOD FORMULAS/SUPPLEMENTS

I believe using green superfood formulas and supplements is so crucial because they provide the body with a large combination of all the green vegetable superfoods mentioned above and more. You don't have to purchase them all individually; you can have a balanced array of nutrients all perfectly combined in one bottle. You can add them to your soups and smoothies or dips and desserts. So many are out there to try, so just google "raw green superfood supplements" and you will come up with many that are great to try. If the ingredients include seaweeds, wheatgrass, and spirulina, they're worth a try. I have also listed my favorites on my website at www.ReawakenYourAuthenticSelf.com if you would like to take a look.

MSM

MSM stands for methylsulfonylmethane, a naturally occurring form of dietary sulfur found in fresh, raw foods and rainwater. It all starts when tiny plankton in the oceans give off a gas called dimethyl sulfide (DMS). DMS rises into the atmosphere where it reacts with sunlight and oxygen. The DMS is oxidized and MSM is created. Water droplets in clouds absorb the MSM and return it to earth in the form of rain.

Sulfur is a vital mineral needed by the body for normal structure and function. It makes up the protein and connective tissue that comprises our body mass, assists enzymes in performing chemical reactions, and protects us from oxidative stress and toxicity's harmful effects.

Sulfur is an element essential to human health and it is required by every cell in our body and makes up part of nearly all of our tissues, especially those highest in protein, such as muscles, skin, hair, tendons, and ligaments. A lack of sulfur in the diet can lead to serious health consequences so its a good idea to supplement. Bodily conditions associated with a lack of sulfur range from arthritis and allergies to acne and memory loss.

One important benefit of MSM softens internal tissues by rebuilding connective tissue with elastic sulfur bonds. MSM increases flexibility, hastens recovery time from sore muscles, and is excellent for recovery from athletic injuries.

It has been common place that MSM has come into the human diet by drinking rainwater or by eating foods watered mostly by rain. It has also been taken as nourishment through skin by direct contact with rainwater. Present day living and food production leave most people with very little contact with rainwater. Most crops are watered by irrigation or are grown in greenhouses, so it certainly can leave foods lacking natural amounts of sulfur.

Make sure that when you buy MSM that it is extracted from natural sources and that has been tested from toxins. Some low quality MSM is created using solvents that can result in toxic byproducts.

MSM has gained much of its reputation as a natural solution for pain especially after attaining soar muscles from working out. It is frequently used to alleviate back pain, headaches, muscle pain, athletic injuries, fibromyalgia, tendonitis, arthritis, and much more. Also, MSM can help to reduce inflammation, and it can speed recovery from injury anywhere in the body. Interestingly enough, MSM helps to make cell walls permeable, allowing nutrients to flow freely into cells and the cells easily to expel toxins. For those who love beautiful skin, Sulfur is essential for collagen formation and detoxification, and it also helps in repairing and maintaining the immune system and balancing blood sugar.

One of the top ways to activate our full potential for ultimate beauty and health is to be sure that our diets contain sufficient amounts of a bio-available form of sulfur. When increasing MSM, many health seekers have witnessed their skin and joint problems all but vanish, sometimes within weeks. Increased intake of MSM has also been know to help with to lustrous hair, radiant skin, and strong, fast-growing nails. Many adults in the U.S. suffers from arthritis, which is the main cause of disability. Arthritis is characterized by acute or chronic inflammation of one or more joints. Some very common areas affected are the hands, wrists, elbows, and knees, but it can also cause pain in the back, hips, pelvis, and toes. MSM beneficial because goes to work on arthritis by reducing inflammation and increasing blood flow to painful joints. It has also been know to help reduce muscle spasms around arthritic joints, offering even more pain relief. Many lives have been changed for the better by taking MSM.

Bee Pollen

Pollen has been said to be one of the most complete foods on the planet. Be pollen are tiny, dust-sized seeds, found on the stamen of all flower blossoms. As honeybees and other insects like butterflies travel from flower to flower looking for nectar, the pollen collects into little clumps on their legs. This situation normally results in pollination, and it is through this connection with bees and other insects that many plants reproduce. When a bee returns to the hive and crawls in, small clumps of pollen fall from its legs into a pile.

Pollen contains from as much as 24 to 35 percent complete protein, twenty-two amino acids, more than twelve vitamins, twenty-eight minerals, eleven enzymes, fourteen beneficial fatty acids, and eleven carbohydrates; it is also low in calories as well as rich in antioxidants. Fortunately, bee pollen is considered by many to be the most complete superfood available in nature because it contains more than ninety-six different nutrients, including every nutrient known that our bodies need.

One of the most significant facts about bee pollen is that it is an alkaline and energy-rich source of complete protein. It is approximately 20 percent easily digestible protein and contains twenty-two essential amino acids, meaning that by volume, pollen contains about five times more protein than cheese, eggs, or meat!

Here are just a few of bee pollen's many qualities:

- More than fifteen vitamins, including many B vitamins and vitamins C, D, and E
- Twenty-eight essential minerals, including iron, magnesium, potassium, zinc, calcium, and copper
- Bio-available enzymes, all of which have been shown to help with digestion and assimilation of other foods (could also help with weight loss and digestion issues)
- Can help balance hormones for improved reproductive health and libido
- 15 percent lecithin, which supports the nervous system and brain
- High levels of nucleic acids, which help protect against radiation

Royal Jelly

Royal jelly, is a superfood which is secreted from the salivary glands of the worker bees and serves as food for all young bee larvae and is the only food for larvae that will develop into queen bees. It contains a nutritious mix of vitamins, minerals, proteins, and fatty acids. Half of the dry weight of royal jelly is protein rich. Royal jelly contains vitamins A, B-complex, C, D, and E and it is particularly useful for its B-complex contents, including B1, B2, B6, B12, biotin, folic acid, and inositol. Royal jelly is high in the B vitamin pantothenic acid, which is known for its ability to reduce stress in the body. It also supplies the minerals calcium, copper, iron, phosphorous, potassium, silicon, and sulfur. Studies in animal testing indicate royal jelly has anti-inflammatory and anti-tumor benefits.

Here are just some of royal jelly's benefits that have been scientifically proven:

- Thanks to the amino acids it contains, it slows the effects of aging and helps to produce collagen in the skin as well as improve longevity.
- The amino acids help to improve the immune system and, therefore, protect against infections and diseases such as arthritis.
- Royal jelly benefits from hormone content are effective in balancing and regulating the female hormone system, reducing the symptoms of PMS and improving female fertility.
- It has proved very effective in treating Graves Disease, which is related to thyroid function in the neck area.

- It has been shown to help to prevent conditions such as Parkinson's and Alzheimer's.
- It has been known as a longevity superfood because the queen bee consumes royal jelly and lives longer than all of her bees that do not consume it.

Turmeric

Turmeric is an ayurvedic antioxidant herb that is yellow in color. The raw version is super bright orange compared to the cooked version; please choose the cold pressed raw version because it is higher in nutrients. It is a member of the ginger family and it is an earthy herb growing in hot, moist, tropical climates where microbial attack would be standard. Because it has developed a chemical defense system from these attacks, turmeric can defend us from parasites, carcinogens, and oxidation when we use it. Botanists believe turmeric is probably indigenous to Bihar, which is the North Indian state. It also still grows there to this day, and it also grows effectively in Hawaii and Orissa.

This powerful yellow herb helps in normalizing and regulating the immune system by boosting it in times of need and calming it when it is working too hard in stressful situations. It is a great addition to your food because it is one of the most purifying herbs in Ayurveda, helping to cleanse all the bodies, including physical and subtle, and any of the muscles and energy points in the body that are worked on in acupuncture medicine.

Turmeric is also beneficial for all the yogis because it helps increase flexibility in the body. It makes the tendons and ligaments moist, flexible, and strong to perform better in yoga. Strengthening your muscles and tendons helps reduce injury, swelling, and pain, and it definitely accelerates healing for arthritis. The anti-inflammatory effects are said to be even more powerful than any drug in Western medicine with no side effects.

Not only does turmeric help heal your liver and detoxify it, but it is also a great herb with powerful antioxidant properties. Daily use maximizes its antioxidant effects. Oxidation from pollution, stress, and bad food can cause serious damage to the body; however, turmeric is one of the most potent antioxidants because it contains the hydroxyl molecule, which is the most effective oxidant.

The best way to intake turmeric is by mixing it in smoothies, pudding, drinks and soups. It is also a great addition to salad dressings, sauces, and dips.

Tocotrienols

Tocotrienols is usually presented in a white powered form and a member of the vitamin E family, and it's said to be a lot more potent than vitamin E itself—up to sixty times more potent. This amazing superfood provides a large variety of essential nutrients for feeding a healthy body. This superfood is also a full protein; found in rice-bran oil, this whole-food is highly beneficial for those looking for deeper nourishment for their bodies.

Tocotrienols are also known for containing vitamins, minerals, and essential fatty acids necessary to enhance overall health. Besides being a potent source of vitamin E, tocotrienols are also a rich source of B vitamins which is also essential for the body. Their benefit of aiding the body use of vitamin A maintains the health of cell membranes. Tocotrienols are also a great contributor to strong, silky, healthy soft skin and hair and popular among women who want beautiful hair. Finally, it also acts as a powerful antioxidant, protecting healthy cells from free radical formation.

Recent tests with Vitamin E suggests it is composed of several tocopherols, the most powerful form of which is alpah-tocopherol. Vitamin E is of great nutritional importance in the function of the human body. All body tissues, have high concentrates of Vitamin E, but storage is mostly in the muscles, fatty tissues, and liver. If you're going to supplement Vitamin E, try the raw tocotrienol version as its more powerful.

Coenzyme Q10

Coenzyme Q-10 is one of the most important nutrients and superfood for good heart health and a strong cardiovascular system; it's an essential supplement for anyone taking statin drugs to reduce cholesterol levels. Coenzyme Q-10 is also important for its ability to regenerate other members of the antioxidant network, specifically glutathione, vitamin E, and vitamin C. The benefits of Coenzyme Q-10 also include improvement of brain function, increase of energy and stamina, and prevention of gum disease, as well as overall health.

Enzymes

Enzymes are the sparks that start the essential chemical reactions in our bodies that we need to live. They are essential for food digestion, stimulating the brain, providing cellular energy, and repairing all tissues, organs, digesting undigested particles in the blood and cells. Although enzymes are not really a food, I include them in the superfood section because they are critical and essential, especially in a society where we traditionally cook our foods and kill the enzymes in them. Even a 100 percent raw diet would benefit with some enzyme supplementation to help make it easier to break down. If you have been on a cooked diet all your life, chances are your body has been depleted of its own enzyme storage. Enzyme therapy helps break down food in the bloodstream that has not been properly digested. Enzymes should be taken especially with heavier foods such as nuts, grains, seeds, and legumes.

Flax Oil/Hemp Oil

Flax and hemp oils in cold pressed form contain high levels of omega-3 fatty acids, which are essential for the body to function properly. It's important to take about two to three tablespoons of each daily when eating. Some call these oils one of the most powerful plant foods on the planet. There's some evidence they may help reduce your risk of heart disease, cancer, stroke, and diabetes.

Hemp oil benefits are plentiful and are raising quite a stir in the medical community. Although the farming of hemp is still controversial because of the legal implications, there is no denying that hemp oil delivers a health punch to any regime. Consuming omega-3s and omega fatty acids have also been proven to be an effective anti-inflammatory, which aids those who suffer from rheumatoid arthritis. Ideally, one should consume the right dosage of omegas to get the full benefits. Most Americans and the world consume too much omega-6, which can have negative effects, but by incorporating foods that offer the right balance of omegas, your health improves dramatically. Hemp seed oil provides an excellent ratio of 3:1, which is recommended.

EATING LOCALLY-GROWN FOOD

Eating locally-grown food is recommended in *The Essene Gospel of Peace*, and it is one of the key components to good health. All of your land fruits and vegetables can be bought locally grown at your farmer's market, and some health food stores carry many or some locally-grown food. The only exceptions are superfoods—which might not be grown locally, but their nutrition content far supersedes this recommendation of eating locally—and coconut water, which is so beneficial for hydrating your body. I recommend you get all your other foods, especially your produce, from local farmers.

Local food is fresher and tastes better than food that has been trucked or flown in from thousands of miles away. Trust me; you can taste the difference between lettuce picked yesterday and lettuce picked last week, factory-washed, and sealed in plastic.

When you buy and eat locally-grown food, you're eating that season's produce, which gives you nutrients to keep you strong. Eating locally also keeps you in tune with what your body needs from the particular location where you are living. A strong link exists between where you live and the food that grows there.

NOURISHING YOUR OUTER BODY

It's important to keep your body as clean on the outside as on the inside. Buy yourself a shower filter to filter out all of the chlorine from your shower; then you will notice that your skin get smoother. Use only natural soaps, shampoos, day creams, hand creams, and face cleansers from health food stores because they don't contain any harsh chemicals. I have found coconut oil, shea butter, and cold pressed almond oil to be the best oils for the body after a shower.

Spraying yourself with lavender spray after every shower has a cleansing effect on your aura and removes negative energy from the energy field around you. I have also found skin brushing once every two weeks to be effective in the removal of old dead skin on your body. You can buy skin brushes at your local health food stores.

BONUS: QUOTE FROM *THE ESSENE GOSPEL OF PEACE*

Here are Jesus' guidelines for eating, as recorded in *The Essene Gospel of Peace*. I want to include it so you get a better idea of the language in which this gospel was written; in my opinion, the language has a subtle effect on how you take in the message and go about applying it. I also wanted to include it because I want everyone to read this gospel, so hopefully, reading a little bit will inspire you to read more of it. Again, I remind you that you can get the entire manuscript for about one or two dollars online. It is a quick read, but I recommend you read it more than once:

Eat only when called by the angel of appetite.... Cook not.... Neither mix all things with one another, lest your bowels become as steaming bogs.... Be content with two or three sorts of foods, which you will always find around you.... Never eat unto fullness..., Satan and his power tempt you to eat more and more, but live by the spirit and resist the desires of the body.... You're fasting is always pleasing in the eyes of the angels of God.... So give heed to how much you have eaten when you are sated [satisfied], and eat less always by a third.... Let the weight of your daily food be not less than a "mina" [a Hebrew weight approximately 99/100ths of a pound], but mark that it not go beyond two....

[i.e., between one and two pounds of food a day]. Trouble not the work of the angels in your body by eating often. For I tell you truly, he who eats more than twice in the day does in him the work of Satan.... Eat only when the Sun is highest in the heavens, and once again when it is set...and if you will that Satan shuns you afar, then sit but once in the day at the table of God.... Eat not unclean foods brought from afar, but eat what your trees bear, for your God knows what is needful of you, and where, and when.... Eat not as the heathen do, who stuff themselves in haste, defiling their bodies with all manner of abomination. Eat always from the table of God: the fruit of the trees, the grasses and grains of the field, the milk of beasts, and the honey of bees. For everything beyond these is of Satan, and leads by the way of sins and diseases unto death...breathe long and deeply with all your meals, and chew well your food with your teeth, that it become water, and that the angel of water turns it into blood in your body.... And eat slowly, as it were a prayer you make to the Lord. For I tell you truly, the power of God enters into you, if you eat after this manner...but Satan turns into a steaming bog the body of him upon whom the angels of air (breathing long and deeply at meals) and water (chewing food into a liquid) do not descend at his repasts.... Put naught upon the altar of the Lord when your spirit is vexed, neither think upon anyone with anger in the temple of God. And enter only into the Lord's sanctuary when you feel in yourselves the call of his angels, for all that you eat in sorrow, or in anger, or without desire, becomes a poison in your body. Place with joy your offerings upon the altar of your body, and remember every seventh day is holy and consecrated to God. On six days, feed your body with the gifts of the earthly Mother, but on the seventh day sanctify your body for your heavenly Father. On the seventh day, eat not any earthly food, but live only upon the words of God.

PUTTING IT INTO PRACTICE

- Change your mindset about your health, make it a necessity and extreme priority in your mind so that you can follow through with the tools in this chapter. Write down what needs to change in your mind.
- Write down all of the health affirmations along with visualizations of perfect health and practice them daily.
- Explore yoga as a daily workout routine, such as doing Bikram yoga six times a week. Add rebounding, dancing, and deep breathing daily during your rest hours after long hours of work.
- Don't cook, freeze, or rot your food.
- Go vegetarian, preferably vegan, since milk is not so great these days. The Essene diet is milk, honey, grains, greens, and fruit.
- Do several colon cleanses until your colon is mucoid plaque free.
- Eat once or twice a day, once at sunrise and once at sunset.
- Practice increasing your food intuition. What is your intuition telling you about what to eat?
- Fast once a week, preferably Sundays.
- Do not eat until fullness.
- Do a colonic at least four times a year during the change of seasons.
- Alkalize your body with fresh-squeezed green vegetables and green superfood powders such as wheatgrass.
- Juice daily, at least 16 ounces of dark leafy green veggies.
- Mix your juices with superfoods such as superfood green powders, tocotrienols, royal jelly, flax oil, bee pollen, lecithin, blueberries, and goji berries.

- Find your local farmer's market and always buy your produce from the local farmers.
- Take care of your outer hygiene. Get a shower filter to filter out chlorine when you shower. Always buy natural soaps and lotions from your local health food store. Spray yourself with lavender spray because it cleans your outer body and aura.

Chapter Five
The Divine Diet for
The Spiritual Body

"Renew yourselves and fast. For I tell you
truly, that Satan and his plagues may only
be cast out by fasting and by prayer."
— Jesus Christ
from *The Essene Gospel of Peace*

FASTING: OPENING A DEEPER MORE INTIMATE CONNECTION TO YOUR SPIRITUAL BODY

This chapter is one of the most important, and it alone is worth the entire investment of this book. If you have applied everything I taught you in the earlier chapters, you will soak in the benefits of this chapter a lot more quickly and easily. You can meditate all you want, or attend seminars by top speakers and gurus, but this one diet change of adding fasting to your lifestyle will alone make all the difference in your life because it makes the body vibrate at such a high frequency. The absence of food (which is the lowest vibration your body takes in aside from negative emotions) allows this higher frequency to happen. I'm not joking here—you can reach a deep connection with your authentic self so much faster than going to meditation retreats for years on end or just making the effort on your own to think positive thoughts, take silent vows, practice yoga, etc. I'm not saying these spiritual practices don't have tremendous value because they do, and I still practice them. But few things I know of are more powerful than fasting.

Please note the quote from Jesus Christ that begins this chapter: "Renew yourselves and fast. For I tell you truly, that Satan and his plagues may only be cast out by fasting and by prayer." That's a very profound statement. Do you really get the profundity of what it's saying and how important fasting is? Dark forces have a grip on you; they can dwell in your body without your conscious realization, and they won't be cleansed out of you unless you fast and pray. Jesus didn't say, "Meditate and you will be free from Satan's grip." He didn't say, "Become a vegetarian." He didn't say, "Attend some famous guru's seminar." He didn't say, "Do yoga." He didn't say, "Become rich." He said, "Start fasting!" Is it any wonder that Jesus was tempted by the Devil to turn a stone into bread so he could eat after he was guided by Spirit to fast for forty days in the desert. I myself have battled a few dark entities on the spiritual level that were trying to enter my space, and I got rid of them by aligning myself fully with my Divine Diet and fasting every Sunday as well as reducing my food intake so my body could have a higher fasting rate on a weekly basis.

Right now, you are being limited in your potential to think better, to have the most beautiful ideas, talents, and creative abilities come to you because lower vibrations from junk food and not following these Divine Diet principles right now are consuming the light from you. If that doesn't disturb and upset you, I don't know what will; you have to get your warrior hat on and claim your territory. Don't let any dark energy have any sort of control over you. One of your biggest weapons is fasting regularly on Sundays or once a week and juicing and blending your food. If you want to grow in consciousness, then fast. If you want to connect more with your authentic self, then fast. If you want to be happier, then fast. Fasting is the fastest way to God. Please make sure you read Chapter Three so you're well-equipped for your fast and nourishing your body so you detoxify correctly, but I want you to understand the profundity of what was stated before you continue; otherwise, you're less likely to adopt fasting as part of your lifestyle.

If the inner world of Spirit is what reflects in the outer world, then it's important that things are in order in this area of your life. Most people are so disconnected with the spirit world and with their souls or highest selves that it's no wonder their lives are not where they want them to be. To be aligned with your spiritual body is more important than anything you will ever do. All of your power resides with your highest self. The more aligned you are with who you really are, the more easily prosperity will come to you, and the more aligned and happy you will be.

Look at how everyone wants to come see some of the most magnetic people in the world; people want to pay to attend their shows and seminars, read their books, and purchase their CDs and clothing. They want to be around their light. Being in the presence of people who are closely aligned to their highest selves, whether they know it or not, is beneficial to your evolution. Fasting will turn on that inner light at a higher level for you, and it will make you more magnetic. I will add here that I recall an interview with Michael Jackson where he said he would eat once a day and dance and fast once a week. When I saw that video, I thought he was somehow consciously or unconsciously connected to how powerful fasting is, and I do believe it strengthened his connection to his talent as an artist.

So this chapter is dedicated to fasting—the most powerful part of the Divine Diet to nourish your spiritual body and reawaken your authentic self. It's no coincidence that I have addressed this tool at the end of this book. You must first address all of the topics in the earlier chapters before you really tackle this one.

Many ways exist to align yourself with the spiritual world, but this is by far one of the most powerful and comprehensive for most people. This lifestyle is for everyone, but not everyone is for it. Fasting may not be something you want to do at this time in your life; it might be something you will resist or reject. And that's okay. You are not being forced to do anything; I am simply providing here what I believe to be one of the most powerful techniques to unlock euphoria and ultimate happiness in you. I believe that because fasting has helped me immensely in my transformation.

Before I get into proper fasting, let me tell you that fasting has miraculously transformed my life. It has changed my appearance and added so much light to my body in so little time. It is better than any workshop I have attended, better than any soul-activation meditation CD I've listened to, and better than any laying on of hands or reiki practice I've experienced. You can literally see mountains of difference after a month of fasting, and I have been fasting consistently on water, teas, or coconut water on a weekly basis. I've had bitterness issues, anger, sadness, and depression taken out of me, all of which I struggled to get out on my own for years without success. I've lost so much weight the correct way because of it where I previously failed while trying to diet and exercise on my own. My skin cleared up, and I look years younger than you would ever imagine possible just from doing water fasts or juice fasts alone. Finally, I was reawakened to my true path and journey. So, if you're clueless about your purpose here on earth, my fasting and prayer method can only guide you to your path, and God will let you know when you reach it.

If you're a singer, your singing will improve; your voice will sound so much sweeter. If you have trouble concentrating while you read, your focus will be a lot better. You will be able to hear, taste, feel, see, and smell a lot better as the ties to dark unclean energies leave you. Fasting is the best tool for ultimate transformation.

The more you fast, the more you will feel what it is to be really alive. The more you fast, the more you will feel what it is to be really present in your life and incarnated in your human body.

Fasting will help you understand the natural order in which God wants you to live your life, if you just open your mind to it. You will be able to sense more clearly what is right and what is wrong for you. All your talents that you were meant to have and share with humanity will be awakened and freely available to everyone.

I can tell you about all the miracles that have happened to me since I started this lifestyle. I remember all of the struggles I went through just to get good grades in school; my energy was scattered and I had the hardest time focusing; I didn't realize that everyone takes on family karma that gets passed down, and I carried a large karmic burden on my mother's side that was weighing me down.

During a healing ceremony, as I fasted, I was letting go of all this burden, and I cried intensely, remembering how much I loved my mother and wanted to carry the karmic burden for her, but it was killing me, and I was literally not letting her pick up her own karma, which is everyone's own responsibility. I was finally taking responsibility for only my own karma and learning how not to be a doormat, how to love the right way, how selfish it is to take on other people's karma, and how unselfish it is to stand up for yourself and say, "No, I'm not doing this anymore for anyone; go pick up your own trash." As soon as I started to do that, it felt like a ton of darkness just left my body during the fast. It was unbelievable. I remember when I later walked into a restaurant to pick up some food, my friend who worked there was dumbfounded by how amazing I looked. From that moment, from that miraculous experience, I had people just naturally coming up to me because of the light I was starting to shine. People were telling me that I looked one thousand times more beautiful than I did before. My friend at the restaurant told me it was as if something dark had been lifted off my body.

I was so grateful for all the responses I was getting. I personally didn't notice it as much since I was with myself all of the time, but one thing I know for sure is that I definitely felt the difference. The amount of presence in my body was astounding. I felt so euphoric and alive. And my level of gratitude for this lifestyle just keeps increasing. I can never grow tired of fasting and will do so at least once a week until the day I die.

One of the neatest things I have discovered with fasting is that it can be a very fast vehicle for integration of the soul into your body. You may also call it enlightenment, ascension, etc., but it's all the same. It can integrate you into your soul more completely. I could not imagine doing this type of work and integrating into my body on my own. Most of us are so lost and clueless most of the time; we might even think we are right, but the more you fast, the more you realize that things you didn't even know were possible are because you are fasting. You can walk through life as one person, but several years down the road, if you start fasting, you can suddenly become a completely different person.

I also want to say that fasting, by itself, is not enough for the complete integration of your authentic self in your body; it is one good tool you must integrate into your lifestyle if you want faster results, but it all starts with the mind, so please read Chapter One and also include prayers in your fast; pray for guidance and for the strength to stay with it. Mindset is everything. It takes a certain kind of person to keep fasting as part of an ongoing lifestyle. You need to be able to stand up and say, "I'm bold enough to go through the discomfort. I'm going to do it because I'm fighting for me." Not everyone is in that type of state. I have had people come up to me who were so shy and scared about doing a fast when the opportunity presented itself to them; they ended up not doing it because they were scared of the unknown, so they missed out on profound miracles wanting to be born through them. So I tell you this: Work on your mindset daily; work on some affirmations to give you some courage. It is important to be courageous and go for what you want in your life. If you want to discover how astounding it is to reconnect back to your authentic self, then you're going to have to roll up your sleeves, muster up all of your joy, enthusiasm, and excitement to grow, and get ready to channel that energy into some good old-fashioned hard work. And massive action doesn't just come; it comes from passion, urges, desire, and usually extreme hunger for something better. And that usually comes from extreme poverty disasters in people's lives. I'm not going to go through much more here of the psychology of mindset, but if you skipped the chapter on mindset and you feel this is an area of your life that you need to work on, please go read Chapter One so you can more easily accomplish your goal.

One of the most profound things I have been privileged finally to be ready for is my mission on this planet as a performance artist. If it were not for the fasting, I would have been so lost in terms of knowing why I was here on the planet; my soul was so far removed from my body that only a small portion of me was really built into my body; therefore, I didn't even remember what my purpose was here in this life. So many of us are in this situation. You are on this planet for a specific purpose; everyone has a specific purpose, and the more you raise your energy with this lifestyle, the more you are able to awaken your talent and let God remind you of what you came here to do.

Don't be afraid. When you are searching for your purpose, and even when you find it, there are usually tests—hard tests; you will have all kinds of people trying to block you and get in your way to prevent your purpose from happening. Don't pay attention to it; don't let it anger you in the slightest. Anger is a trap that can get you stuck. (I have fallen into it many times.) Just take it as a compliment that people actually bother to rain on your parade. It is a sure sign that you are going in the right direction in your life and that the beauty of being in union with God is in the near future. So congratulations in advance.

I can tell you that practicing the spiritual lifestyle is a revolution, probably one of the most advanced, if not the most advanced, systems to correcting and nourishing your spiritual body to its maximum. If I may say so boldly, it is better than any cigarette, alcohol, painkiller, junk food, or drug you will ever try. Your authentic self becomes present at a level you never dreamed of when you fast. If you decide to fast, but you don't even believe that full transformation can happen the first time, then when it does, you'll think fasting is the greatest thing ever.

When I started, I hated fasting; I felt only the suffering and was tormented and tired. Little did I know that two years later, after I adopted fasting at least once a week, I was going to love every single aspect of it. Sure, some really awful cleansing experiences will get on your nerves, or there might be some temptations to stop earlier than you planned, but those tests and lessons are meant to happen to make you stronger. Just forgive, be strong, and move on.

If fasting does become part of your life, you might decide to travel to do group fasts. Traveling and attending fasting retreats or visiting people and communities can be one of the most profound healing journeys you will ever encounter. I am in the process of building my own fasting retreats, so please check for those being offered through my academy. So many slightly different perspectives exist on the fasting lifestyle, and there are so many different teachers within the community, but it's all wonderful. Do your research online for different juice fasting retreats if you want to try one. I want you to listen deeply within your heart for what's good and not good for you. Some retreats might value the idea of fasting and don't consider alkalizing and nourishing the body properly, which is why I included Chapter Four on the physical body in this book for you to read before you start a fast.

One of my favorite things to do right before a fast is to clean up my house and burn sage or palo santo. Your house truly is a reflection of what is going on inside you; if you clean the outside, it's like giving the fast the opportunity and space to clean you more quickly on the inside. Your very essence and your invisible angel helpers like clean spaces and can enter your residence a lot more easily to assist you when it's clean. Cleaning goes to an even deeper level to include your eating. Eat lightly—fruit, salad, or fresh-squeezed juice— so your body is not clogged down with anything too heavy before you undertake a fast.

Make sure you take a shower daily, even twice a day, and pray to your creator to clean you of anything that needs to be removed from your body. Believe me; prayer will make all the difference. I wish I knew that when I started fasting, but I had to learn the hard way. It might be scary or strange for people to hear, but it is worth mentioning that there might be dark energies or entities attached to you already that do not belong there, so you want them ejected and sealed from reentering your body. What I want you to do is ask the Universe, your creator, God, or your guardian angel to help you seal your body and protect it from any negative energies that might want to attach to you from other people or that are already attached.

If you do feel dark energies that need to be released, then once you take a shower, preferably with natural soap from a health food store, take a rosemary and basil remedy with cold water and pour it on you after your shower. Not over your head because you don't want to seal off your crown chakra—you want that to stay open. Pour the cold water with the basil rosemary essence over your chest and back. I'll give you the basil and rosemary preparation methods below, but first let me explain that the cold water you pour on yourself repels all entities from you that do not belong in your body because they don't like cold water.

Rosemary and basil water wards off dark energy and seals and protects you. I swear I didn't believe in this at all until I started doing it twice daily. Then I could not believe how much cleaner I felt. I no longer felt so many dark energies because they had no power to come since the rosemary-basil water removed them and sealed my energy. Then after a while, if you want, you can just take a shower and use cold water at the end. Then spray the rosemary-basil water on you after you towel off. You're supposed to air dry after you pour the mixture on you, but it's a little faster if you just spray it on after a five-second cold shower before you towel off.

Okay. So here is how you make the rosemary and basil. First, buy the rosemary and basil, preferably organic, at your local health food store. Then tear the leaves into little pieces and place them in a filled pitcher of water. Put the pitcher in the fridge overnight. In the morning, remove and discard the leaves. Now you can use the cold water after your bath (which can be a warm bath).

Those are the basic steps for outer cleanliness so your fasting can work more efficiently. Also be sure to do a short peaceful meditation during your fast, and avoid trashy television or media. Being peaceful will help center you so you are able to receive more efficiently from the fast.

Fasting tip: Whenever you fast, make ice cubes out of pure water. Buy fun-shaped ice trays, stick them in your freezer, and crunch on them throughout the day. That way, your mouth has something to chew on and your jaw muscles can chew if they miss chewing after long periods of not chewing. Juice can also be used to make ice cubes if you're doing a juice diet or juice fast.

Fasting tip: Whenever you fast, limit the amount of time you spend watching junk television or being around negative people because they will contaminate your fast. Surround yourself as much as you can with positive friends and nature. Make sure you spend time reading empowering books or books to transform your life in positive ways.

THE ESSENE GOSPEL OF PEACE ON FASTING

In this section, I would like to break down for you the passages of fasting from *The Essene Gospel of Peace*. I will explain how these passages helped me and how they can help you to understand fasting in a new light that may make you want to take action in this new lifestyle you're about to take on.

Let me start by saying that the answers to all your problems lie in the reconnection to your highest self. If you follow what I have to offer, based on the Essene teachings, you will be rewarded with an amplification of your true self. If you give in to eating habits that are not in harmony with the teachings here, you will have a stronger disconnection to your authentic self and dark energy can set in. This dark energy is very real and can be seen in gossiping, judging, fighting, and killing other people. Do you think people who behave that way are really showing their true personalities, or is it some darker force or ego that has silently taken them over? Be cautious and present; you don't want disconnected energy from your authentic self controlling your body or speaking through you because you have not taken action to cleanse all areas of your body, including through fasting. Part of having a body and incarnating into it is to do the work of cleansing. You have this body to accelerate your spiritual evolution, so don't waste it.

Below, I want to talk about the following three types of water fasts:

- Alkaline Juice Fasts
- Semi-Water/Semi-Juice Fasts
- Long Water Fasts

Alkaline Juice Fasts

If you have never fasted before, start with an alkaline veggie juice fast and some juiced fruits. Basically, it's a fast of freshly juiced fruits and vegetables mixed with superfoods such as raw wheatgrass, which is highly alkaline. Ideally, about two to six tablespoons of wheatgrass powder a day will be alkaline enough for your body to start detoxifying and dropping acid waste that otherwise you would not be able to drop without a high alkaline juice fast.

Blend in the alkaline superfood into your daily smoothies and drink anywhere from two to six 16 ounces of juice daily. I recommend mixing about two tablespoons of raw wheatgrass powder every day. Another alternative would be a blend of green superfood powder. Ideally, buy a raw organic version of it.

If you are really overweight, start with six glasses of this juice a day. If you don't have much weight to lose, drink one for lunch and one for dinner. Thirty days of following this juice fast is unbelievable for your body. You might consider adding some flax oil if you like, or for a more rigorous fast, go without the oil.

I recommend starting with this type of fast instead of a water fast because you will get so much more out of it, and it's an ideal step for beginners and even more advanced fasters. If you have never fasted before and are eager to try a water fast, it might be too dangerous; you might have too much accumulated in your system, and if it feels too uncomfortable for you, chances are you might not want to do it again.

An alkaline juice fast is much more gentle. And you will really be able to lose excess weight and balance your pH levels. Your blood's normal pH level should be about 7.4, but most people's levels are so acidic that they are leaching their bones from alkaline calcium deposits. An alkaline juice fast not only supports and strengthens your bones, but it gives your organs a break so they can recover and heal themselves to optimal levels; that way, when you do eat again, your digestion is much faster, quicker, and more efficient. You may also notice that you feel tired during the fast because so much energy is going to detoxification, but not to worry—you will notice an increase in energy after the fast.

Here are some alkaline vegetables you might want to juice during your fast:

- Kale, dinosaur kale, regular kale, green kale, purple kale
- Collard greens
- Parsley, Italian and regular
- Cilantro (metal detoxifier)
- Green onions
- Green and rainbow chard
- Spinach
- Dandelion greens (liver cleanser)
- Baby broccoli
- Arugula
- Watercress
- Beat Leaves
- Dill
- Chinese broccoli

The following vegetables are not as alkaline as the ones above, but they are still a good addition to your alkaline juices:

- Lettuce
- Brussels sprouts
- Purple and green cabbage
- Mustard greens
- Celery
- Broccoli
- Bok choy
- Baby bok choy
- Turnip leaves
- Carrot leaves
- Mint leaves
- Cauliflower (white, purple, or yellow)

- Leeks
- Chinese cabbage
- Endive

Your alkaline juice fast doesn't have to be fruit-free. Here are some fruit suggestions:

- Cucumber (great diuretic and perfect for fasting)
- Tomatoes (cherry, wild, or regular)
- Apple (green, red, or yellow; breaks down gallstones)
- Oranges
- Tangerines
- Lemon
- Grapefruit
- Lime
- Cantaloupe
- Watermelon
- Honeydew melon
- Pineapple
- Pears
- Seed-bearing grapes
- Strawberries
- Blackberries
- Kiwi
- Papaya

Semi-Juice/Semi-Water Fasts

This is the second step for you. It will go even deeper into your fasting and detoxification process. I would recommend to keep adding alkaline foods daily into your diet to prepare for this fast and for the longer water fasts you will be doing.

For this one, you drink alkaline juices for three days as instructed in the section above on alkaline juice fasts. Then for four days, you drink coconut water or lemonade with honey or raw cane juice.

For three days, you are alkalizing your body and building it up with minerals with alkaline superfoods. Then for the next four days, you are diving deeper into a longer fast so the body can detoxify at a deeper level. Then at the end of those four days, you start the alkaline juices again to make sure you are alkalizing again and not dropping to low acid levels. Doing this entire process for thirty to sixty days is a great experience, and you will experience profound changes. I don't recommend water for the next four days; instead, I recommend coconut water or lemonade with raw honey because it will sustain you so you can go to work or do whatever it is you need to concentrate on. I believe also that coconut has the ability to detoxify at a deeper level than water and can penetrate deeper into your cells and remove toxins.

Long Water Fasts

For the long fast, the instructions in *The Essene Gospel of Peace* are to go fast on your own and not show your fast to anyone. I know finances may be a problem for some people. The ideal is to go to your vacation home, rent a cabin in the middle of nature, or fast in nature, as directed in the scriptures. Alternatively, you can just fast in your apartment or home and not go out anywhere. If you don't have the time and you need to work, pray to God to show you a way where you can find time for a week, two weeks, three weeks, or up to forty days. If you haven't fasted that long before, maybe a seven to twenty-one day fast would be a good first try. It really depends on your level of commitment to the process, your desire for change, or whether you have cancer or some disease that increased the level of urgency you're feeling to heal yourself.

The next instruction in the scriptures is that while you fast, it is important that you pray fervently for God to heal you. Now, it is very easy just to keep reading and skip what I just wrote, but fervent emotion is necessary during your fast because fasting is probably the hardest thing you will undertake in your life. You will probably have temptations to eat all sorts of things, things you haven't even thought of for years to eat. It's going to be hard.

Especially if you are a beginner, and this is a battle against unclean energy and darkness, you better get your fervent on! You can adopt an attitude of "This is going to be a fun, passionate fast," and it will be if you say so, even if it's challenging. You better think about everything in your life that is limiting you because you are not free from the grips of dark forces, so they will get you wound up. If you don't have a clue of what fervent looks like, I recommend you watch the fasting YouTube videos of Mr. Jentezen Franklin. This man is on fire, so take on his initiative. Write down some prayers if you'd like and read them daily with all the emotional intensity you have. Read *The Essene Gospel of Peace* while you're fasting; read this book while you're fasting; read books that inspire you, and make sure you pray for help from God's angels while you fast. And be mindful about what you read; don't focus on television, or magazines; they will contaminate your fast. Fasting is a time of meditation, silence, peace, prayer, affirmation, inspiring music, and cleansing showers.

In *The Essene Gospel of Peace* is a paragraph I thought would be worth mentioning here:

> If you will that the living God's word and his power may enter you, defile not your body and your spirit; for the body is the temple of the spirit, and the spirit is the temple of God. Purify, therefore, the temple, that

the Lord of the temple may dwell therein and occupy a place that is worthy of him.

I love this paragraph; I think it's the epitome of what I want to accomplish in this book. It reflects what the power of fasting can do for you. Remember, the scripture also mentions, "Renew yourselves and fast. For I tell you truly, that Satan and his plagues may only be cast out by fasting and by prayer...except you fast, you shall never be freed from the power of Satan and from all diseases that come from Satan." If you want a miracle in your life, fasting is it! For most of us, we do not yet remember the glory of our own souls because they cannot inhabit our bodies completely with all the uncleanness. The highest and most complete vibration of your soul is so pure it can only come into the body when the body's vibration is a match to it. Again, cleanliness is next to godliness, so you need to clean your body through fasting if you want a transformation in consciousness.

Have you ever had a disorganized room in your home, or worse, been in a home that's so messy there is dirt everywhere and food laying around growing mold? Have you ever started to feel depressed or had low energy because you were inhabiting a place like this? What happened when you cleaned up the mess? Did you feel a lot better, a lot happier, and more productive with a sense of ease and peace of mind? Did you feel as if you were able to function a lot better within that environment? Cleanliness is so important because it invites clarity, the angels, and God's presence into your home if it's clean. Cleanliness is truly next to godliness. The same goes with your body; when you're clean within, you're inviting the entirety of your soul to integrate itself within your body, and you are able to function better and give insights and actions that you weren't able to when your body was unclean.

As a last note on water fasting, I recommend that you do it once a week for the rest of your life, than for forty days once in your life. If you are eating twice a day and fasting once on weekends, you are already starting to increase your detoxification levels by increasing your rate of fasting. Especially for beginners, I wouldn't focus on extreme fasts like these. Try at least five to ten years of fasting on Sundays, eating twice a day, and not having breakfast, and you're on your way to training to higher levels in the future. Personally, I am on a liquid-blended soup diet permanently, I eat once a day, and I fast on Sundays.

The Angel of Air

For the long water fast, it's important, as *The Essene Gospel of Peace* describes, that you seek the angel of air as the scripture calls it. Ideally, you are fasting in or near nature in a place with clean air where you can take your clothes off and let the air surround your body entirely. Breathe deep breaths every day of your fast. I recommend that you do this during your daily meditations and you focus completely on deep breathing exercises. Air will remove all uncleanness that inhabits your body and cause it to rise out of you.

The Angels of Water

Take a shower! Daily, even twice a day! Your body will be ridding itself of toxins, which cleanses your auric field, and you will automatically feel a recharge in energy every time you take a shower. But, more importantly, commit to drinking plenty of fresh water during your fasts to flush away the majority of your toxins and the uncleanness within your body.

The third purpose for using water is cleaning your bowels. The scripture recommends using a long gourd, the size of a man, filled with water to put up your bowels; however, I think it's best to consider getting colonics since we're in modern times now, and I think a colonic by someone who is certified is far more capable of cleaning you out than what you can do on your own (although it's worth a shot after you learn how to do it during your alone fasts). Research colonics clinics within your area.

The colon is the ultimate gas drainage outlet. In conjunction with an improved diet, colon hydrotherapy is *the most powerful tool* anyone can utilize for detoxification.

Colon hydrotherapy is a miracle! As soon as the 100 percent raw food eater reaches that heavy, toxic state, a session of colon hydrotherapy can transport him into a state of *clean*, light, spiritual, vibrational *bliss*. Zits (pimples), rashes, hemorrhoids, psoriasis, and other skin blemishes created from this toxic state will disappear, the nose and bronchial pathways will clear of mucus, breathing becomes easier and deeper, body odor leaves, infections disappear, your brain functions better, and you are catapulted on the "Super-Sonic Jet Plane" pathway to health.

If a 100 percent raw food lifestyle and periodic colon cleansing are continued, you will rapidly seem to become younger; you will become more beautiful; your skin will become silky smooth, shine, and glow; you will heal the body from degenerative disease; all foul odor will leave your body, and you will experience heightened spiritual receptivity.

Ironically, someone who is truly 100 percent raw should do colon hydrotherapy more often than someone who is not, due to how the body cleanses with this kind of lifestyle. If you are truly 100 percent raw, you can "get away" with less and yet...for optimal health, I recommend doing a minimum of four colonic irrigations a year, for the rest of your life. In my opinion, if you periodically practice colon hydrotherapy, you could potentially add more than a decade to your lifespan.

Ninety-five percent of the people I talk to who have drastically improved their diets claim that they have more gas now than before the improvement. That is because the toxins are leaving your body. How many times have you tried to go 100 percent raw? Why do so many raw food eaters have cooked food "slip-ups"? Have you ever seen a heroin addict sent to the hospital, forced to abstain from the drug? It's not a pretty sight. Although not so extreme, abstaining from cooked/processed foods will cause a similar withdrawal, resulting in cravings and desires to get your fix. Colon hydrotherapy can be a highly beneficial tool for relieving the system of those toxins being released during withdrawal, which lessens the impact of cravings. It helps us to clean out our systems more quickly of all the accumulated waste so we can move onwards into more vibrant health. Though our detoxification will never truly be over, we can help ourselves to get through the harshest part of the initial detox from cooked/processed foods with the tool of colon hydrotherapy.

The Angel of Sunlight

Again, like being nude and partaking in the healing energy of air, so you will want to be nude with the sunlight. Unless you're in the woods alone or in a rented cabin away from every one, it'll be hard to do this since you have to consider your neighbors. If you're fasting at home, the best you can do is wear a bikini or bathing suit at your pool, or on your roof; just take as much clothing off as you can so the sunlight can heal you. Do this daily.

Remember to take air, water, and sunlight within and without during your fast. They are more powerful and miraculous than you might realize.

One last tip on fasting: a seven-day coconut water fast is ideal to start with. The more you fast, the longer you will be able to sustain it. Make your body use to it and start with seven days. A month may pass by, and then you might choose to do a longer fast; follow your intuition as much as you can. The scriptures talk about seven days of fasting equaling seven years of sin being resolved. That's not a bad deal considering it just takes seven days to resolve so much time spent on incorrect ways of living.

THE POWER OF ENTHEOGENS

After you read this section on entheogens, I want you to read Daniel Pinchbeck's *Breaking Open the Head* to understand more about the different experiences people have on different entheogenic medicines. He has experimented with more of them than I have, so he can give you a greater understanding of where to direct your spiritual path. His book is a must read. That said, this section on entheogens is pretty powerful so don't skip it! Please enjoy!

So what are entheogens? Here is the description:

A term derived from the Greek "entheos," directly translated to mean having "God (theos) within" and also translated as "inspired" and "genesthe" meaning "to generate." "Entheos" was usually used to describe poets, musicians and many other artists who were believed to receive their divine talents and gifts of art from the divine. The word entheogen then gives itself as signifying "that which generates God/the divine expression in a person." The term was first coined in the late 1970's as a replacement for "psychedelic" and "hallucinogen" which both carry with them certain negative connotations. Entheogen is a concept to be used in firm reverence of agents that act as divine sacraments and facilitate transcendent experiences for a higher connection with the universal creator of all that is.

I do not recommend any particular type of entheogen because I believe these plant teachers choose you, so I don't want to stand in the way of that. I will say, however, that these plant medicines do play a great role in reawakening your authentic self and the overall consciousness of humanity so they are worth mentioning. Very few of us are born with our full talent and potential, so a little help from these plants to reawaken our full potential doesn't hurt. These plant teachers can condense and quicken your spiritual evolution a lot faster in addition to all of the teachings I have mentioned here. You are going to have to do your own research and figure out which ones you are called to or whether you are called to do this type of spiritual healing. This path is not for everyone, but what I can say from my experience is that it can result in a profound spiritual awakening and the integration of your soul within your being. Please note, entheogens are not recreational drugs; they must be taken very seriously just like fasting must be taken seriously; entheogens are used in ceremonial settings with a shaman. Nor are they addictive drugs; they are medicine and can lead to a profound, difficult, yet transformative healing experience. Currently, legality issues exist in certain countries with entheogens. Some countries legally allow their use in healing ceremonies, so please check for current legality issues in your country. Many people fly to Peru to do ayahuasca, where it is legal to practice it among the natives. I recommend going to a country in Africa or to Peru where the government has legalized these types of spiritual ceremonies; it's worth the trip.

Although there are other entheogens that you can research more about if you choose, here are the three most popular entheogens, their history, background, and a bit of what people say about them:

- Peyote
- Ayahuasca
- Iboga

Peyote

I have never done peyote personally, but I have heard great things about it. It has a grounding effect and is connected to the earth; it's a very slow medicine to activate within the body compared to ayahuasca. Peyote is a hallucinogenic entheogen prepared from a small, soft, blue-green, spineless cactus native to Mexico and the southwest United States that contains mescaline. It is used in the Native American Church, a religious denomination that practices Peyotism or the Peyote Religion, which originated in the U.S. state of Oklahoma and is the most widespread indigenous religion among Native Americans in the United States. Peyotism involves the use of the entheogen peyote. From earliest recorded time, peyote has been used by natives in northern Mexico and the southwestern United States as a part of their religious rites.

The Native Americans in the Native American Church describe the peyote medicine as a grandfather energy, very masculine, that has sun energy attached to it. Its effects have been described as very dreamlike and drifting; you can

234

reach almost a state of delirium during the first few hours of using it. That said, it is connected to the earth and has a very grounding effect.

Peyote buttons are consumed in both dried and fresh form. People typically chew them, although they may be stewed in teas or cooked with other foods to mask the bitter taste. As with many natural hallucinogens, peyote usually causes a feeling of nausea and discomfort before its effects set in. The effects include visions, disorientation, and various physiological effects, which are caused by the body as it tries to express the alkaloids in the peyote.

Among Native Americans, peyote or divine cactus is used to bring on visions said to connect the user with his or her ancestors and the spirit world. As the visions take place, the user can search for lessons, meaning, guidance, and divine messages to share when he or she emerges from the hallucinogenic state induced by peyote. This religious use is protected under United States code, which protects the freedom of religion.

However, recreational use of peyote is not protected under United States code, and it can be penalized with jail time and hefty fines and can be dangerous without correct supervision. As with any hallucinogen, peyote has its risks in use. The medicine can contain some impurities, depending on how it was handled and where it was grown, and the strength of the alkaloids can vary depending on the location. In various cases, this entheogen can cause severe reactions, which can be very dangerous in users who are unsupervised or unfamiliar with its sacred uses. The ceremonies using it can go up to fourteen hours in a teepee setting, so you must develop discipline to be able to stay firm during your journey and healing experience.

Ayahuasca

Ayahuasca's lineage is closely tied to Peru and the natives living in the forest of that country. It is a sacrament in the form of a drink that activates the vision of the third internal eye, which is used by the body to activate the visions of the dream state. It is made from the stem of the ayahuasca vine and mixed with other plants such as chacruna, sameruca, ocoyage, chalopanga, chagraponga, and huambisa. Ayahuasca is derived from a tropical vine native to the South American and Latin American forests, including along the Amazon and in Peru, Ecuador, and Costa Rica.

The term *ayahuasca* comes from the Quechua language. The word *huasca* is the usual Quechua term for any species of vine. The word *aya* refers to something like a separable soul, and thus, also, to the spirit of a dead person—hence the two common English translations, "vine of the soul" and "vine of the dead." The word *ayahuasca* can apparently have either connotation, depending largely on cultural context. Quechua speakers in Canelos or on the Napo, as well as mestizo shamans, translate the word into Spanish as *soga del alma*, "vine of the soul"; people on the Bajo Urubamba often translate the word as *soga de muerto*, "vine of the dead."

The Quechua term ayahuasca is used primarily in present-day Peru and Ecuador; in Colombia, the common term for both the vine and the drink is the Tukano term *yagé* or *yajé*. Many additional words for ayahuasca exist in other indigenous languages, but this is the most popular name.

The Ayahuasca Experience

Ayahuasca is often associated with cats and has a snake-like, sensual, feminine energy. It's very connected with the astral and the heavens. Using it for purging is very common; it helps to get rid of dark energies and entities within you that do not serve you.

Using ayahuasca can be a very visual experience, through the third eye, and also very intense. For beginners, it can be a scary experience that they resist, yet very rewarding if you let it be. The medicine can dance in you, it can sing through you, and it can teach you things you would have never seen without it. It has the power to help transform your being into your authentic self. I believe it is nearly impossible for any outside teacher to transform you at that level.

Personally, I have been blessed to have negative entities removed from my body that I didn't know were lodged in it through the power of this medicine. People would be astounded by the number of negative energies and entities they carry. Once they drink the medicine, they can see where the blocks are and where the dark energies are leaving them while they purge.

Ayahuasca showed me my authentic self during the first few ceremonies I participated in. In one of the ceremonies, I saw a huge soul floating above me. It was very familiar; it had my essence, and it was waiting for me to clean myself out in order to enter my body. The medicine told me I was so disconnected from myself that I was unable to be fully expressed in my present physical body. After I looked up and saw my soul floating, I looked down and saw all the karma, all the dark energy, that I had accumulated and that needed to be transformed. I was so humbled to be able to be shown this and to have instruction from the medicine on how to purify and expand myself so I would be able to expand more to my highest self. Years later, the same medicine planted the foundation, the very essence of my authentic self. It can do this and more for you if you let it.

Here are some interesting facts about ayahuasca:
The ceremonial use of ayahuasca has a very intertwined connection between the religion and spirituality of almost all the indigenous peoples of the Upper Amazon but usually connected to shamanism. It's very likely that the shamanic practices of most of the Upper Amazon—Brazil, Venezuela, Colombia, Ecuador, Peru, and Bolivia—form a single religious and or spiritual cultural area. Ayahuasca use is also found as far west as the Pacific coastal areas of Panama, Colombia, and Ecuador, and southward into the Peruvian and Bolivian Amazon and is no spreading worldwide. It has also been originally used by the Indians of Colombia, aw well as the Quichua, Waoroni, Shuar, and other peoples of Ecuador and in Amazonian Brazil. As many as seventy-two indigenous groups in central and south america have been reported to have used ayahuasca.

Iboga

Iboga is used in what is probably the most intense and longest entheogen ceremonial experience, which goes on for about ten days. Use of smaller doses allows the experience to be shortened. I personally have not experienced this entheogen, and I only recommend it as a medicine for people who have severe drug addictions to cocaine, heroin, or other addictive drugs, and whose lives may depend on its use. This medicine is very intense, the most intense probably of all entheogens, but it will cure and transform anyone who has struggled with any type of addiction.

Although I don't agree at all that iboga is the best medicine, as some people involved in it might think who are involved with it, I still want to mention here some more information about this powerful Iboga entheogen.

Some people believe Iboga to be the godfather of all plants on the earth. There are many powerful entheogenic plants out there that people use for visions and for healings and every plant on the planet has great healing properties, but you just have to know them. Iboga is a very powerful plant, like the chief father spirit. You can have the spirits of the earth, the spirits of the sun, the spirit of the moon, the spirits of the fire, the spirits of nature, the spirits of the water, and the spirits of the wind. Every element has a chief spirit and Iboga is considered by many a chief godfather spirit.

One Iboga journey can equal 100 times the intensity of a peyote or ayahuasca journey. Many people with addictions have healed from one iboga journey alone compared to taking ayahuasca. Once you come to Iboga especially for your addictions, it usually takes one time to get rid of that addiction. Many people prefer to take iboga instead of ayahuasca specifically for addiction purposes. I have no need to do any other medicine plant. Some people believe that whatever you need, you can have it with iboga and that it can take you to the beginning of time. They also believe that it is the master of all plants and that it understands all other plants on earth. Many people also say that iboga is probably the most intense experience they have every had compared to other entheogentic journeys.

Let me tell you more about Iboga's abilities to cure addictions. The alkaloid of ibogene has the capability to mimic all types of neurotransmitters and, therefore, effortlessly goes into the nervous system where it does its magical work. Ibogene is said to have the capability to produce a bihemispheric reintegration and restore proper feedback between the left and the right hemispheres. Addiction itself is the vicious communication loop between the hemispheres due to "corrupted" neurotransmission front he addiction. The ibogene experience is a deeply therapeutic one in which you are confronted with everything that is not right in your life and it is important to surrender to that experience for a more gentle experience. Ibogene completely cures heroin, cocaine or any other drug addiction overnight without any symptoms of withdrawal. It even repels your system to want to be addicted to any drugs.

Iboga is a shrub that is born to Central West African lands. It originated in the South of Gabon where it was first known by the people called the Bobongo Pygmies. Tribes have been working with iboga for thousands of year. Iboga has been used for healing many illnesses, such as inability to be fertile for childbirth, cellular detoxification, emotional healing, anti-herpes treatment, fibromyalgia, lupus, mental illness and it is often used in spiritual ritualistic ceremonies.

Summary of Entheogens

Before we go further, I'm going to mention it one more time. I highly recommend Daniel Pinchbeck's book *Breaking Open the Head* so you can maximize your understanding of entheogens. For those that have the eyes to see and the ears to hear, you must purchase this book and read it in its entirety because there is something very special there for you and I hope that it calls out to you as you read it. All I can say here is that ayahuasca has helped me tremendously in reawakening and activating my soul body into my physical body. The most important thing to remember is to do your research and talk to people who have tried these three medicines to see which one calls to you and fits you the most or to see whether there are other similar entheogenic options to these you might want to try. The other option is not to use entheogens at all. Using them might not be the path for you, and using the other tools in this book might be enough for you to integrate your spiritual body and all aspects of your authentic self. Primarily, tune in to your intuition and what it's telling you. If it feels good, it's an indication to explore. If it doesn't, then it's not for you. With that said, I wish you the best path on your journey.

SOUL-ACTIVATION MEDITATIONS

Soul-activation meditations are meditations in which one vocally calls forth spiritual work from the spiritual plane of existence to accomplish with the help of angels, archangels, spiritual ascended masters, enlightened beings, the Holy Spirit, God, and the entire spiritual hierarchy of light. I hope you are already familiar with the concepts of the spiritual plane and that while we are existing in this world, we actually come from the spiritual world. If you don't believe that, use these soul-activation meditations anyway since you don't have to believe in or understand the spiritual plane to heal and expand your soul body into your physical body. This spiritual practice, done on a regular basis, will expand your consciousness, remove negative entities or energies from you, and transform and expand you a lot more rapidly and faster than if you did not do these at all.

At one point, I performed these meditations a lot. Then I stopped for a while; then all of a sudden, I heard my highest self speak to me during a ceremony and tell me how powerful these soul-activation meditations are. Therefore, I have created a super-mega, over-the-top, soul-activation meditation series that will transform you completely and expand your soul body so much. It is one of the most powerful meditation series on this planet today! It is available and sold as a package at my website www. ReawakenYourAuthenticSelfAcademy.com and also practiced through the first and second year of my academy program. I cannot recommend this enough because it has dozens of soul activations within one meditation session.

Soul-activation meditations are so powerful because they allow you to call in the help of so many light beings on the spiritual plane to work on you. You literally can call in so many soul activations in one sitting that by the end of the sitting, you will have activated so much light within your being. Silent meditations are very powerful, but when you use them in conjunction with asking for light and soul activation, it becomes a powerhouse for building your soul body in your physical body like nothing else. Ask and you shall receive applies very well in this case, and all this is for the asking. You just have to be willing to pick up the soul-activation meditation tapes.

Some people might not feel very much happening during a soul-activation meditation. Others will feel very subtle energies working and moving through them. I have felt my pituitary gland and my thyroid gland pulsate a few times, but generally on the subtle side. Please don't be discouraged if you feel like nothing is going on; the work is still being done, so do your part by being present with the meditations and do them on a consistent basis. You will not regret it.

PUTTING IT INTO PRACTICE

- For beginners, start with an alkaline juice fast and work your way up to coconut water fasts. Start with a smaller number of days and work your way up to increase the number of days to forty days. Also remember to do live juices, soups, and smoothies daily, even if you're not fasting.

- Explore peyote, ayahuasca, and iboga ceremonies as forms of healing to create a deeper connection with your authentic self. Reread what's written in this book about them and extend your research by reading up on them online and buying books like *Breaking Open the Head*, or talk to people who have had the experience.

  Note: Always follow your intuition; you may or may not be called to do these forms of ceremonial healing. It is important only to practice with a qualified shaman and in a ceremonial setting. These are not recreational drugs; they are sacred plant medicine and must be treated with respect.

- Do at least one spiritual soul-activation meditation a week.

Chapter Six
Overview and The Story of Reawakening

"Your Authentic Divine Highest Self is within
you and waiting to be reawakened."
— Divina

In the entire journey of this book, we have learned that there are primarily four Divine Diets: mental, emotional, physical, and spiritual. They all should be worked on and addressed in that order because thoughts affect emotions, emotions move the body, and a clean body reawakens the spirit.

For the mental diet, we learned:

- The power of creating habits
- The power of purpose
- The power of affirming and visualizing
- The power of meditation
- The power of associating with positive people

For the emotional diet, we learned to:

- Understand that you are only positive emotion
- Set the rules and beliefs in your mind so you can be happy
- Remember happiness is in constant personal growth
- Add emotional intensity to your daily affirmations, prayer, spoken word, and daily action
- Use focused visualization to create positive emotions and the powerful emotion of certainty
- Embrace the power of gratitude, enthusiasm, love, and passion
- Set the intention to enjoy every day
- Use food and physical movement to create positive emotion

For the physical diet, we learned several techniques on diet and cleaning the body:

- We explored the mind-body connection, how the power of a great mental psychology influences action toward a healthy body, and how to use affirmations and visualization to create massive energy, health, and wellbeing.

- We learned about the power of yoga, rebounding, dancing, and deep breathing to activate our authentic selves
- We learned the Food Principles:
- Do not cook, freeze, or rot your food
- Eat vegetarian: milk, honey, grains, greens, fruit
- Do a colon cleanse
- Eat once or twice a day, once at sunrise and once at sunset. Ideally once a day, but no more than twice
- Practice increasing your food intuition
- Fast once a week; Sunday is my recommendation
- Do not eat until fullness
- Do a colonic at least four times a year with the change of seasons, and when you do long fasts or colon cleanses
- Alkalize your body
- Understand the power of protein and authentic nutrition
- Use the power of juicing and liquids
- Take superfoods
- Eat locally-grown food
- Nourish your outer body

For the spiritual diet, we learned about:

- The power of three different fasts: 1) the alkaline juice diet, which was the much milder fast, 2) the semi-juice/semi-water fast, and 3) the completely water fast.
- How plant medicines can aid in the transformation and the calling in and awakening of our spiritual selves. Among those medicines are peyote, ayahuasca, and iboga, which are all different and powerful

healing modalities to accelerate spiritual growth and awakening.

- The power of spiritual soul-activation meditations.

Now that you have finished this book, the first thing you need to do is focus on the second chapter on mental diet because, as I mentioned several times, it all starts with the right mindset. After you understand your purpose for life, you must adopt a daily habitual routine of affirmation and visualization of what you want in life to move toward your goals, and you must adopt a daily meditation practice. Read that chapter entirely again, until you really get it, because it will help you take action and have the will to move on to taking the suggestions in the following chapters.

I now want to tell you a story that is part-fiction and part-reality; the dreams in it were based on my own dreams and encounters with my highest self, which touched me deeply in my journey of reawakening, so I would like to share them with you. It is the story of all of us who are on this journey to reawakening our authentic self, which will happen eventually, in this lifetime or another one to come. May this story teach and inspire you to reawaken your own. I hope you will read this short story many times to deepen the lessons or your reawakening and to inspire you to become more of who you really are.

The Story of Reawakening

Hello, my name I will leave anonymous. I am writing to you today as an enlightened being. I have rare and secret wisdom I will reveal to you today, but it will remain a secret to those with closed minds. If you are reading this, you are ready to open your mind. My years on this planet are done now and I feel called by Spirit to pass on to the spiritual world and leave this life here on the earth for you and new beings to come to. My life here has been grand; I have lived it full of wealth, divine guidance, prosperity, fulfillment, happiness, and peace. Everything I have asked for has come to pass, and everything I am has integrated fully. I am not anything more special than you, for when I was born here on this planet, I started with struggles and suffering just like many of you. I started on this planet by struggling with money and being homeless many times. I suffered from attracting the wrong people into my life and horrible addictions. I couldn't understand why I couldn't manifest the things I was hoping for. I am sure all of this sounds so familiar to you. This darkness that sets in is some of your karma, the karma of the thoughts and lifestyles of the world instilled in you grow up, and your genetic karma has been passed down by your mother and father from centuries of human existence. Your blood bears the sins of all your past ancestors and all their victories. Many hold a deeper burden here than others in their family bloodline, but nonetheless, it's yours to clear. If it is bad karma, you have the power to put a stop to it and not pass it down to future generations, whether its cancer, overeating, stealing, anger, rage, etc. Behind all of this, like a closed door, lies who you really are.

By the time you read these words, my spirit will have already left this planet. But before I leave, I write these words to you so my life experiences may serve you in your own journey to finding your success. Everything you experience in your outer world is the sum total of how little or how much you have merged with your authentic self. May my journal of my own life path as written below inspire you, teach you, and become part of you; it is my gift to all the people who follow to be born in this world; may you savor the lessons in the following words.

* * *

I was born in 1969. My parents were middle class. My father was a carpenter, my mother a seamstress. I was born in Pennsylvania, and I was brought up in a middle class neighborhood. My childhood was average. I wouldn't say that I was very happy, but I was not overly sad either. I had food on the table for lunch and dinner. We, as a family, sometimes were frugal as living on my father and mother's earnings was sometimes hard; nonetheless, we got along just fine. I shall not spend too long talking of my childhood, for I think it wise to begin where the real test of my life started and that is when I finally moved to New York and got my first job. I realized that after doing woodwork with my father, I wanted to enter the construction field, so I got my first construction job in my early twenties. The labor was long and intense, but I was content that I had made the first step in being independent from my family and able to stand on my own away from home.

After a few months of starting my job, everything was going well for me, and after a few years, I moved into a comfortable home. Things were going well until a disastrous event occurred. I was robbed of all my fortune, my home was wrecked, and I was blamed for being responsible for theft at work also. No one believed that I was innocent, so I was left with no job, and no one in town would hire me because of my reputation. I was beaten in the streets and forced to beg for food. I couldn't believe the immense suffering that I went through. For some reason, it all started to happen after I got bitter and took my life for granted. I started to change; the happiness in my heart started to change; I had no more hope for the future, and my sense of confidence started to leave me. For the first time in my life, I knew what it was like to be depressed and suicidal.

My life went like this for many years, and I stole and became drunk and mingled with the wrong crowds on the streets. One day, while I was begging on the street, a man stopped and looked at me. Then he reached down in his pocket and gave me all the coins he had. But then for some reason, he stopped, and he looked back at me again and gave me a dollar and said, "I hope you have faith that you can get out of this." I looked down at the dollar, turned it over, and for some reason, the words written on it, "In God we trust," stuck out like a diamond in a haystack. I took a deep breath and something started to breathe life in me again. I felt an essence inside of me saying that my life was not over and that I still had the opportunity to make something of myself, no matter how bad things had gotten for me. Somehow, I felt the presence of God still there, watching over me, and that man who gave me that dollar was a sign of renewed hope. That day, I learned the most important lesson, which I had forgotten. I had let myself be too soft with what had happened to me when I could have chosen to fight even stronger, and I was still breathing so I had not failed because I was not dead yet. I never spent the dollar that man gave me. It might have been a dollar, but to me, it could have been a million because I felt handed an energy of hope, a sign of the love God had for me, and a sense of knowing that I could trust that God would help me out of this.

When I made my decision to change, I had only a few coins in my pocket, some dirty garments on my back, old soiled shoes, and that lucky dollar, but a fire that was worth tons of weight in gold had struck in my heart, and it was now guiding me to get my life back together. After all, I had been a skilled workman before the entire disastrous incident had happened.

I noticed, however, that the people I had surrounded myself with in the streets thought it crazy of me to pursue a better life. They thought it impossible, and they began to poison me with thoughts of disillusionment. I realized right then and there that it was the people of misfortune I associated with and me thinking like them that had kept me far behind and caused my miserable life.

It was a mischievous person who had stolen my goods at home and pinned that stealing on me at work, and it was the people in the streets who had kept me behind with less hope than ever. And so I decided to take caution and proceed without them. I did not care anymore how alone I was. If I did not find anyone who wanted to help me or make me advance forward in life, then I was going to stand alone until I found people to surround myself with who would bring me up. I spent the next few weeks determined to find those who wanted me to get ahead in my life.

I finally got a job; it was one where I had less wages than ever, perhaps because of what I looked like at the time, but I couldn't get anything better. Things seemed to drag by like this for a long time. I was too poor to get a new home, but I found the old home I used to live in. Now it was an old shack with no roof, so I dwelled there as I went to work for my new job. Although my hope was set in place, I still dwelled with sadness on my broken life. One cold night, as I lit a fire to stay warm in my roofless home, I said a prayer and asked for a miracle in my life to happen. Then I realized I had never prayed before, but that I was going to mean it and have complete faith that my life was worth more than I had attained, and once I decided to change, I was not willing to give up.

Well, I do remember that night very clearly because it was the night everything changed for me. That was the night

I reawakened to my highest enlightened self. That was the night I had my prayers answered, but I didn't even realize my prayers were to bring me the most powerful thing I could ever possess, but which wasn't present in my personality—my highest self. I didn't realize what the highest self was at the time, or that everyone had one, and everyone's purpose in this life was to attain a higher expression of it in their physical bodies.

As the fire I built that night grew dim, and I cozied myself up with all the blankets I owned while I drifted to sleep, I had a profound dream, if that's what it was. It was more than a regular dream. There was a profound realness to the presence I felt, and my entire body started to vibrate; it felt like I was filled with a liquid light, which was almost unbearable, but its essence was so transformative and full of goodness. I was sleeping, yet I was wide awake, like I have never experienced in a dream before. Then I saw a familiar face; it looked like me, yet it was stronger, lighter, happier, more confident, and commanded much power and knowing.

This presence before me didn't speak to me, but telepathically communicated to me. This communication carried high vibrations of love that were so uncomfortable for me to experience, yet I was open to them. The energy of this presence gave me a most profound message: I had been living my entire life apart from who I was, and I had given in to the lower egoic self I was expressing. All my negative outer circumstances were a reflection of all the negative choices I had made in this life and karma from past lives, so it had brought me great sorrow and poverty. There were two identities that were mine: my highest self and my lowest egoic self. It showed me my life and how I lived back and forth between thoughts of my highest self and thoughts of my lowest self. The moment I had attracted negative energy and egoic thoughts, I became a magnet for forces of negativity, and as a result, my life was ruined.

During this experience, so much pain was being transmuted and sorrow in my heart was being cleansed. I was shown my future, and the presence was smiling with joy and inviting me to move forward to the choices that would help me bond with it. It told me we were going to be one very soon, and I should not lose hope.

The energy changed quickly; everything went very quiet, and I felt this presence that was my highest self become very still. It looked at me intensely, and for some reason, my entire being froze. I started to have memories of what it was like to live like this soul lived, what it was like to have a great complexion, skin that was soft and unwrinkled and alive, and in the twinkle of an eye, flashes and memories of joy came to me as I was somehow locked into my authentic self's eyes and felt a filling in my heart of a new energy of enthusiasm, joy, and love. He grew calmer, more confident, and his light around him seemed a hundred times brighter now; it was as if he were infusing me with his presence, yet a part of me was scared to let go. I was resisting this change; it was somewhat painful and uncomfortable, and somehow, I had grown accustomed to this lower self person that I had become. I started to shiver as my body grew cold. I couldn't understand why I felt like I was freezing; it must have been the energy being transmitted to me. I was confused; my fear grew, and somehow, I wanted it to stop and so it did. Everything went blank and the presence disappeared. When I awoke in the morning, I felt a certain part of me was very different, yet I still felt resistant to what had happened. I remember regretting the fear. Why had I let it get to me? It seemed to have turned away the very essence of what I asked for.

The following night, I lit a fire again and prayed, but that night nothing happened. I was disappointed in the morning, and I realized how much I wanted to change and know more of who I really was. I decided to choose the thoughts and ideas that would guide me to my highest self as instructed in my dream, and I worked hard to follow the essence and instruction of my true being. But somehow, I couldn't let go of this fear of my lowest self I embodied.

I was growing tired of asking for this presence to come to me, and it never did again. Then one day, I realized that the moment I let go of my resistance and fear of change, my highest self would come back, and all of a sudden, I felt at peace in my heart; I didn't fear whatever was coming for me, so I let go. I pulled out that dollar bill I had in my pocket and kissed the words "In God we trust," and I started to believe in them with complete love.

All of a sudden, I wasn't asleep; I felt the energy and the presence while I was awake. I could see this presence in my third eye as if I were dreaming while awake. It told me that it was waiting for me to have complete faith and love, and that was the way it would approach me. From then on, I agreed, and almost every night while I slept, I had my training and encounters with my highest self. Then weeks went by, and the more I encountered this presence, the more I was transformed, and the more it could merge with me during the daytime.

A strange thing started to happen. I could sense that my lowest self was getting weaker and that my highest self was now taking control. I would be inspired in the daytime to do things it would tell me to do. It taught me about cleanliness, fasting, and it told me to keep not only my internal body clean of alcohol or any junk food, but to keep my home clean as well because that would help my highest self enter my body. That was one of the most profound lessons: to keep a mind clean of negative thoughts, an emotional body clean from fear, a body clean from all junk food and alcohol and to do constant fasting to cleanse it; then the spiritual body of my highest self could more easily merge with me.

These practices were so uncomfortable, but they were worth it because they were very transformative. Every day, I worked hard to expand my highest self and presence. The more I did so, the more I could sense my own power of whom I really was rising within.

Then one morning, a strange feeling came over me as I heard the inner voice say, "You're ready." I couldn't understand intellectually what it meant, but my body knew. I got up and dressed myself. My intuition told me to go back to my old job that I'd had years ago, but this time, it wasn't telling me just to pursue that job; it told me to go for being the head of the company. It was the strangest feeling as I mustered all the courage I had to walk into the place where I had been fired. All my thoughts of the hardship that happened after I got the blame for the theft came back, but there was no fear; there was courage and a sense of power that swept over me. It was as if someone else were guiding my steps; it was familiar, yet unfamiliar.

I stepped into the old place and said, with the biggest courage and confidence, "I am starting to work today with my old job. I shall go to my old desk. I expect to start getting my work schedule as soon as today." The manager looked at me as if I were crazy, yet he was taken aback by his own sense of willingness to help and participate. He seemed baffled by his own helping me, but he smiled and handed me the papers for the day.

Everyone stopped and looked at me in surprise, and one of the workers there told me that two days earlier the real criminal who had stolen from the company had been discovered. I found it funny that I had the courage to go back after the news of who was really guilty had surfaced. He was going to prison. That night when I went home, it was if an old part of me came back to my being; a sense of peace was establishing itself in me, and I felt a strong sense that I was getting ready to dream deeper that night with my highest self and presence.

I was excited. I knew that night was going to come with amazing instruction, so I prepared by being as peaceful and still as I possibly could. As I fell sound asleep, here came again the lucid dream. The presence that was myself was bigger than ever; it looked twice my size. It was as if my growth and integration of it had welcomed in a higher and larger essence of my presence. The energy I felt from my presence was twice as strong and twice as loving and transformative. It proceeded to speak to me telepathically. It told me that my fear had kept me away from my highest self, and that the only thing that unified me with him was consciously creating the presence of love. It showed me visually how fear scatters all my energy and makes it difficult to be present in my body, but love and feeling it and lovingly doing things is like a magnet that unifies all aspects of myself into my body. When I felt this as true, I felt an immediate shift within my heart. I felt myself consciously loving myself and everything around me, and as I did, my presence took a step closer; it spoke in front of me, yet I felt it speak louder from inside of me.

Then I asked this aspect of myself, "What are you exactly?" He smiled and responded, "I am the universal presence of all that is. I am all that I am. I am he who you

256

were. I am he who you will be, and I am in the now that you truly exist in. You have denied me in this life because you chose the pleasures of illusion of your lowest self. I am the essence of your soul made in the perfect image of God, who once took complete command of your body. You and I were one; we lived in harmony with the laws of God, and soon enough, I walked away when you chose sins that separated us. The more you deny your lower self, the more I can integrate myself within you. The more love and actions of love you call forth, the more I can guide you. It is up to you to decide for me to dominate in your flesh or let the lower self take control. You have led your whole life temporarily without me; that is why you have suffered greatly with so much poverty in all areas of your life. It is time for you to dig deeper into a cleanliness that will call me in completely to your body. You have done well so far, and I ask that if you want to know me and remember who you are again completely, to let go into the cleanliness that will magnetize me completely to you. All of me cannot enter unless you do the work of cleansing all four of your bodies—the mental, emotional, physical, and spiritual."

"Why did you decide to come to me now and not earlier?" I asked. The presence replied, "You were not ready for me, and you never asked for me. I cannot come to you unless you ask for me either consciously or unconsciously. Everything that came to you before me was of a downward spiral, but now that you have called me in, your life is being filled with life and growth on all levels. Your external world reflects now the growth of your internal world. You are at a greater level of contact with me, but you must surrender your will completely to me so I can guide your life to the fullest. In the presence of your highest self, all your desires are possible, and abundance is your natural state. Your highest self, which you have seen before is unstoppable, does not fear; it commands and leads with strength, confidence, and faith in its decisions."

That night, I slept well, but when I woke up, everything was different. The world I lived in had the same things, but everything looked brighter, and my life seemed to have a different meaning. My remaining fears had seemed to disappear, and I was no longer doubtful. I was filled with confidence and certainty that my life was about to shift at a deeper level. I had never felt this elated. I felt as if I had transformed so deeply.

I thought my highest self would come to visit me, and I called for it, but somehow, I felt the absence of it, as if it were no longer going to pay me visits, but there was something else that night that paid a visit to me, and it was then that I realized I had become my highest self. What paid a visit to me was an energy form that was lying in the ground; it was an old form of my lowest self that I was carrying that had finally left my body. As I looked at it, I could sense the old energies of fears, doubt, and darkness around it. In the dream, I saw water melting it away and transforming it into light. I was elated to realize that who was in me now was my real self, and it was as if I remembered all of a sudden what it felt like to act like the divine essence that my creator made me to be.

The next morning, I woke up and went to my job. It was as if a new force were guiding me. I walked up to the manager and said, with no effort whatsoever in my thoughts of what to say, but just kind of blurting it out on its own, "I wish to be the president of this company. I can take this company and double it in size. I have been working here for several months now since I got my old job back, and I have seen the company increase in business because of my ideas. If you allow me to take this position, I shall do it. I only ask for a raise in salary when the company doubles in business." The manager, to my surprise, was impressed, and with no hesitation, he spoke to the owner, who gave me the job. Within six months, I felt the energy of my highest self-guiding me, and I was able to make the company's profits double. I got a raise, bonuses, and commission for doubling the company's size. Everyone in the company praised me and asked me how I knew what to do to bring about such success.

I soon moved to a higher income neighborhood and had well-to-do people as my best friends. I couldn't believe that my outer world could change so drastically as I worked so hard to change and transform myself to my highest self. I couldn't believe how people would react to me on the street and treat me so differently; they could sense the difference in energy in my presence, and they seemed to want to be around me. I soon became a teacher and started to teach others how to do what I had accomplished. I started an institution that grew to millions of dollars. Where I was once ignored, I now commanded attention, respect, and abundance.

To those who read this, please pay close attention because in what I am about to say lies the key to your success in all areas of your life. All your goals, dreams, and desires that are of the light and in harmony with what is good are yours for the taking—all you have to do is open yourself up to the power and presence of your highest self. No matter how much or little you possess of it, it is always there for you to command; command with love and you will attain it. This consciousness of your highest self is a power within you that makes all things attainable. But when you operate from a fearful place, which is the essence of your lower self, you block the way for your desires to be attained, so only cultivate and have love; then you will create it. With faith in God, you need not have fear.

Seek guidance only from your highest self; intuitively let it guide you and inform you. It always speaks through you, so consciously call it forth in every action of your day. Rely only on the power and guidance within; do not let any man misguide you or tell you that you can't do something; you can because you have imagined it. The abundance that the Universe has in store for you is waiting for you through your every step that is being guided by your highest self, so don't wait another second and start now!

This life is an incredible opportunity to find yourself. You have taken on a body to reawaken. When you go to the spirit world, it is hard to reach enlightenment, so make use of this lifetime to expand and find your highest self and cleanse yourself on all levels. Work hard on cleansing yourself on all levels, and your highest self will take possession of your body once more; it is waiting on you. If you seek wealth, work harder on expanding your highest self than you work at your job; then you will possess it.

My instruction to you now is to start on your new path to find yourself. Always be hungry for it, and do whatever it takes, no matter what. Those who fail to have their highest selves take possession of their bodies are those who are not willing to do what it takes because they are letting fear rule over them. Those who are always attentive with their thoughts of positivity and negativity will always cancel the negative ones in their minds and consciously choose the positive so they move forward with ease toward their highest expression.

Don't delay. Start now. Be on guard as to who is controlling the game of your life in the present moment. Are you angry and hating someone? Your highest self is now hovering above you and not in control because you have given your power to your lowest self. Are you treating someone with kindness? Your highest self is in control then and your lowest self is losing the battle. Always be aware and present to your thoughts and emotions. Don't let negativity enter your present moment, not even for a second. Here lies the great secret to your success. If you do all this, you cannot help but attract your highest self to you and expand it within your body.

You are the next generation. As I commented earlier, I am far gone from this planet by the time you read this. I wish to tell you now that it is in your hands—not just the responsibility of awakening yourself, but to pass on the wisdom of your own experiences and these teachings for future generations to come. The prosperity of this planet depends on it. Have confidence in yourself; God created you, and with strength and immense power, He made your soul. Take this knowledge with you now and prosper. Good luck, and I wish you well!

THE END

This story moved me to my bones when I first wrote it. It was something that I felt very close to home. I hope it moves you as well, and you feel and sense the profundity of it. When I wrote the first draft of "The Story of Reawakening," I was intrigued by the idea of two entities in a person. While growing up, I had a sense that some people were taken over by a dark force or a force of the light. I saw both expressed within myself and others. Some had a stronger sense of one or the other. I had yearned for a very long time for the full expression and reawakening of my authentic self to take full and complete expression within my being. When I finished writing this story, I had a new insight and a sense that writing this story at the particular time when I did was not a coincidence. If you are reading this book, I truly believe it is not a coincidence for you either. At the time I first wrote it, I was very close to the new rebirth I experienced that I mentioned in the first chapter, and I felt that my highest self was surrounding me, calling me, and excited to reconnect with me, due to all of my hard work and the efforts I was putting forth to reawaken. It really is our choice; we can choose to call in our authentic self and reawaken!

This is a very exciting time for you, me, and everyone on this planet because information and tools are readily available for us to grow, and our ability is limitless. You are more powerful than you think; your ability to transform yourself with applied extensive action is easier than you think because you are a divine creation of God, and the entire power of the Universe is here to back you up; you just simply have to do your part.

Never forget that the most Divine created you, so your ability to express your authentic self and to accomplish great things has no limits. This is your time to do it—to shine, to detangle from the web of what is not serving you! Shake off the idea that you cannot demonstrate greatness because you are greatness! I have given you the foundation of what I know that has transformed my life in all areas, and I know you can do it, too! Go out and get busy; give your all to awakening your authentic self so you may feel what is truly yours to feel, so you may have all the abundance that is rightfully yours and be able to give back to the world to awaken others. Be bold! You really can do it. Start enjoying every moment of this new journey; your reawakening has already begun!

If you have enjoyed this story, and this book, I also want to mention now that while you have come to the end of this book, it is only the beginning for you. I would love to continue my relationship with you in expanding your journey to greatness! I want to extend an invitation to you to dive even deeper through my academy's yearly programs. Experience the academy with our coaching, our soul-activation meditations, transformational meditations, our audio programs, our recipe books, our membership sites, and our live events. This is just the beginning for you of a new level of experience, and all I can say is that the deeper you immerse yourself in different avenues of what we offer, the more deeply transforming your experience will be. Please do check us out and experience us with our free three bonus training videos by opting in at our site www.ReawakenYourAuthenticSelfAcademy.com. I can't wait for you to introduce yourself to me and tell me about your amazing transformational story at one of our events. I look forward to connecting with you through our yearly membership programs and events. Until next time, live the courage to reawaken your authentic self!

ABOUT THE AUTHOR

Divina, bestselling author of *Reawaken Your Authentic Self*, is a certified Law of Attraction life coach and the founder of Reawaken Your Authentic Self Academy, a program that helps individuals maximize their talents and life purposes to their fullest potential so they can generate an abundant lifestyle. The academy is all about teaching people how to reawaken their authentic selves to get ahead in their personal and professional lives.

After a period of six years of intensely following the teachings written in her book *Reawaken Your Authentic Self* and used in her academy programs, Divina experienced a profound transformation where the essence of her highest self merged back into her physical body. Since then, she has dedicated her life to reawakening others into their authentic selves so they can realize their dreams through their own artistic talents and messages. The powerful teachings in her book *Reawaken Your Authentic Self* had a profound effect on her journey in rediscovering and reawakening her authentic self within and sharing and teaching this message of reawakening to others.

Meet Divina and her talents and gifts at:

www.ReawakenYourAuthenticSelf.com
www.ReawakenYourAuthenticSelfAcademy.com

YOU CAN REAWAKEN YOUR AUTHENTIC SELF!

In this radically life-changing book by Divina, founder of Reawaken Your Authentic Self Academy, you will discover:

a. The science and psychology behind a great mindset to prosper financially with your life purpose
b. The real truth about how to have real happiness to attract more prosperity with your life purpose
c. How to manifest abundant energy, an ageless body, and permanent health
d. How to anchor more of your authentic spiritual body into your physical body

In *Reawaken Your Authentic Self*, certified Law of Attraction life coach Divina reveals the top and most life-changing tools and techniques for reawakening your authentic self which is key to the blossoming of your divine mission on earth. These tools will maximize your God-given talents and generate and attract greater prosperity into your life. Divina breaks down this process into four major chapters addressing how to activate the mental, emotional, physical, and spiritual bodies to create an integrated authentic self that will attract to you the life you were born to live. The Divine Diet of those four bodies, as revealed in this book, will profoundly change your life and become your greatest gift in achieving your true personal success.

www.ReawakenYourAuthenticSelf.com

Printed in the United States
By Bookmasters